The Art of Preservation

Also by Victoria Loalou

The Science of the Sacred Secretion

Law of Attraction in a Week

Saint Claustrum

The Art of Preservation

A Sacred Practice From Ancient Roots

VICTORIA LOALOU

Cover design by Jevgenija Bitter
Illustrations by Victoria Loalou
Printed and bound by Amazon

First published in Great Britain 2019
Reprinted in 2020

This book is written as a source of information only. The information
contained in this book should by no means be considered a substitute
for the advice of a qualified medical professional, who should always
be consulted before beginning any new diet, exercise or other health
practice.

All efforts have been made to ensure the accuracy of the information
contained in this book as of the date of publication. The authors and the
publisher expressly disclaim responsibility for any adverse effects
arising from the use of application of the information contained herein.

www.victorialoalou.com

ISBN 9781675122051

For Lily,

Whose love is preserved in us all.

Contents

List of Figures

Acknowledgements

I would first like to thank my closest friends and family, who have had to hold me in mind and not in sight whilst I hibernated away to complete this book. As humans are designed for social connection, having this physical support available has been an essential foundation in completing this text.

To my Instagram family, thank you for being so patient with my lack of connection during my time of writing. I would like to particularly give personal thanks to Victoria Marshall, my soul-sister by name and energy, Karen Hall for always thinking of me when discovering a gem of knowledge and Tim Bailey for making me question the stars. Thank you also to every single truth- seeker who has messaged me their questions and testimonies, enabling me to know what knowledge was needed in the mainstream.

My gratitude will forever be owed to John St Julien Baba Wanyama who brought an awareness of the sacred secretion into my life. I know he has awakened many souls to this practice by way of his inspiring words which are a work of art in their own right. Anyone reading this who has not yet subscribed to John's YouTube channel is asked to do so in order to gain a full understanding of the strength and insights true commitment to such a practice can enlighten. Without John these words would not be in your hands right now.

Charlie, my soul-mate, thank you for supporting me during my dark times and for your critical understanding of human homeopathic health which steered my search for deeper truths.

Gaia, the mother of all life on Earth, has my continuous gratitude always. The power and determination of this macrocosmic being we call home to heal and regenerate, regardless of how historical people have plagued its body, is both admirable and inspiring. Thank you for trusting us to develop this level of awakening, again. In the same way, I give thanks to the universal father energies which have laid my spiritual path and guided me along it towards this current level of awakening. I look forward to the future journeys you have in store for me.

Last but not least, I thank you, the reader, for the loving vibrations you send out to the collective consciousness in order to heal our planet's past traumas. The collective is rising and ascension is unstoppable.

Victoria Loalou
THE ART OF PRESERVATION

Introduction

Like many people, the psychic world was always one that fascinated me. Before the age of ten I already had more crystals than I could count and my first Tarot card deck. Unfortunately, during my training and years as a teacher, work life dis-connected me from the spiritual and I got caught up in the Rat-Race. Forgetting the true motives as to why I wanted to teach in the first place, I became depressed and burned out. After a recommendation to watch *The Secret* by Rhonda Byrne and listen to *The Art of Exceptional Living* by Jim Rohn, I decided to take a gap year from work in order to preserve my sanity. Later, as an adult travelling Australia, I reached an intense state of bliss during a deep meditation. The feeling was of immense joy, love and energy, and one I had never felt during a meditation before. Knowing the pineal to be the throne of consciousness and craving to feel that state of bliss some more, I began searching for the reason behind such experiences.

Seeking deeper insights into the mysteries of the pineal, I came across a string of videos by the one and only John St. Julien Baba Wanyama. He was addicting to watch as his tone and manner were so pure and beautiful. During my YouTube binge, I heard John explain his theory of an all-healing spiritual essence, a phenomenon new to me: The Sacred Secretion. The description resonated with me instantly, as if every cell in my body was screeching with excitement. Following this awakening, I searched frantically for books and studies that could answer my endless questions. Unfortunately, there was very little to be found, at which time I received my first sign. With my mind away in thought and my body scrolling through social media on autopilot, I came across a quote by Toni Morrison: "If there's a book you really want to read, but it hasn't been written yet, then you must write it". Since then my obsession has continuously elevated as more and more signs were given to me. At the time of publication, I have attempted to preserve this spiritual essence referred to as the sacred secretion countless times and have experimented with a vast range of strategies, from meditation to yoga, diet to sexual abstinence. I believe that I have now found the methods which work for my unique body and wish to share these, as well as the mountain of research discovered along the way, with you.

In short, the sacred secretion is a way of bringing sacred union into yourself. For too long the world has seen the masculine and feminine as opposites; now, we are waking up to the balance, the equality, the sacred royal marriage of both. This historic torment and splitting, however, has left scars in our energy fields and genetic print in what is commonly referred to as our 'shadows'. We each have built up vast amounts of shadows, from inherited ancestral trauma to past life karma to modern social conditioning. Preserving the sacred secretion is just one way of working with the laws of nature to actively awaken the light body. The more you transmute your shadows into light, the more in touch you will be with the divine and you will synchronise more easily to your soul mission.

The preservation of this spiritual essence has not only improved my ability to read my food cravings and feel oneness with the world and nature, but I am increasingly able to manifest my futures at faster rates and find myself speaking to people using wisdom I was not even aware that I had. Have you ever watched the film 'Limitless'? The way Bradley Cooper felt after taking that shiny pill is the most real description that I have found so far. Today, I will begin to communicate this channelled information as well as correlations within scientific research to you. With every atom of my being I hope that these words find you well and that, together, we can collectively alter the consciousness of our planet for the greater good. For now, let's begin with a general explanation of what this secretion is. (Do not worry if this reads like a foreign language, all will be clarified.)

As well as following natural biorhythms (such as sleep-wake cycles), the human body is also protected by biomechanical mechanisms, such as throwing up rotten fruit or immune system responses. The sacred secretion is a biomechanical mechanism and, like all aspects of survival, is dependent on a healthy environment. Due to being discovered and re-discovered over and over throughout time and across the globe, the Sacred Secretion has been given many names over the millennia, including Heaven On Earth, Christ Within, Christ Oil, Oil Of Gladness, Chrism, Christos, Kundalini Energy, Serpent Energy and Sacred Secret. During my own research, I also discovered that magnetic influence pulls apart ions (charged particles in the body) and changes the chemical composition of these. For example, within water exposed to magnets, salt ions changed and dissolved, creating purer water that could be absorbed more readily. A similar molecular process is used to create the substance referred to as the sacred secretion. Consequently, the phrase sacred secret-ion (an adaptation of sacred secretion) can also

13

be used as a term to describe how cosmic magnetic influences stimulate one's awakening through the production of Christ Energy. All of these terms will be used interchangeably throughout this book.

According to George Carey (2013), the Essenes (early Christians) taught that Christ (Greek for 'anointed one') was a substance contained in the spinal cord, which connected all parts of the body like a river. After receiving signalling from lunar (magnetic) energy in your star sign, the spiritual substance undergoes crucifixion (meaning 'increased in power') before resting in a 'tomb' within the brain for 2.5 days. Carey claims that the Essenes were persecuted by the priesthood for their teachings, so had to meet (and write) is secret. It is reported that the Dead Sea Scrolls were the true words of this ancient civilisation, and the original Gnostic religions. As a result, it is widely believed that the sacred secretion is the hidden story of the Bible, with the Old Testament being the wisdom passed down through the ancestral line and the New Testament being how this wisdom was put into practice. Hence, it is this anointment that is considered the 'true christening'. See, where the Bible discusses the use of Olive Oil on the forehead of a Christened person, metaphorically we now know this to be a representation of the Christ Oil (sacred secretion) passing the Olives (hence Olive Oil) on each side of the Medulla within the brainstem. Thus, the preservation of the sacred secretion can be seen as a biological upgrade; the act of becoming holy (whole). As this alchemical reaction is triggered monthly, it is classified as another natural rhythm of the body, and one of the most important as it is the rhythmic link between our physical and spiritual selves.

Historically, Western mystery school hermeticists have long been practitioners and facilitators of *endocrine anatomy*- the science behind the enchanting and magical fluids of the human body. These knowledgeable elders understood that when our endocrine alchemy was activated, it created the fountain of life, also referred to by others as the Holy Grail, which enhanced healing, longevity and upgraded one's magical powers. Preserving the sacred secretion is one of such endocrine alchemical practices.

As hinted previously, this sacred secretion happens once a month, 12 to 13 times a year, when the Moon rests in the zodiac sign that influenced the biorhythmic energy of your body at the time of birth. Ergo, the body receives differing levels of electromagnetic energy at different times depending on cosmic influences. Another interesting point to make here is that Jesus began his Father's work at 12 years old (the time of day that the Sun is highest in the sky and at which age the Christ Oil can begin to be preserved within the body as the pineal has fully developed) and was baptised at 30 years old- the number of degrees in each star sign's constellation: 30x12=360, and also the point (the 30th vertebrae, counting up) at which spinal energy reaches the throat chakra, responsible for speaking higher truths.

This spiritual essence is first awakened within the vital fluid network of the nervous system: the cerebrospinal fluid (CSF). The process of CSF pumping up and down the spinal column actually occurs every 12 hours. The only difference here is that when lunar energy empowers our sun energy (star sign/ zodiac sign), the minerals within the body vibrate in correspondence, which enhances the production of the spiritual essence. In this way, the daily secretion becomes sacred.

The validity of the sacred secretion is questioned by some scholars due to the fact that it has not actually been fully studied yet, with all areas considered, within a clinical setting. This text hopes to have this ideology reconsidered and, I pray, physically confirmed by neurologists. Until that day, I give you the words of this book, the words of God and the words of researchers.

Part 1 of The Art of Preservation can be read in any order. My aim here was to put all of the components of the mystifying equation together in order to focus my own personal experimentation each month. At the end of each chapter within this section I have included not only a reference and bibliography list, but also my personal recommendations for further research, encase this is an area of particular interest to you. The purpose of this part of the book is to provide some context and background knowledge to aid the comprehension of and validity of this sacred practice.

Part 2 of The Art of Preservation focuses on the evidence of the sacred fluid itself. This section includes references to a range of integrated messages from the Bible and various areas of science, so may be worth re-reading in order to tie all areas together. There are references to vast sources of evidence, both modern and historic, to appease all brain areas and types of learners.

Part 3 of The Art of Preservation brings us to the end of this book but the beginning of your own journey to self-discovery. Here, I sum up everything I have discovered and provide details of my own practices during the time of preservation each month, which can be seen as a starting point for anyone who is unsure of where to begin. There is also space provided where you can make your own notes and ideas.

Please note that the repetitions and cross-references made throughout this text to essential concepts are intentional. This is for consolidation and link-making purposes in order to make the science and philosophies underpinning this practice comprehendible to all who are seeking this path. If you are new to the philosophies behind the sacred secretion, then it may be worth taking the opportunity to read the short summaries of each chapter in Part 1 first so that a basic understanding of the theory is gained before delving into the deeper science, or read the blogs available on my website (www.victorialoalou.com).

I sincerely hope that these words resonate with you, or at least open the doors to words that do.

Enjoy!

V.L

Victoria Loalou.

Victoria Loalou
THE ART OF PRESERVATION

Part 1

What Makes A Human

Victoria Loalou
THE ART OF PRESERVATION

Chapter 1

Evolution:

And the Philosopher's Stoner

As far back as modern discoveries and technologies can take us, humans have been very spiritual beings, from the Stone Age worship of animal spirits to the mighty Zeus of Greece. Graham Hancock speculates that the spirit world has used evolution to manifest physical entities, in which consciousness can emerge and express itself through, learning lessons along the way. Basically, consciousness was first and the physical realm, our world of projections, followed. Consequently, spiritual evolution through the plant and animal kingdom is seen by Bruce Lipton as a means of this consciousness simply upgrading its 'vehicle'. This means that, as humans, we are fortunate that universal energies have manifested into us, as conscious beings rather than a rock or jellyfish. Evolution in this way has made us a social species who crave freedom of thought and awareness, requiring trust and connection to feel truly happy and to live a long life in a healthy body. Please note, however, that like all areas of science and philosophy, there are very differing opinions. The theories presented here are my own and are based on my own interpretations. For example, the involvement of psychedelics in human evolution is a concept supported by such influential figures as Terence McKenna, Dennis McKenna, Jordan Peterson, Professor Guerva- Doce and Doctor Paul Pstamets, to name a few. Yet I am sure that it is an idea that appals most Darwinists. But even Galileo was once imprisoned for suggesting that the Earth orbited the Sun, so it is the birth of these new ideas that potentially inform our future understanding of the world. All I ask is that you keep an open mind and conduct your own study. Now, let's consider some key theories of human evolution.

Advanced Technology and Wise Men

The concept of evolution currently taught in mainstream schooling is that, during the phases of advancement from apes, several different species of human were conquering the world. Whilst other species such as the Neanderthals and Heidelbergensis occupied Europe and Asia, archaeological belief to date claims that wild apes began the evolutionary process to form the DNA of homo-sapiens within the depths of Africa. Apparently, Homo Sapiens ("wise men") stayed in Africa for at least 100,000 years before migrating and becoming the dominant species of the planet. Yet more recent evidence is coming to light which is suggesting otherwise. In fact, more and more scholars are accepting the idea that ancient civilisations were far more advanced, using such technology as gravity-defying machinery and extra-terrestrial communication. The commonly accepted reasoning behind why we lack evidence of this is because the ancients are said to have been more in touch with the Earth, so used biodegradable and sustainable materials that did not withstand time. Scholars such as Graham Hancock (2015) also suggest mass catastrophic disasters, such as a colossal flood. In fact, Hancock's extensive research describes a flooding extremely similar to that of Noah in the Old Testament. (Interestingly, many other creation stories also hint towards a kind of watery chaos as the start of the new world.)

Graham Hancock (2015) researched human evolution for decades and has recently concluded that: there were advanced civilisations pre-20,000BC predominately in America; a cosmic impact caused drastic changes in weather, including a mass flood; this flood destroyed lands such as Atlantis; survivors from the flood migrated to other lands and taught other tribes, much like modern humans still do today; these survivors who taught all they knew became known as 'magi', 'gods' or 'sages'. Thus, there were very likely advanced, ancient human civilisations who were very psychic, connected and knowledgeable. After surviving the harsh ice-age conditions, the world began warming up again. However, catastrophe occurred following a comet collision, which triggered the onset of a further cold period and mass flooding, known as the Younger Dryas Period. (The comet from the 'heavens' could have been viewed by the ancients as an act of God to punish humans who may have lost their way, only leaving those holy enough to have foretold the catastrophe and sheltered accordingly.) Those who survived would have naturally sought shelter upon high mountains, or even built boats to travel to distant lands with better conditions for life. Once finally reaching these new countries, these humans would have met other tribes who potentially were less advanced than themselves (just like many modern humans see the tribes of people still currently living as hunter-gatherers deep in the Amazon rainforest). After having their own legacies destroyed by 'natural' disaster, such knowledgeable survivors would have likely sought ways to pass on their understanding of enlightenment and oneness with other humans, and possibly even had children with the people of these tribes.

Consequently, all humans alive today are said to have descended from 'Mitochondrial Eve', a population of around 10,000 individuals from the planes of Africa. From here, the ancients likely encouraged the recording of their knowledge on stone tablets and within large structures such as pyramids, which had more durability against the test of time and catastrophe than most other materials. In this way, ancient human teachings and legacies could be preserved and understood by those who acquired the ability to do so.

Within Hancock's research are images from ancient sites depicting these sages holding a bucket of holy water in one hand and a pinecone purifier in the other, beside a sacred tree. Could this also be representation of the focus of this book; the sacred, internal baptism, practiced over 20,000 years ago? Personally, I think so. These people are believed to have eventually migrated to Britain, where they taught the native tribes and, thus, contributed to the formation of Celts and Druids. Joanna Van Der Hoeven (2014) believes Druidry to be the "native" spiritual tradition of Britain and Ireland. Their laws centred around the concepts of personal responsibility, truth and service to Gaia (the name given to the consciousness of Earth). Unfortunately for us, the Celts used oral tradition so there isn't much written, except the accounts by Julius Ceasar who claimed that the Druids were prolifent in astronomy, biology and theology. With this is mind, the vast awe-inspiring stone circles around Britain that attract hundreds of thousands of visitors each year must have had an important, magical purpose beyond our comprehension. As an obsession with the cosmos and their influence on us is an ideology that has survived hundreds of generations, and one we are still chasing to this today, there must be some truth that resonates within our DNA.

The proof of this advanced technology that is even beyond the comprehension of scientists today is not only evident in the fact that the pyramids are filled with quartz crystal, which is renowned for its electrical properties and even used in computers to this day, but the pyramids are also supported by ramps and tunnels which appear to have used flowing water to create an electrical output. Incredibly, energy produced in this way also does not generate pollution or by-products such as radio waves and electro-smog like most modern electrical appliances, proving that a more advanced understanding of energy and health must have been at work. Further evidence of ancient knowledge is undoubtably still concealed within the man-made tunnels under Egypt and the buried pyramids which are yet to be excavated.

So no, the pyramids were not tombs. In fact, this theory is regarded as 'childish' by modern Egyptologists, especially as no mummies have ever been found in the Giza pyramid complex. Similarly, it is claimed that slavery was not used to build the pyramids. Instead, they are said to have been built by willing workers who were motivated by the potential energy it would supply to their families and future generations. One could even speculate that the Earth-and-cosmic-energy-rich darkrooms within the pyramids could have been used to stimulate DMT production (a psychedelic drug that can be synthesised endogenously within the human body, detailed in Chapter 12).

The pyramids, as well as other megalithic sites all over the world, are overwhelmingly built on grounds where there is high electromagnetic activity so that the buildings can concentrate these energies. In England these are commonly referred to as ley lines, although the Chinese call them Dragon Lines. Surprisingly, Stone Henge of England was constructed of the same materials and in the same way as the Great Pyramid; with aquifers. An aquifer is an underground layer of water-bearing permeable rock that, as a result of friction and ion content in the water, generates an electromagnetic field (frequencies and wavelengths). As flowing water generates an electric charge, which creates a corresponding magnetic charge, it is not only physical electricity that can be produced but also a magnetic connection to the cosmos. Interestingly, this phenomenon was not an intelligence unique to ancient civilisations as this can be likened to how planet Earth generates its own magnetic field via the dynamo theory.

The dynamo theory states that the abundance of free electrons in and around the planet become excited by the flowing motion, generated by the Earth's rapid spin upon its axis. As a result, the electric currents in the liquid outer core of the planet generate the magnetic field. The phenomenon of being able to harvest energy in this way was classically proven by Nikola Tesla, who, in 1899, managed to set up an experiment whereby light bulbs were placed in a field and were lit up by transmitted power alone; no wires!

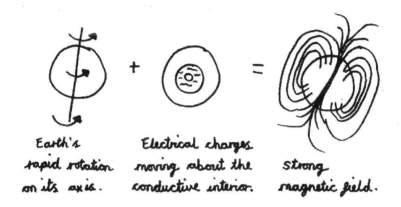

Earth's rapid rotation on its axis.   Electrical charges moving about the conductive interior.   Strong magnetic field.

FIGURE 1 – Earth Generating a Magnetic Field

Fascinatingly, many scholars have shown that the pyramids are not only wide-spread, accessible energy generators, but also astrological clocks and observatories. For example, the pyramids along the Nile of Egypt relate to the constellation Orion, with the Great Pyramid at the exact centre of the belt. Furthermore, Giza points towards the rising sun during Winter Solstice, Gaia's own macrocosmic, annual equivalent to our microcosmic, monthly sacred secretion. Based on the vast evidence presented throughout this book, I personally think it is very clear that these ancient civilisations knew of the human connection to the cosmos and worshipped this truth through action and intent.

Could those advanced humans who survived the catastrophes of America have reached Africa in their search of refuge? Here, could these knowledgeable ancestors have shared their wisdom of the stars with the endogenous people at that time, thus portraying themselves as 'messengers of God'? Maybe they even used stories and pictures as words to describe their teachings in ways that these tribes could understand? One can only speculate at this time, but one thing is for certain: the stars led the way. According to Graham Hancock (2015), there is evidence of star worship all over the world, from El Castillo in Spain, to the Pleiades in the Cave of Lascaux in France, to Gobekli Tepe in Turkey.

Star Cults

The human brain seems hardwired to seek, find and make sense of patterns. It is no surprise, then, that particular interest was taken to the stars, which seem to appear and disappear at different times of the year as the Earth spins and orbits. Naturally, this would have generated stories that satisfied the human need for pattern seeking as well as imbed this within living memory (as the brain is able to remember stories with great ease), such as tales of certain constellations going to the underworld and being born again.

Noticeable differences in the sky, then, would have sparked particular interest and the worship of specific constellations which influenced life on Earth. An example here could include the pre-dynastic Cattle Cults, whom worshipped cattle as earthly representatives of God. Unsurprisingly, this cult is said to have thrived during the Age Of Taurus (details of astronomical 'Ages' are explained later in Chapter 5).

To early humans, the cow would have been seen as sacred. It provided meat, milk, clothing, manure for fertilising land for crop growth and even access to the Gods via the 'as above, so below' phenomenon provided by the constellation (sky god). People could literally use every part of the animal. It was a gift from the universe that deserved to be worshipped (as those of the modern Hindu faith do) and so did the godly representative of this sacred animal residing in the heavens above: Taurus. Ralph Ellis' (2002) historical research proposes that the followers of Moses were in fact an Egyptian star cult whom were in disagreement with another Egyptian star cult, demonstrating the shift from the Age of Taurus (cattle worship) to the Age of Aries (shepherd kings). The Bible is full of symbolism related to the sacred secretion and so referencing to these will be made throughout this text.

Fruit From The Tree Of Knowledge

Following the creation of the world by God, the Bible presents the first man and woman: Adam and Eve. The story of Adam and Eve describes a river flowing out of Eden (the garden in which God created for humans) that splits into 4 branches. In Africa where these biblical stories are believed to have manifested, the river Nile fits this description. (Note, though, that so does the Amazon river in the Americas. See the blog 'Evidencing Eden' on my website for more details on this.) The Nile is the longest river in Africa and was worshipped by the Ancient Egyptians due to the fact that its annual flooding brought about fertile soil, and so was essential for survival. Other Biblical symbolism that derive from Ancient Egypt include that of the crucifix, winged sun- disc and the scarab beetle, all of which are also star constellations. Therefore, one could assume that the story of the creation of man and woman originates from Ancient Egypt, where the wise-men who survived the flooding shared their knowledge.

Following the introduction to man and woman in this beautiful garden provided by God, readers of the Bible are told that humans disobeyed God when, after some temptation from a serpent, ate forbidden fruit. From the Book Of Genesis:

When the woman saw that the fruit of the Tree [Of Knowledge] was good to eat, and that it was pleasing to the eye and pleasing to contemplate, she took some and ate it. She also gave her husband some and he ate it. Then the eyes of both of them were opened and they discovered that they were naked... [The Lord God] said, "The man has become like one of us, knowing good and evil; what if he now reaches out his hand and takes fruit from the Tree of Life also, eats it and lives forever?" So the Lord God drove him out of the Garden Of Eden... [God] stationed the cherubim and a sword whirling and flashing to guard the way to the Tree Of Life.

It is interesting to note that in the Egyptians consider the Acacia tree as the Tree Of Life and it is under the Acacia tree that all of the Egyptian gods were apparently born. What's more, the Acacia tree is potent in DMT (the significance of which is detailed in Chapter 12) and is found abundantly along the Nile. Later in the Bible, God communicated with Moses (a biblical prophet) through a burning bush, which was apparently an Acacia (the burning of the plant would have released an incense with psychedelic properties, which Moses likely inhaled).

Moses was then given direct instruction to lead the Israelites out of Egypt and to freedom. Eventually, after a long and treacherous journey, they finally reached The Promised Land, 'flowing with milk and honey'. Soma (sap from the soma plant) mixed with milk (a reference to cattle) is apparently an all healing fluid, which can also be paralleled to Honey and Milk, and is even said to enable communication with the gods (with psychedelic properties, too). [INTERESTING NOTE: The grey, bulbous cell body of a neuron, which contains the oval-shaped nucleus and DNA, is also aptly called the 'Soma'].

If accurate, the information presented here would support the Stoned Ape Theory proposed by researcher Terence McKenna. McKenna (1992) suggested that it's the psychedelic alkaloids in plants that catalysed the emergence of human self-reflection, thus enhancing information processing activity, environmental sensitivity and the development of the imagination, which led to religion and even language. The development of voice would have had a double positive effect as vibrations of the human skull, produced by vocalisation such as chanting, exerts a massaging effect on the brain, which facilitates the elution of metabolic products from the brain (such as DMT) into the cerebrospinal fluid (brain cushioning liquid) to promote physical and mental well-being (Jindrak and Jindrak, 1988).

By tying this knowledge in with the symbolic teachings of the Adam and Eve story, a number of theories are currently circulating.

One is that modern man evolved from barbaric tribes that began consuming psychedelic plants. Due to the fact that the women were the gatherers of fruit and vegetation, whereas the men were the hunters, it

31

was *Eve* who found the fruit. During the natural cycles of a year, when food sources were scarce, the ancients would have been starving and likely recognised the vast source of fungi that thrived from the manure of cattle. Hungry pre-historic humans may have consumed this wealth of vegetation and, upon eating these, it is speculated that they would have had a psychedelic trip. The symbolic use of a *tree* of knowledge could have arisen from the fact that mushrooms and other plants communicate via colossal fungal systems under the earth and that many mushrooms grow in, on and around trees.

Interestingly, neurologists have proven that psychedelic drugs actually increase neuroplasticity (meaning that the neuronal structure within the brain would have been more susceptible to re-wiring to new beliefs, as well as being more creative when problem solving and able to better remember new skills). This makes way for faster learning. Consequently, as a result of these trance states, early humans were better equipped to develop speech and language. From this, the 'messengers' (advanced people), with a deeper understanding of DNA (evident within the animal-human hybrid depictions of Gods) would have told stories to the emerging tribes as a way of educating them on how to produce these psychedelic states endogenously, with potentially less risk of a bad trip.

If we look again at the story of the fall of humans from Eden, it clearly states that a *"cherubim and a sword whirling and flashing"* was positioned in the East *"to guard the way to the Tree Of Life"*. Seeing as the Sun rises in the East, it could be argued that the warming climate may have forced human migration away from these planes and closer to the Nile, where the Acacia tree grew. However, as the Bible has been translated and altered vastly, the Cherub (light) may have in fact led the way *towards* the Tree of Life, rather than prevented access to it. The advanced humans from the Americas, who found refuge in Africa and used stories and imagery to pass on their knowledge, could have told the story of Adam and Eve with a symbolic interpretation. That is, that we can return to God and the Garden of Eden [creation], by means of the internal sacred secretion, whereby the fruit [seed] is given life by God [the Sun] and edibility [internal use] by the snake [Moon] and guarded by the angel/ cherubim [stars] (if this doesn't make sense now, it will later).

If read at face value alone, it's easy to see how these stories of astronomical visions and health hacks would have been distorted over time in order to suit those in power. An understanding only just being re-learned is that the meaning of hieroglyphs varies depending on the context around them. For example, the word 'Sin' could mean 'without' or it could mean 'moon'- both very different and can vary the implications of such phrases as "Born in sin". On the flip side, the image of an egg can mean 'one', 'atom' or 'fertility' depending on the context of the other glyths around. Another example is the spoken word 'hyk', which can mean either 'king' or 'captive' depending on how it is pronounced (Ellis, 2002). Just these few example alone could turn most Biblical stories on their head!

If we fast forward into more recent history, it can be seen that, over time, the Christian church grew in power and, by 325 AD, was the official faith of the Roman Empire. With their strength and influence (and extreme violence), the faith spread like wildfire. As a result, the written memory of our evolution and experiences, passed down through the generations, was almost completely destroyed by authorities who required a mass population of worker-ants. To preserve the ancient knowledge of humanity, other means were sought for teaching the progression of internal alchemy.

Let's really throw a spanner in the works now and say, for example, a story was created which told of a man, both human and God, who performed miracles and foretold the future. Let's say this man was called Jesus, and at birth this babe was given three gifts by three wise men: gold (a key conductor of electricity, which is the connector of all life on Gaia), as well as frankincense and myrrh (both of which have psychedelic properties). This child could then have been educated in Egypt and learned the way of the cosmos and internal alchemy ('alchemy' means 'from Egypt') and became a messenger of God who taught the way of the stars and the laws of nature.

Unfortunately, even knowledge preserved within the oral traditions of a family line from such times were almost completely destroyed during the Dark Ages. At such a time, all believed to be using 'magic' were labelled as witches and murdered, alongside any acquaintances, written records and respect. This led the way for religious texts, such as the Bible, to be taken far more literally; to be believed as fact rather than a cosmic story of connection. A speculated theory is that the top families who want to control the world actually sectioned this inhumane act of witch-hunting as a way of ridding the world of ancient knowledge in order to gain more power.

The final nail in the coffin for psychedelic freedom was struck during the 1960s when Western governments banned the use of psychedelic drugs altogether, even for scientific purposes. Yet, in some tribal civilisations, the use of powerful psychedelics, particularly plant based DMT, to enhance communication with the Gods is still common. It is predominately put to effect by Shaman (healers), who use rituals to practice healing, divination and natural magic. The Shaman are commonly seen as dimensional explorers by their tribes, who are able to access trance-states, shape-shift into animals and see the path options for the future, enabling them to make decisions about when the group should move, hunt or go to war.

Through the manipulation of sound vibration, breath, illusion and sexual energy, these practitioners commonly enter higher trance states. The Shaman also watch over others who consume plant medicine (psychedelic brews) to experience altered states. During these 'trips', people regularly interact with beings who are usually humanoids of varying colours and sometimes made of animal-parts. This is particularly interesting when referring back to the Bible as messages from the Gods are often received from Angels or other higher beings, such as shape-shifting entities that take the form of animals. Entities in this form are particularly renowned within the Egyptian and Hindu faiths. Within the Bible and other religious texts, these messages also tend to occur within the 'dream' state. It is no surprise, then, that the brain waves typical of sleep, meditation and psychedelic tripping are very similar.

By combining religious stories with the still-modern advocation of psychedelic plant consumption for spiritual connection to the gods, I personally do not doubt the role of such compounds within our evolution. Over millennia, these spirituality- enhancing plant molecules would have literally ingrained into our DNA and re-wired the neuronal structure of the brain. Unfortunately, years of distortion have made such knowledge a distant memory. However, the overwhelming need for meaningfully spiritual experiences still pulsates through our biological body, waiting to awaken. Plants provide us with large hits of psychedelic molecules all at once, yes, but we do not need them to reach these states. As conscious beings, we are able to work with nature, with our own biological rhythms and the astronomical energies, to increase our ability to access and interact with these higher levels of existence.

Like a video game, for early humans these psychedelics may have acted like a cheat code, allowing the players to reach higher levels and achieve further advancing missions. Nowadays, however, we are better at playing the game and no longer require the quick- hit codes. We can become conscious (aware of our awareness) through natural means. Through the sacred secretion. And, as evidence is continuously increasing to prove this evolutionary theory, strict religious practitioners in the future may have to accept the fact that it was hallucinogens that modelled the way for all religions to follow; that their book of worship was written by communities of men who were able to access these other realities through drug manipulation. Or even just that humans have been caring for the Earth for much longer than science currently likes to admit. Another theory worth briefly exploring is that the written accounts of these prophets were, in fact, of extra-terrestrial origin.

Hybrid Humans

Much of what is currently known of Egyptian hieroglyphs etc is thanks to the knowledge preserved within the still thriving Dogon community in West Africa. The Dogon report that their distant ancestors left Egypt because they did not like how it was going (much alike the story of Moses and the exodus from Egypt reported within the Old Testament). According to Laird Scranton (2006), ancient Dogon knowledge that has been passed down includes an understanding of how thoughts can change atoms. Thus, it can be inferred that the ancients not only were aware of astronomical phenomena, but also immediate physics.

Scranton's work with the Dogon presents a historical awareness of correctly defined key components of matter, from atoms, quarks and even the string theory. Intriguingly, the Dogon claim to have learned this from the Nommos, an alien race who visited Earth from the star of Sirius many millennia ago. The Dogons claim that the Nommos (half human, half fish beings, which could possibly indicate a connection to submarine/ water travel) gave them knowledge of the solar system, including the fact that the planets orbit the Sun (long before the days of Galileo).

Maxim Makukov and Vladimir Shcherback (2015), whom spent 13 years working for the Human Genome Project, mapping out human DNA, concluded that the human species were designed by an alien civilisation, with 97% of non-coding sequences in human DNA being the genetic code of alien life forms. Similarly, Francis Crick, renowned for his discovery of the double helix DNA structure, also suggests that it is reasonable to suspect that the first life on Earth was deliberately seeded.

Daniella Fenton (2018) recently conducted some interesting research on the topic of extra-terrestrial influence on the development of human DNA. Fenton believes that the human DNA double-helix is in fact a library of information from aliens that spored the planet hundreds of thousands of years ago in order to preserve their own genetic information.

A similar theory is that of panspermia, the hypothesis that life travels around the universe and lands on planets by accident, distributed by space dust, meteoroids, asteroids, comets and even spaceship contamination. These bacteria then influence the developing DNA of other organisms on that planet. Therefore, it could stand that life on Earth has some extra-terrestrial strains. Mushrooms, which are genetically closer to animals than vegetation, are believed by Terence McKenna to be a perfect example of this, as mushroom spores are able to survive space travel. Hence, consumption of these psychedelic alkaloids could in fact be awakening alien memories and communication abilities within our genetic library. Another interesting point to consider is that it is through the use of fungal systems that trees are able to optimise survival and communicate. So mushrooms may not just hold the genetic memory of extra-terrestrial life, but even of terrestrial life forms which are unable to speak to us via our verbal tongue.

Beyond the scope of this book, but worth mentioning, is the idea of Simulation Theory. This hypothesis proposes that all of reality, including Earth and the universe, is in fact an artificial simulation, like a computer game simulation. If true, the craving for spiritual advancement and altered states could be a result of boredom generated by the prolonged experience of this state of awareness.

Nonetheless, if we re-consider the story of the fall within the Old Testament, the idea that Adam and Eve (humans) had their eyes opened by the forbidden fruit, technically provided by the snake (strands of DNA), could indeed be the story of the double-helix- extra- terrestrial-DNA library which enables humans to realise their god-like powers. In this story, it is written that humans were now like the gods in power, thus were creators by genetic design. As Dr Berit Brogaard (2016) claims we can access specific skills of our ancestors through the activation of genetic material coded within our DNA, both the theories of terrestrial and extra-terrestrial DNA origin can plausibly support the role of psychedelic compounds, whether external or endogenous, in advancing homosapien potential.

Epigenetics

Everything a human has ever achieved is, in one way or another, encoded within our DNA. DNA is the hereditary material from our ancestors, which responds to environmental stimuli. Sitting above these

DNA strands are flags and tags that are waiting to accept information from the environment. These stimulate changes in genetic expression, such as the development of type two diabetes. The term 'epigenetics' is used to describe this phenomenon, which literally means "above genetics" due to the positioning of these flags and tags. The purpose of this is to promote survival rate within fluctuating environments. Therefore, epigenetics is the biological action that allows us to pass on information that has been gained over many generations, like an internal library that can be referred back to later. Cultural beliefs, individual ideas, phobias and fears, emotional control and even food preferences are passed on to offspring. As a result, it is speculated that psychedelic plants sped up evolution, which would have otherwise taken much, much longer, as they provided humans with enhanced neurogenesis, creativity, problem solving ability, sex drive and access to universal information such as tool manipulation, the invention of fire to advance food nutrition, natural laws, etc. As evolving people repeatedly operated these experiences, their own ideologies and philosophies would have altered. Naturally, these would have also been passed down. Interestingly, as the increased expression of particular genes manifests as proteins, neurotransmitters, etc, the cell receptor sites for these would have also increased, making such activations easier and faster in the future (which will be detailed in Chapter 12).

In some humans, specific aspects of cosmically influenced DNA could be activated or more dominant than other strands, which is why some people may feel more connected with specific alien entities. In particular, Mary Rodwell, author of *The New Human*, has concluded from her studies that it is more and more common for children nowadays to be speaking to these alien entities whom they are genetically connected to. Such children also claim to be taken to 'schools' at night and taught skills such as telekinesis and telepathy. These humans are believed to have incarnated and been genetically awakened by these cosmic entities in order to help the planet and deliver particular teachings, such as how to speak/ connect with Mother Earth/ animals, etc.

Summary

In short, whether you believe that our DNA holds extra-terrestrial influence and is drenched in psychedelic compounds or not, the fact is we inherit vast arrays of potential genetic coding, which is covered in tiny receptors, from our ancestral line. These stick out above DNA strands awaiting environmental input, such as proteins from food, which would then signal specific genetic expression. It is not only nutritional intake which influences the genetic expression of our cells, however. Environmental factors such as light exposure, toxic air, temperature and electromagnetic fields also effect this DNA-communication. Proof of our connection to the Earth can be seen within the research of Schumann Resonances, which are natural frequencies that show a correlation between the electrical pulses of the human brain and the Earth's field (detailed in Chapter 7). Astonishingly, the human body is also able to produce bio-photons. These are photons of light produced by a biological system; a type of bioluminescence generally reserved for higher luminance luciferin (more in Chapter 6). Such light photons are even emitted from the DNA itself. Therefore, within our DNA, we all literally hold the potential for emitting 'inner light' when exposed to a genetically adequate environment.

The idea that humans evolved in conjunction with nature and that the conscious connection between them enabled the development of the spirit within, which is able to connect with other realms by way of endogenous psychedelic enhancement, is one that resonates with me, personally. Billy Carlson states that it only takes a few generations for a civilisation to forget their roots. For example, if an alien species were to conquer the planet now, it would only take a couple of generations for all humans to be speaking the language of the aliens and have no ability to speak their native tongue. Consequently, it is commonly believed that humans are a species with amnesia. However, as DNA stores knowledge and abilities within its genetic structure, all of the understandings of our ancestors are evident within us, waiting to be re-discovered.

You are literally a walking, talking library!

As already hinted, if the Old Testament is evolution in the stars, the New Testament is how we can reconnect. Through the use of technology, the scale of human societies has increased, from the family group, to the local group, to regional polity, to a global society. Personally, I believe that there were advanced civilisations on Earth, that may or may not hold cosmic DNA, who travelled and contacted tribes, providing them with knowledge of plant medicine (including psychedelics). The most well- preserved of these reside in Egypt. The Bible even shows that Jesus was educated in Egypt, where he learned all the wise ways of the elders who were educated by the knowledgeable messengers of God. This wisdom was then encoded within the Bible for "those with ears". An apt example is the use of 'bread' to represent knowledge and 'fish' to symbolise the stars. Thus, when the Bible speaks of Christ feeding thousands of people with scraps of bread and fish, he is actually simply providing knowledge of the constellations and our connection to them ('As above, so below'). This leads to our next area of focus: biorhythms.

Top Recommendations

Website: http://grahamhancock.com/blog/

Books: 'Magicians of the Gods' by Graham Hancock and 'Food Of The Gods' by Terrance McKenna

Articles: Brogaard, B. 2016. *Can We Access The Memories Of Our Ancestors Through Our DNA?* Available online at:
<https://www.vice.com/en_au/article/ypv58j/genetic-memory>

Brogaard, B. 2015. Q&*A: Berit Brogaard on Unlocking Your Brain's Superhuman Abilities.* Available online
at:<https://www.inverse.com/article/5716-q-a-berit-brogaard-on-unlocking-your-brain-s-superhuman-abilities>

Podcast: Earth Ancients with Cliff Dunning

Video: 'The Pyramid Code' documentary on Netflix

Bibliography and References

Allegro, J. 1970. *The Sacred Mushroom and the Cross*. Hodder and Stroughton Limited.

Ancient Code. N.d. The great pyramid of Giza: A Tesla-like power plant built thousands of years ago? Available online at: <ancient-code.com>

Bauval, R. and Hancock, G. 2011. *Keeper of Genesis*. Cornerstone Digital.

Brogaard, B. 2013. *Remembering Things From Before You Were Born*. Available online at: <https://www.psychologytoday.com/intl/blog/the-superhuman-mind/201302/remembering-things-you-were-born>

Brogaard, B. 2015. *Q&A: Berit Brogaard on Unlocking Your Brain's Superhuman Abilities*. Available online at:<https://www.inverse.com/article/5716-q-a-berit-brogaard-on-unlocking-your-brain-s-superhuman-abilities>

Brogaard, B. and Marlow, K. 2015. *The Superhuman Mind*. Hudson Street Press.

Brogaard, B. 2016. *Can We Access The Memories Of Our Ancestors Through Our DNA?* Available online at: <https://www.vice.com/en_au/article/ypv58j/genetic-memory>

Ellis, R. 2002. *Jesus: Last Of The Pharaohs*. Independently Published.

Faulkner, R. 1969. *The Ancient Egyptian Pyramid Texts*. Utterance 412-442. Oxford University Press. Aris and Phillips reprint edition.

Fenton, D. 2018. *Hybrid Humans*. Independently Published.

Hancock, G. 2001. *Fingerprints of the Gods*. Century.

Hancock, G. 2015. *The Divine Spark*. Hay House UK.

Hancock, G. 2015. *Magicians of the Gods*. Coronet.

Makukov, M. and Shcherback, V. 2015. **In**. Discovery CSC. *The Planetary Science Journal Karus, the 'Wow' signal of intelligent design.*

McKanzie, C. 2017. *Mystery of Our Coded DNA- Who Was The 'Programmer'?* Available online at: < http://www.messagetoeagle.com/mystery-of-our-coded-dna-who-was-the-programmer/>

McKenna, T. 1992. *Food Of The Gods.* Rider.

Redd, N. 2017. *What Is a Wormhole?* Available online at:
<https://www.space.com/20881-wormholes.html>

Rodwell, M. 2016. *The New Human: Awakening to Our Cosmic Heritage.* New Mind Publishers.

Scranton, L. 2006. *The Science of the Dogon.* Inner Traditions.

Scranton, L. 2014. *China's Cosmological Prehistory.* Inner Traditions.

Scranton, L. *2018. Decoding Maori Cosmology.* Inner Traditions.

Van Der Hoeven, J. 2014. *The Awen Alone.* Moon Books.

Chapter 2

Biorhythms:

And the Order of the PEMFs

Since the dawn of time, all manner of life has adapted and responded to the natural cycles that influence the universe. Everything follows cycles and rhythms: orbits, hormones, water, the Sun, the Moon, day and night, seasons, harvest, seed germination, organ regeneration, and so on. Even the Earth follows a cycle of grow and rest, where it goes inside itself to re-absorb energy that can begin the cycle again, in the form of seasons. According to Randall Carlson (2018), there is also evidence of cyclical patterns and cycles of cosmic catastrophe (such as meteor impact). Carlson exerts that there is an order to the galaxy, a tempo and wave pattern that moves up and down, above and below the galactic plane. Within that there are sub-orbital cycles, too, and a tempo of delivery of cosmic impact into our solar system. It is for this reason that mass extinctions, ice ages, global warming, etc, happen continuously, and why ancient civilisations were such avid recorders of celestial events. Interestingly, these events would occur during certain 'Ages' of the planet (evidenced by the background of stars during certain times of the year- detailed in Chapter 5). Thus concluding that nothing is random and we are all part of a cosmic timetable.

All of these cycles follow smooth, repetitive waves and are governed by the atoms that combine to create the basic building blocks of all matter. It is matter that makes up all that is physical. If you were to break down the human, you would first find organs, then their chemical cells. Even further, it would be seen that these cells are made of molecules, that these molecules are combinations of atoms, and that the atoms are formed from a construction of sub-atomic particles (electrons, protons and neutrons). These sub-atomic particles can be split further into fermions, bosons and quarks, which are non-physical (pure energy). Even here, at this microscopic level, we see an eternal search for balance. Atoms link electron orbits as a way of seeking balance, which form molecules. Each atom will have an equal number of electrons, protons and neutrons, and the very energy that is the building block of all matter will seek likewise energy, as dictated by the Law Of Attraction (described in Chapter 7).

Due to the fact that everything in the universe is a combination of this energy, all is entangled and united; allied, whether we know it or not. Even the stars are inter-connected by electromagnetic fields which have been discovered spanning deep space and connecting distant galaxies. Therefore, the astronomical energy furnaces are not scattered randomly, as some may assume, but actually occur in communities referred to as "stellar clusters" where they often live in couples. So the pictorials of constellations, such as the ram for Aries, may not have occurred by

47

chance. A current emerging theory is that the binary star to our star is that of Sirius (see Chapter 16).

Interestingly, each star also sends its own unique signal into space, confirming its individuality and influencing the distant energy fields of other cosmic bodies. In 2008, NASA discovered that our closest star, the Sun, is connected to the Earth's geomagnetic field via a magnetic portal, the same diameter as the planet, through which high-energy particles pass at 8-minute intervals. This phenomenon is known as a "flux transfer event" (Basically, there are magnetic portals that connect the Sun and the Earth). As a result, the Earth and all life on it are affected by the pulsating energy and positioning of the Sun. It's worth noting here that it is proven that this influx is more prominent during the equinoxes. This phenomenon, known as the Russell-McPherron Effect, even causes temporary 'cracks' in the Earth's atmosphere, which make the famous Northern Lights more visible. It is very likely that the ancients knew of these higher influxes of energy during the equinoxes, which may explain why initiation ceremonies into such groups as Druidry took place during these. Moving on, as other cosmic energies from such signals as distant star constellations and planets interact and communicate with our own Sun, which then relays that information back out to us on Earth via the magnetic portal, it is clear to see how varying background influences could alter one's energy field.

These forces and others have even been proven to affect the physical body. Dr Percy Seymour (1988) demonstrated how the foetus in the womb is influenced by the Earth's magnetic field at the time of birth and that the birthing process causes the foetal nervous system to code geomagnetically to that time and place. This is supported by the work of Frances Nixon (1960s), who discovered that, at the moment of birth, every living creature creates a spherical wave field of rotating magnetic energy which anchors itself into its magnetic and physical location. This is why many animals, such as frogs and birds, migrate back to where they were born and why we can feel at home in other countries, influenced by past life memories. Similarly, Richard Gerber (1988) concluded that, at the time of birth, the chakras become magnetised by the surrounding fields, becoming fixed and influenced by the alignments of various planets and stars.

A slight variation is the idea that, when energetically setting your soul's mission before incarnation, you would have attracted your specific time and place of birth in order to have your physical vessel synchronised in a way with the cosmos that best supports this alignment. What's more, it is commonly accepted nowadays that fertilisation is not a mere 'random' phenomena, whereby a lucky sperm *'wins the race'*, but, instead, it appears that the mother's egg *choses* which sperm to connect with. Thus, it seems that spirit adapts the physical world in order to encourage the procreation of a body that is most aligned, based on the DNA blueprint that the incoming soul has chosen or needs in order to embody and journey through the lessons of this particular life on Earth.

From these theories it can be seen that, at the moment of birth when a body becomes singular from its mothers, the magnetic forces of the galaxy which are set within that specific moment of time generate an electromagnetic imprint. This internal, cosmic imprint then follows the cycles of these external influences, creating what is referred to as 'biorhythms'.

Biorhythms are innate rhythms in our body. Almost all of the body's physiological processes have a rhythm that varies throughout the day, month, year, etc, in response to both the internal timer and external stimuli. These rhythms are predominately regulated by the endocrine system of the body, which is responsible for hormone release. Some hormones, such as insulin, are secreted every few minutes, whereas others, particularly those of the pituitary, are usually at hourly intervals. These hormonal secretions regulate a range of biorhythms within the body, including shorter cycles such as the wake-sleep cycle, and longer ones, such as a woman's menstrual cycle.

The purpose of these biorhythms is that all parts and elements of the human body have opportunities to rest, repair and replicate in response to changes within the environment; for the greater good of the whole organism. By responding in this way, the DNA is able to silence or awaken thousands of years of inherited genetic potentials, such as a quick temper in a perceivably dangerous world or a euphoric calmness in a more silent one.

A similar theory has been adopted by Richard Rudd, although he refers to this ideology as 'Gene Keys'. According to Rudd, the energetic influences on a person at the time of birth influences core universal archetypes of their genes. That is, that cosmic frequencies effect the coding of our DNA, which fluctuate throughout our lives based on the frequency of consciousness. Rudd explains that it is this phenomenon that holds the secret to us being able to, scientifically, map out our purpose and reason for incarnating as human. If one is interested in looking further into this, a free hologenetic profile can be made on www.genekeys.com using your date, time and place of birth.

In a similar way, due to the fact that unborn children are constantly tuned into their mother's energy, every action, thought and feeling produces a chemical response within the blood that flows through both hearts. From the moment of conception, the experience in the womb shapes the brain and lays the groundwork for personality, temperament and the power of higher thought. Then, from the day of birth, as a person is disconnected from the flow of their mother's blood and rhythms, their individual body (blood, organs and all) adapts physically to the universal energy field, creating a unique vibration. This is influenced by the astronomical and planetary alignments and the energy fields of nearby matter, as well as the natural patterns of the human body, as previously explained. Individual connection with life energy in this way is what generates our relationship with the cosmos (horoscopes) and the physical (biorhythms), thus dictating our sensitivity levels to outside frequencies and the vibrancy of our energy systems.

In short, both cosmic energies and physical secretions work interchangeably, adapting the body for survival until such a time that it is ready to reach higher states of being. By manifesting consciousness in this way, Gaia (the spirit of Earth) can preserve its own life by way of improving the communication between the organisms responsible for maintaining it. [For future reference, it is worth noting that the terms 'macrocosm' and 'microcosm' are commonly used to describe the relationship between smaller organisms like humans and larger living things such as solar systems. 'Macro' (meaning very large scale) obviously refers to the larger manifestation of life, whereas 'micro' (meaning small) is used to describe similar manifestations but on a tinier scale, with 'cosm' meaning world. Thus, macrocosm literally translates to 'very large world' and microcosm means 'small world'.]

Human Energy Systems

The chakra system is the title given to the collection of energy centres within the body. These are responsible for the colours and buoyancy of a person's unique aura, which can be felt, and sometimes even seen, by others; hence the word 'human' meaning *colour man*. As beings with God-like power, we are able to consciously change our energy system using our electromagnetic thoughts, which alter our physical chemistry. Although there are vast energy centres throughout the human microcosmic body, the main chakra system is an alignment of 7 energy centres that run through the central nervous system [see FIGURE 23]. These 7 each radiate a particular colour and are strengthened by specific organs and plexuses of nerves, as well as thoughts and actions that are linked to these. When aligned, the body enters a state of homeostasis (balance). Some facts worth knowing for now are:

The Crown Chakra

This chakra vibrates violet, is centred at the top of the head and is associated with spirituality. This energy centre acts like a funnel, transferring and receiving information from the universal energy field.

(An interesting point to consider here is that the light of vibration higher than violet is Ultra-Violet. UV can be felt and affects human physiology even if not seen physically, like God's angels of light. Hence, one could conclude that angels are in fact beings that are only one light-grade higher than awakened humans.) Although referred to as the 'third eye', the pineal gland actually has a stronger resonance with the crown chakra due to its ability to transmute cosmic energies.

The Third Eye Chakra

This is located in the middle of the forehead and is linked to psychic ability. It is connected with the colour indigo and controls the pituitary gland and optic nerves. During the first days of gestation, the pineal and pituitary glands are one, hence the intense connection and synchronicity between them being central to spiritual awakening and higher levels of consciousness; a phenomenon commonly referred to as the 'sacred royal marriage'. This chakra is very vulnerable to blockages from negative thought patterns and pineal calcification (detailed in Chapter 20), which would prevent adequate communication between the crown and third eye chakras.

The Throat Chakra

Obviously, this blue chakra vibrates within the throat and is responsible for communication. It is linked with the thyroid gland (the 'shield' of the body) and carotid plexus. The activation of this chakra is key for speaking higher truths with confidence and ensuring that one is heard by those who are ready to hear. The most common cause of blockage to this chakra is iodine deficiency, which is an essential component within hormone production that should keep the thyroid gland healthy.

The Heart Chakra

This is located in the chest and is associated with giving and love. It vibrates green and responds to the thymus gland and cardiac plexus. The heart chakra is the bridge between our lower and higher levels of consciousness. Thus, once the lower, animal energies are conquered, our sacred-self can cross the bridge of love and compassion to reach our higher states of awareness. A blockage of this chakra typically manifests as physical illness and disease due to the thymus gland's role in supporting white blood cell production within immune system maintenance. Interestingly, the heart has more than 5000 mitochondria ('the force'- emphasised and explained throughout this text, particularly within Chapters 4 and 20) per cell, making it the most energy dense tissue in the body and the centre of the our electromagnetic field.

The Solar Plexus

This yellow chakra sits just above the navel and is linked to confidence and power. It is also connected to the adrenal glands. When preserving the sacred secretion, it is here that the 'son' (hence the title of this energy centre literally being the 'SUN' plexus), after being protected by the mother (pituitary hormones and corresponding felt emotions), begins his father's work by ascending back to the temple of God (the brain). However, as the adrenal glands are responsible for cortisol production (the stress hormone- King Herod), the seed can often be spoilt before it can ascend when born within the body of a person who is feeling negative emotions, such as fear, anger, jealousy and guilt.

The Sacral Chakra

Located within the lower abdomen, the orange chakra is responsible for creativity and emotions. This energy centre balances with the hypogastric glands (AKA lymph nodes) and the sacral plexus. Here, there is a five-bone fused vertebrate which looks like a small house, or manger (where the spiritual seed of the sacred secret-ion is born). The inguinal lymph nodes within this physical area act as filters to prevent harm to the body, much like the Biblical reasoning behind (and probably the true metaphorical interpretation of) the controversial circumcision.

The Root Chakra

The final chakra is red and lies at the base of the spine. It is associated with feeling safe and grounded. It is also part of the pelvic glands (testes and ovaries) and the coccygeal plexus. When clearing the path for the sacred secretion to ascend, this is the first energy centre that must be healed and purified (as a 'virgin') in order to allow mother-earth's energy to ground us in preparation for the birth of the 'son'.

In sum so far, these chakra energy centres seek natural balance and alignment. If any of them are out of sync, you will know about it through manifested pain and mood. Energetically, the bottom three are our lower, ego-tistical, animal- selves responsible for survival. The heart, then, is the bridge between these lower three chakras and the higher three, which are our spiritual energy centres. Most commonly, it is due to our perceived lack and desire for materialism that blocks our base chakras. Therefore, if any of these base chakras are blocked, then limited energy will be able to pass along our heart- bridge to the higher spiritual ones.

A key indicator that there is a blockage (or potential blockage) is our emotional state. Therefore, emotions are biochemical reactions to our thoughts that even affect our heart's rhythm, thus 'rocking the bridge'. However, when these energy centres are balanced, the corresponding glands are free to secrete their natural hormones and chemicals that lead to a state of ease and a vibrant energy field surrounding the body; the aura. It is for this reason that the all-loving mother-hormones of the pituitary gland in the brain are so important in ensuring that the internal- Christ consciousness is kept safe from destruction.

Emotion Altering Rhythms

Like the chakra system, all energy flows in circular cycles as a way of eternal movement. Sigmund Freud, a renowned Austrian neurologist, famously followed the biological cycles of his patients when investigating psychoanalysis and found a correlation. Similarly, Alfred Telcher, a teacher in the 1920s, discovered that the abilities of his students also followed clear patterns. These proposals contributed to the foundation of understanding with regards to Biorhythms.

At this time, among our vast bodily rhythms are three clearly defined cycles that affect our behaviour patterns. These indicate potential physical ability, emotional sensitivity and intellectual acuity. The three key biorhythmic cycles that are studied and affected by our physical age (and are therefore measurable and predictable) are aptly titled the Physical Cycle, the Emotional Cycle and the Intellectual Cycle.

All rhythms (Yin and Yang, day and night, good and bad) flow from positive to negative and back to positive, repeatedly, and biorhythms are no exception. During the negative state, that biological energy is regenerating, just like Earth's winter. Fortunately, the biorhythms are not synchronised, so we don't have to worry about super negative days as, for example, when the physical is low and we're lacking energy, the intellectual could be high, allowing us to concentrate better on paperwork. The time when a cycle crosses over from positive to negative, or vice versa, is known as a Critical Day. During this time, our biological vibration is adjusting which can cause an array of behaviours, such as mood swings. The main, primary biorhythms include:

The Physical Cycle

There is a strong health factor involved with this phase. During a positive state, skin feels good, energy levels are high and we feel physically well and prepared. The negative is always the opposite, resulting in a lack of energy and tiredness. This follows a 23 day cycle and is associated with the red (root) and orange (sacral) chakras.

The Emotional Cycle

The emotional cycle is governed largely by the nervous system. When positive, we feel optimistic, creative, cheerful, confident and friendlier. Reversed during a negative state, we tend to be less cooperative, moody and as if we are against the world. This is a 28 day cycle and is linked with the yellow (solar plexus) and green (heart) chakras.

The Intellectual Cycle

On the positive days of an intellectual cycle, concentration is at its peak, memory is more efficient and understanding is stronger. The negative days that follow, however, can leave us feeling dull and lacking effort. It has also been linked to higher crime rates. Intellectually, our bodies flow in a 33 day cycle, which is connected to the blue (throat) and indigo (third eye) chakras.

The secondary cycles include Spiritual, Intuitive, Awareness and Aesthetic, which are supported by the violet (crown) chakra and associated with higher order thinking and our connection with spirit; however there is very little research supporting the philosophies behind the secondary cycles, to date. Naturally, biorhythms can also affect our compatibility with others as it can contribute to contradicting energy fields, hence why biorhythms can also be used as a tool for understanding how our natural self affects our mood and preparing for it. For example, if you're feeling emotionally high but your friend is emotionally low, then you may find their negative energy irritating.

In the past, these were difficult to calculate as they require an understanding of the exact number of days a person has been alive. Fortunately, with today's technology it is simple. Just internet search 'biorhythm calculator' and use your birthdate to generate your own bio-gram (I use www.biorhythmonline.com). This can then be followed day-by-day to plan events etc to your advantage by seeing when these cycles overlap or are critical. Interestingly, biorhythms can also affect a recipient's reaction to drug-producing plants. So historically, the art of medicine depended on not only alchemical knowledge but also astronomical and divine timing.

It is important to remember that these cycles can be affected by energetic disturbances, such as universal energy shifts from the Sun, Moon and also planets. Interestingly, the appearance of the Moon changing is in fact due to its position in relation to the Earth and Sun. It is the angles between the Moon, Earth and Sun throughout the month that cause a different amount of the Moon to be lit up (reflecting solar energy). Thus, the solar energy from the Sun (masculine energy) is reflected and empowered in duality by the surface of the Moon (feminine energy). For example, as we are succumbed to the energy shifts of a New Moon, detoxifying power is at its peak, making it easier to throw out old habits. This would be particularly effective if our intellectual cycle was in a positive state. Similarly, a Waning Moon's frequency makes it easier to lose weight and be active, which will compliment a positive physical rhythm.

The Moon also influences a female's menstrual cycle. Both the Moon's monthly cycle and a woman's are synchronised at about 29 days and follow similar patterns of ebbs and flows. Historically, the women used the Moon phases in order to calculate their cycles; thus informing them of when they were ovulating and when they were due to bleed. According to Bertrand and Bertrand (2018), it is the womb that is the secret *Holy Grail* of Jesus Christ, which was metaphorical for his wife and lover: Mary Magdalene. There is now overwhelming evidence that

Mary Magdalene actually taught women how to cultivate the energies of their menstrual cycles and was a descendent of a special lineage of powerful women who held ancient womb knowledge; gifts of which were highly sought after by men of higher caliber, such as Jesus/ Yeshua. Magdalene's teachings included how falling into divine union love with someone opened portals to other dimensions and states of consciousness, as well as enabling faster manifestations of desires (as stated by the *law of attraction*). It is also believed that the giving of menses (which is actually very clean and full of stem cells and nutrients) was the original meaning behind the idea of offering blood (commonly misinterpreted as *sacrifice* nowadays). The first step into this was to return the womb to its innocence and purity (the true meaning of 'virgin', hence Mother Mary's ability to birth a Christed child, as her womb was pure and not attached to any negative karma, trauma, etc). When a woman is able to consciously heal her womb and make space for a loving sacred union relationship, both partners can reach higher states of bliss and connectedness. For more information on this, *Womb Awakening* by Bertrand and Bertrand is highly recommended.

Another key cycle within our physical body is our Circadian Rhythm; a 24-hour internal clock.

The Circadian Rhythm

Like all biorhythms, our Circadian Rhythm influences our physical, mental and behavioural changes throughout the day. Our circadian rhythms are able to remain in-sync with the help of Mother Earth, through interaction with natural light, electrons from the ground and temperature maintenance.

Primarily, the suprachiasmatic nucleus (which lies at the crossing point of the optic nerves coming from the eyes) analyses the light spectrum being sent in from each eye and uses this to reset the body's circadian rhythm using the hormone *melatonin*. As night draws in, melatonin is released into the bloodstream by the pineal gland (a small part of the brain), rising steadily after sunset (triggered by fading light and lower temperature) and continuing to rise until the brain signals that it is time to sleep. At which point, melatonin slowly decreases until light entering the eyes signals the pineal to stop releasing melatonin as it is time to wake up. At this point, the adrenals are signalled to drop some cortisol into the system to stimulate alertness and get us up out of bed. Later, as light levels decrease, the pineal begins to produce melatonin again in preparation for sleep.

As we enter REM sleep (the dreaming, problem-solving state), it is speculated by researchers such as Rick Strassman that another chemical called DMT is released, which allows us to dream. By living within the rhythm of our external environment, our brain automatically times the production of these chemicals, generating our Circadian Rhythm. If we move out of this natural cycle, let's say, to another country with a different time zone, we often feel disorientated. This is due to the fact that the brain has to reorganise itself and alter its production of these chemicals.

Moreover, a hormone in the skin known as solitrol works in conjunction with melatonin to regulate mood, circadian rhythms and seasonal reproduction. Solitrol is produced from UV light and influences many of the body's regulatory centres as well as the immune system. It is for this reason that the apparent 'flu season' (when sickness rates increase) falls during the winter months when we are spending less time outside in the natural light. As with all aspects of health, though, we must listen to our bodies telling us when enough is enough. (If you feel your skin burning, for example, it's probably time to seek some shade!)

And the immune system isn't the only thing improved when in contact with natural light. Getting your daily dose of the full spectrum of light is also shown to improve mood and overall mental health. But the full benefits are listed in Chapter 6. For now, it's safe to know that natural light is essential for every aspect of human health optimisation.

Ways of supporting the body's resonance with natural day/ night cycles includes:

- Being outside as much as possible to keep the pineal updated with the time of day. If you work indoors, then 'light-breaks' throughout the day work, particularly at sun rise and sun set.
- Eating food outside when possible. Any ingested substance must go through a series of chemical reactions that are catalysed by a specific portion of the electromagnetic spectrum. Thus, eating outside where the body is exposed to the entire light spectrum will increase nutrient absorption.

- Wearing blue-light blocking glasses after sunset and when looking at strong blue-light, such as computer screens. (It's also good practice to cover the neck due to the fact that the thyroid is close to the skin here, which plays a key role in hormone regulation.)

- Using incandescent bulbs. These have lower levels of blue light and higher red, which is more natural at sunset. Red bulbs, Himalayan salt lamps and candlelight are also better choices.

- Turning the WiFi off at night and putting your phone on airplane mode to not only lower electro-pollution but to also lower the risk of you being woken by a spam messages!

Electromagnetic Frequencies (EMFs)

As the cells within our bodies communicate with one another through chemical reactions and electricity, and as the pineal is particularly influenced by subtle changes in the body's electromagnetic field, other electromagnetic frequencies (EMFs), such as those emitted from mobile phones, WiFi boxes and power lines, have an extremely negative health influence. Unnatural EMFs stress the body by confusing signals, such as those required for DNA regeneration (resulting in degenerative diseases), programmed cell death (leading to tumour growth) and brain development (hence a possible cause of autism). Most commonly, these frequencies cause the cells within the body to open voltage-gated (electrically influenced) calcium channels. These are channels in the outer membrane of the cell (the plasma) that, when opened up, allow calcium ions to flow into a cell. Even very low levels of different types of EMFs cause the voltage-gated calcium channels (like little doors in the membrane of a cell) to open and allow excess calcium to flow into a cell. This over-dose of calcium within a cell leads to vast biological effects, including cancer, heart failure, autism, the breakdown of the blood-brain-barrier and disrupted nerve-cell communication, to state just a few. It can also lead to the creation of free radicals (unstable atoms which stress the cells of the body).

With regards to the sacred secretion, these electromagnetic frequencies which penetrate through the human organism interrupt the electrical communication between cells, thus interfering with normal nervous system functioning. It also disrupts the magnetic influxes from further cosmic bodies, such as the Moon, by smogging the planet with artificial electromagnetic frequencies.

From the above, it can be seen that the effects of exposure to EMFs not only prevent the natural biorhythmic signalling of the physical and spiritual body, but they also damage DNA and cause health- mayhem along the path. This phenomenon, combined with poor diet and too much blue light during dark hours which confuses hormone secretion, leads to poor sleep quality, lack of healing and irregular nervous system response. All of which commonly manifest as disease and mental illness.

It is true that all living things contain plenty of molecular repair experts within their blood stream to remove these mutations, but these also require energy from our environment, which we are deprived of within the modern world. Smart Meters and 5G (the frequency dispersal of which is increased by LED lights), for example, emit these radioactive waves hundreds of times above the scientifically proven safety limit. [NOTE: Scientifically proven, not government stated]. These not only suppress the immune system and aggravate various parasites and viruses that would normally lie dormant and suppressed, thus manifesting a wide range of illness and disease, but it also scrambles the electromagnetic coding of the body, which can lead to a feeling of disconnectedness. Furthermore, very strong evidence published in an abundance of peer- reviewed journals prove that radiation from dirty electricity and radio waves cause infertility, additional learning needs, heart palpitations, insomnia and even cancer. (The actual list of negative effects is far too long to list here but an understanding of it is paramount to the health of our species and the rest of the planet. For further information on how to shield yourself, please look into the work of Dr. Mercola. He has an abundance of information available, free of charge, on his website, www.mercola.com, and even funds research into protecting the world from EMF radiation.)

There is, however, a naturally generated form of EMF from the Earth known as PEMF (Pulsed Electromagnetic Fields), which is essential for optimal health. PEMF increases ATP (energy) production in mitochondria (tiny organisms in our cells which produce energy for us) and maintains the cellular pH of the body, keeping it at optimal levels of alkalinity. This pulse is referred to as the 'heartbeat' of the planet and is responsible for the connection felt between all living things that ground to it. Therefore, from the tiniest atom to the largest solar system, each layer of the universe is connected electromagnetically. The super-interconnected organism that governs all life on Earth is referred to as Gaia. And Gaia, too, is continuously abiding to the natural, balance-seeking cycles. It is this 'pulse' (heartbeat of the Earth) that is known as the Schumann Resonance.

Schumann Resonance

Frequency is defined as the number of waves (or cycles) that pass a fixed place in a given amount of time. For example, if 50 waves pass through a fixed point in one second, the frequency would be 50 cycles per second, or 50 Hertz. Hertz (or Hz) was coined in the 19th century in honour of German physicist Heinrich Rudolf Hertz, and measures the number of waves, cycles or oscillations per second. In everyday life, brain waves stay within this 1 to 30 Hz window, switching between Delta (1-4 Hz), Theta (4-8 Hz), Alpha (8-12 Hz), Beta (12-40 Hz) and sometimes Gamma (40-100 Hz). [Easily remembered using the acronym: Get Better At Thinking Daily]. Similarly, the Schumann Resonances are a set of low frequency, naturally occurring EMF generated by and excited by lightning discharges within the Earth's ionosphere (a layer surrounding the Earth which is powered by cosmic radiation).

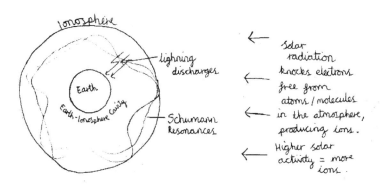

FIGURE 2 – The Schumann Resonance

This 'heartbeat' maintains all life on the planet by allowing for optimal electrical communication between our internal systems and cosmic influxes. Our evolution on this Earth, influenced by such a frequency, is what allows us to connect to the wider consciousness of the planet and universe as a whole. This field isn't constant, though, as it, too, is influenced by cosmic influxes and so typically fluctuates between the primary frequencies (harmonies). These primary frequencies lie between 1 and 30 Hz- the same as the human brain. As living things are tuned to this frequency, it is not surprising, then, that biomagnetic pulsations from the hands can mimic this range that the Earth emits, which is why Reiki and other energy healing practices can be so effective.

Reiki is a term used to describe the divine energy system that resides in all life force. It is the same as chi/ qi and shakti/ prana; they are all simply universal energy. Reiki Healers are those who have learned to channel pure, clean, positive energy for healing purposes whilst protecting themselves from taking on the sick energy, and vice versa. By placing their hands in certain positions, practitioners are able to remove energy blockages from the body, clearing the path for one's energy to move where needed. According to Borang (2000), the essence of Reiki is LOVE because love has no discrimination and no judgement; it just is. In this way, Reiki massage can be seen as a purification process that can even lead to altered states of consciousness as brain waves adapt to the changed and charged energy flow of the body. Because of the healing power of the Schumann resonance, similar results can be obtained from grounding to Mother Earth.

Until a few millennia ago, most humans walked and slept in direct contact with the earth, so were continuously grounded to this global circuit. However, modern insulated shoes and sleeping in buildings with cemented flooring has resulted in most people being electrically isolate from the ground plane, massively disconnecting the body from the mother planet. From the use of plastics, carpets, synthetic soled shoes, cars with rubber tyres and more, we have depleted our body of electrons and become overly charged with unnatural electro-radiation.

During Grounding/ Earthing, a person walks or stands barefoot on the ground (typically dirt in a forest, grass in a field and sand at a beach) or is connecting the body using a conductive apparatus, such as copper-wired shoes. The Earth's surface is electrically conductive and is maintained at a negative potential by solar wind and molten magnetite within the Earth's centre layers, so is abundant in free, life-preserving electrons that will never run short! Thus, when our own bare feet come into contact with the ground, we are able to absorb these negative ions and neutralise free radicals that may have accumulated from, for example, radio wave interference. In this way, the body can use these electrons to optimise overall health. What's more, through Earthing, our electric body is able to equalise with the Earth's natural Pulsed Electromagnetic Field (PEMF), return to synchronicity and maintain its natural, electrical model.

As EMFs can interfere with the natural biorhythms of our physical being, regular grounding is essential for the regulation of these cycles. This transfer stimulates our biological rhythm and resets our circadian cycle to the state of the earth it is exposed to. Hence, Grounding is believed to be helpful when adjusting to a new time zone, curing disease, re-setting the body's natural systems and maintaining healthy mental well-being. Grounding has even been reported to enable previously-paralysed patients to walk again (Ober et al, 2014). [NOTE: As oxygen is one of the best transmitters of energy in the body, thus allowing more energy into each cell, breathing in the clean air of the forest whilst grounding is beneficial for more reasons than one.]

It is necessary, however, for Grounding to be conducted away from strong artificial EMFs such as power lines. This is because electricity is naturally attracted to the earth. Therefore, other nearby EMF sources will use you as an antenna to the ground, which will have the opposite effect to that desired. Personally, I go into the forest behind my house, which has no power lines nearby, and switch my phone onto Airplane Mode and into a Faraday bag. Trees are especially good at blocking damaging frequencies, such as 5G, so ensuring coverage from those is like a protective shield from Mother Earth. In addition, contact with pets who are grounded can also have the same beneficial effects, deeming dog walking beneficial to health for more than just basic fitness!

Whilst thinking about the up-coming rollout of the 5G network which vast numbers of people know to be incredibly detrimental to the health of all living organisms, Magenta Pixie (2019) claims that each human who awakens and raises their vibration provides more collective power to the frequency of the Schumann resonance, thus 'watering-down' the 5G network. This further supports the give-and-take relationship between the macrocosmic Gaia and microcosmic humans as not only does the earth provide us with negative ions to balance our own health, but the human can send out frequencies of empowerment to the ion-rich atmosphere surrounding Gaia which enables her to maintain electromagnetic contact with the rest of the universe.

Geopathic Stress

From the Greek words 'geo' meaning *of the earth* and 'pathos' meaning *suffering*, geopathic can be defined as *the stress generated from the suffering of Earth*. The basic idea is that the resonant energy of the planet affects human health and that problems typically occur when disruptions like underground streams, sewers, water, electric lines, minerals and tectonic faults distort Earth's natal energy. As a result of the electromagnetic pollution from modern technology, the atmospheric layers covering the Earth, enhancing and protecting its individuality and habitability, are altering. Hence, an array of disease is manifesting in all life forms. To prevent collective illness as a result of mass geopathic stress, synchronising one's energy to the Schumann resonances and strengthening each other by raising the collective vibration has never been so essential.

According to David Furlong (2003), by communicating with nature (Gaia) we can use our own thoughts and emotions to empower the planet by offering our own energies. Nature is the living essence of all parts of the web of soul experiences on this planet. Even a simple walk in the countryside, enjoying the sights, smells and sounds, is enough to begin to re-connect and nurture the planet. Furlong claims that, with conscious effort and goodwill, Gaia's past traumas (including those caused by humans) can be healed. Offering the world feelings of peace and tranquillity, as well as visions of health and perfection, begin to shift the balance of energies in favour of regeneration.

Summary

In conclusion, good health is totally dependent on good energy balance and an unhindered flow of energy that follows the path of the meridians. Hundreds of factors can influence and interfere with these systems, thus knowing how to use the electro-magnetic field of energy in order to restore energy flow is paramount. We must become more conscious of the fact that thoughts and vibrations will bring harmony to mind, body and spirit, but can also generate dis-ease in the same way. Through the release of chemical and electrical signals, all of nature's interconnected components interact. Using the sacred secretion, we can increase our biological creation of these chemical signals to act as interspecies and dimensional messengers. As we are conscious beings, instead of automatically reacting to the energetic field around us, that includes the ties and pull of the planets, we can modify our own vibrations and our responses to the vibrations of others, giving us god-like powers without actually trying to become a god. Within our brain, it is the pineal gland that controls the flow of these rhythms.

The sacred secretion is a natural biorhythm. When the Moon's magnetic energy encompasses the electrical energy of the angle of the zodiac belt which encoded our nervous system at birth, the electromagnetic influx from the Earth's ionosphere stimulates the body's endocrine system to re-connect to its spiritual birth-right via the preservation of the sacred oil. This essence, when put to effective use, can increase one's connectedness and sensitivity to other planes of existence by altering our state of awareness.

Top Recommendations

Website: www.biorhythm-calculator.net and www.mercola.com

Book: Biorhythms by Peter West.

Article: Zimecki, M. 2006. *The Lunar Cycle: Effect on human and animal behaviour and physiology.* Postepy Hig Med Dosw. 60:p.1-17.

Podcast: Jennifer Gehl: The return of Planet Sedna. Earth Ancients, 1 June 2019.

Video: Carlson, R. 2018. Cosmic Patterns and Cycles of Catastrophe [YouTube]. Sacred Geometry International.

Bibliography and References

Becker, R. 1998. *The Body Electric.* William Morrow Publisher.

Boland, Y. 2016. *Moonology.* Hay House.

Borang, K. 2000. *Reiki.* Thorsons.

Carlson, R. 2018. Cosmic Patterns and Cycles of Catastrophe [YouTube]. Sacred Geometry International.

DeVries, J. 1989. *Body Energy.* Mainstream Publishing Co.

Furlong, D. 2003. *Working With Earth Energies.* Piatkus.

Gaughan, R. 2017. How Solar Energy Affects the Earth's Atmosphere. *Sciencing.* Available online at: <www.sciencing.com/solar-energy-affects-earths-atomsphere-22463.html>

Leblanc, F. 2008. *Planetary Atmospheric Electricity.* Springer.

Levy, J. *Earthing: 5 Ways It Can Help You Fight Disease.* Dr. Axe. Available online at: <https://draxe.com/health/earthing/>

McTaggart, L. 2001. *The Field.* Harper Collins.

Mercola, J. 2017. *The Harmful Effects of Electromagnetic Fields Explained.* Available online at: <www.mercola.com>

Mousa, Haider Abdul-Lateef. 2016. Health Effects of Alkaline Diet and Water, Reduction of Digestive-tract Bacterial Load, and Earthing. *Alternative Therapies in Health & Medicine.* 22:pp.24-34.

Myers, B. 2013. *PEMF: The 5th Element of Health.* Balboa Press.

NASA. 2013. Impacts of Solar Flares. Available online at: <https://www.nasa.gov/mission_pages/sunearth/news/flare-impacts.html>

Ober, C., Sinatra, S. and Zucker, M. 2014. *Earthing.* Basic Health Publications.

Pixie, M. 2019. *The Black Box Programme and the Rose Gold Flame.* Independently Published.

Rogers, K. Ed. 2011. *The Endocrine System.* Rosen Publishing Group.

Seymour, P. 1988. *Astrology: The Evidence of Science.* Lennard Publishing.

Sutton, N. 2014. What Are Biorhythms? Helping You To Know Yourself. [YouTube] Spiritual-Awakening.Net.

Walker, M. 2018. *Why We Sleep.* Penguin Publishers.

West, P. 1984. *Biorhythms: Your Daily Guide To Achieving Peak Potential.* Thorsons.

Chapter 3

Altered States:

The Body Sleeps & Meditation Helps

As the human brain is trapped within the skull for all of its living days, it requires the use of the senses to navigate its way through life. Through the amalgamation of the senses, the brain is able to adapt and optimise the survival of the whole organism. It is for this reason that if one sense becomes damaged then others strengthen, and also why each person apparently has a dominating sense, which they can use to communicate with higher vibrating spirits. These senses use various techniques in order to read the world. One of these includes the use of circadian rhythms, as discussed in the last chapter. The main purpose of this biorhythm is to enable the whole organism to enter a state of consciousness known as sleep. Evolutionarily, if one was to believe the ideology 'survival of the fittest', being unconscious for such as large chunk of our time seems like a dangerous phenomenon to develop. Consequently, Walker (2018) speculates that sleep must be absolutely paramount to overall survival.

From research, the following has been inferred about the overall purpose of sleep for the physical body:

- For the hippocampus to transfer memories from the short-term reservoir into the long-term context. Walker (2018) discovered that an afternoon nap also refreshed this hippocampus reservoir, thus promoting learning and memory. Therefore, sleep is essential both before learning to make room in the reservoir for new memories, as well as after in order to transfer those memories into long-term learning.

- During deep sleep, the brain removes unwanted memories and tests out different synaptic connections. This is why the "try turning it off and on again" computer hack also works for human beings. During sleep, the brain processes information from the day and, by linking up the appropriate synapses, is able to problem solve. Consequently, good quality sleep is essential when dealing with trauma.

- Sleep boosts the production of human-growth hormone, which is vital for cellular growth and regeneration throughout life. It makes sure that muscles, bones and fat stay in a healthy balance. Hence, sleep has direct anti-aging properties.

- Quality sleep activates the parasympathetic (rest and repair) nervous system. This supports optimal healing and mental wellbeing.

- During sleep brain cells shrink up to 60% so that the brain can flush through cerebrospinal fluid (CSF) in order to get rid of toxins from the central nervous system (CNS). CSF also carries nutrients and chemicals from the blood to various parts of the brain. With such a large influx during sleep, one could speculate a connection between the chemical flush from CSF and dream-states, but more on this later.

- DNA requires adequate sleep to translate their instructional code into materialised action. This is because of stretches of DNA-protein structures (like little protective caps) at the end of each chromosome called 'telomeres'. Telomeres are responsible for limiting cell divisions and also protect chromosomes from deterioration, such as aging. The length of a person's telomeres also determine how long and how well they will live; the longer the telomeres, the more cells can replicate. Thus, shorter sleep = shorter telomeres = shorter life. Interestingly, telomeres can also be grown through meditation. In sum, sleep deprivation alters DNA as a result of shortened telomeres and corresponding cell damage.

- As sleep is the foundation of all other pillars of health, such as diet and exercise, lack of sleep corresponds with low energy levels, motivation and mood, as well as increased sugar cravings, all of which can lead to a cascade of other health issues, such as diabetes and depression. On the contrary, quality sleep allows the body to nurse emotional trauma, aid problem solving and improve creativity, especially the dream state (REM).

In addition to the vast array of physical and psychological health benefits of sleep, the Bible is filled with stories of holy people who came to some kind of revelation during a dream. So what is the spiritual purpose of this state of consciousness?

Carl Jung (1974) believed it was the maturation of the psyche and the development of the 'self' (how you perceive yourself and your place in the world) that connects us to the universe, and that it was dreaming and trance states that contained messages from the 'self' that could be used for personal growth. Jung (1969) also claimed that dreaming is a fragment of psychic activity with an underlying psychological statement, claiming that the unconscious contains everything that is known to be a function of the conscious. Basically, dreaming can be seen as a way of consciously tapping into stored knowledge (both physically and energetically). Saint Germain even claimed that a person can ask to be taken to *soul school* during sleep in order to subliminally connect to the higher forces. From this, one could conclude that quality sleep is not only necessary for optimal health and wellbeing, but also for spiritual advancement.

Whilst sleeping, our brain progresses through a range of brain-wave states, also known as neural oscillations. Such activity is measurable using electroencephalograms (EEG) devices in order to generate a reading of brain oscillations which are measured in Hertz (waves per second). Through practices such as meditation and mindfulness, one can consciously travel through these states of consciousness in order to access the realms available (kind of similar to the movie, Inception). For example, a person can slow their brain waves to a calmer state in order to solve a problem, a practice used by such inventors as Thomas Edison and Aristotle. The stages of alertness/ sleep include:

GAMMA – Peak Performance

These oscillations can read high-frequencies of 30-100 Hertz. Neuroscientists believe that gamma waves are able to link all parts of the brain, providing clarity and high levels of cognitive functioning. Interestingly, meditation has also been shown to increase brain oscillations to a state of Gamma. According to David Dobbs (2005), researchers at the University of Wisconsin-Madison found that Zen Buddhist monks reached Gamma brain rhythms during meditation, which the researchers claim is associated with robust brain function. Gamma brain waves are particularly fascinating as the oscillations produced at such a frequency is surprisingly similar to those recorded of people on DMT.

BETA - The Waking State

This pattern follows a Beta rhythm of around 12-40 Hertz (Hz). Beta waves allow us to focus, problem solve and complete tasks easily. It is the common frequency of music listened to during times of high concentration, such as studying. The higher waves of Beta use a lot of energy, however, so can manifest as stress in the long term. It is for this reason that taking time out within the day to meditate and be calm is so beneficial (maybe even an afternoon nap!)

ALPHA - The Relaxed State

As a person becomes increasingly drowsy, their brain waves slow to around 8-12 Hz, referred to as the Alpha rhythm. At around the age of 7, when children become less susceptible, their growing brains start to function at the higher Alpha state and they begin to develop a sense of 'self' (an understanding that they are distinct from others). Using Alpha waves, we can open the bridge between the conscious and unconscious mind as the voice of intuition is said to be heard during the Alpha state. Interestingly, the gemstone Tourmaline radiates alpha waves, thus is often used to reduce anxiety.

THETA - Sleep Stage 1/ Drowsy State

A state of Theta (4-8 Hz) is often involved in daydreaming and the lighter stages of sleep. Theta is the lowest frequency human consciousness can reach before deep sleep. Whilst in a Theta state, the intuitive and creative parts of the brain become more active. It can therefore be seen that this level of awareness allows for a stronger connection between the physical brain and higher planes as it makes an individual more open to the flow of ideas from both their subconscious mind (suppressed thoughts and ideas) and spiritual energy within the universe. Hence, whilst in this state, it is not uncommon to receive 'messages' or 'guidance'.

The Theta state is known as the 'suggestible wave' by psychologists because of its prevalence when in a trance or hypnotic state. We naturally experience a Theta state just before bed and just before waking up, making these optimal times for our visualisations to be better accepted by the subconscious mind. As mentioned previously, this state can also be accessed during deep meditation. For this reason, many people find it can be useful to meditate with the intention of solving a particular problem, if you have one.

An interesting note to make here is that, during the first few years of life, the brain is predominately in the Theta state, hence why fantasy and reality are often entangled at this time.

DELTA - Sleep Stage 2/ Sleeping

Here, the slowest recorded brain waves are measured (referred to as 'slow-wave-sleep'). Delta rhythms, oscillating at 1-4 Hz, are typically observed during the deeper stages of sleep (or extremely deep meditation) when the body is healing most efficiently. The brain is not able to produce dream-stories at this point as all focus is on healing. Intriguingly, the brain is at the slowest Delta frequency within the womb and first months of life as so much growing and adapting is necessary, which is why babies sleep a lot!

Rapid Eye Movement State (REM)

Patterns recorded during this phase of sleep are similar to those of a waking EEG scan. It takes around an hour for the brain to reach deep, slow-wave-sleep, then another 45 minutes for it to reach REM. During this phase, the brain is more active, simulating Theta and Beta oscillations, but the rest of the body is paralysed. Oxygen use by the brain is tremendous during REM- greater than during the waking state- which could contribute to the production of DMT (note this for later).

REM is believed to be the state of consciousness in which we dream. In REM sleep, brain energy exceeds energy-use in typical waking states. If so much energy is used during this state of consciousness, its purpose must go beyond the basic rest and repair. Moreover, during REM, neural activity is seen to originate from the brainstem (which feeds into the 'Tomb of Christ', discussed in Chapter 11). From this, one could speculate the dream-state's role in allowing possible astral travel between dimensions and access to both higher states of awareness and the subconscious.

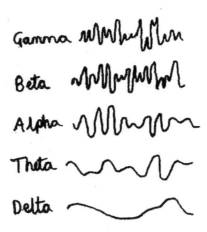

FIGURE 3 – Brain Wave Oscillations

Sleep Supplements

As quality sleep is so critical for all areas of health and optimal physical and spiritual functioning, there is a lot of research being conducted at the moment on how to improve sleep quality, particularly by Dr Michael Van (2019). From this area of research, the following sleep supplements are recommended:

- Magnesium- magnesium deficiency impairs sleep and melatonin production because magnesium activates parasympathetic and GABA receptors in the brain. Basically, magnesium changes physiology and calms mood, which promotes better sleep quality.
- L'Theanine - an amino acid found in green tea that crosses the blood-brain barrier and supports melatonin production. It also increases alpha brain waves whilst awake and encourages the feeling of alertness without the anxiety.
- Valerian Root- a medicinal herb which contains GABA pre-cursors, thus reducing excitability of the nervous system and enabling deeper sleep.
- Ashwagandha- an adaptogenic herb to reduce anxiety and lower cortisol.
- Melatonin- to enhance sleep quality and quantity.
- Typtophan- the precursor to melatonin, serotonin and DMT. This helps you fall asleep quicker and stay asleep, as well as stabilising mood.
- Taurine- inhibits excitability of the brain and stimulates growth of new brain cells.

Finding a good, organic supplement sourced as locally and fairly as possible is key, however, to ensure minimal contamination toxins. Other bio-hacks for optimising sleep quality include turning off all electro-interferences such as Wi-Fi, cooling the body before bed, not using artificial lighting or phones (or at least applying a red-light filter if you do), consuming foods high in tryptophan (such as raisins [not coated in sunflower oil!]) which is also a precursor to serotonin, exercising earlier in the day (particularly strength exercising as the body will force itself into a deeper sleep after in order to aid repair), as well as activities that calm brain waves, such as meditation, controlled breathing and listening to binaural beats (on airplane mode to prevent EMF interference) later on in the day.

Clearly, getting adequate sleep is necessary for providing an environment in which the internal body is able to repair and regenerate. It also gives the mind time to process information from the day and store memories into the long-term bank. With regards to the sacred secretion, it is important to keep the brain at slower wave-states in order to reduce cortisol production and allow the body time to rest. Like Christ in the tomb conserving his power, the days of preservation are a time for focused attention and rejuvenation. Meditating as much as possible is key not only for calming the mind into a slower state of consciousness so that it is in a better position to connect and develop intuitively, but also to increase oxytocin (the love hormone) levels that will keep the internal Christ saved as well as allowing for better overall communication with the body through the power of visualisation.

Visualisation

Visualisation is the act of imagining future desires. It is a process put into practice by many professionals and successful inventors, such as Einstein and Tesla. For best results when visualising, Dispenza (2017) advocates using all of your senses to make the image as real as possible. The brain then releases corresponding chemicals into the blood, which relate to appropriate glands and energy centres, thus emitting the related aura (energy field) that will attract likewise energies, including that of which is being visualised. This is how the phenomenon known as the Law of Attraction works (detailed in Chapter 7).

Though visualisation is not always easy as the brain naturally wanders, it is through use of a developed imagination that creativity spikes in the human mind, allowing the brain to become more alert and receptive to outside vibrations. Even Einstein said that his greatest discovery was that imagination is more powerful than knowledge because that was the source of all his discoveries. In science, this is known as Gedanken Experiments; experiments of pure thought. Consequently, every scientist, really, is just a person with an exceptional imagination. They are visualisers. Yet, when asked how it felt to be the smartest man alive, Einstein said, "I don't know. You'll have to ask Nikola Tesla."

Now, Nikola Tesla tends to be at the root of every technological invention we have at hand today. The young Tesla discovered AC current, which does produce EMFs that are bad for our health, but the older, wiser Tesla was focussed on free, unlimited and renewable energy naturally sourced sustainably from Mother Earth, without cell-damaging EMFs. Obviously, such projects were not funded as there was little profit to be made. Thus, Tesla's work remains unfinished. The reason I have mentioned Nikola Tesla in this section is because he was a huge advocate for visualisation. Before every invention, he would visualise it in his head, first. He would visualise overcoming any difficulties and arriving at completion. Only when he had perfected an invention in his mind would he go ahead and act upon it in reality, consistently working towards the greater good for mankind and the Earth, regardless of any negative views of others. He knew how to use his mental power and went ahead to say: "The practical success of the idea, regardless of its inherent advantages, depends on the attitude of the people. If it suits the time, it is accepted... Let the future tell the truth... The present is theirs; the future, for which I have really worked, is mine."

Therefore, an important point to make here is to not concern yourself with *how* it will happen. Focus on the outcome. You don't need to visualise money for a holiday, just visualise the holiday and the universe will bring it to you in the quickest, most efficient way, abiding by the natural laws of physics. In the words of Tesla: "Nature may reach the same results in many ways."

Everybody visualises, whether they know it or not, so a key aspect of the Law of Attraction is training your mind to visualise consciously and repeatedly until a desire becomes subconscious and is constantly released through your aura energy field, in turn, attracting likewise energies. Visualisation can be happening at any time in any place, but I would suggest making amendments to your daily routine for a specific ten-minute slot at least two, even three times a day. The visualisation process works best during the theta frequency, so putting this into practice within meditation or just before bed when the body is relaxed and the mind is calm and ready to receive messages from the universe, is effective. The reason visualisation works so well is because the subconscious mind does not have the ability to tell the difference between physical-reality and imagined-reality. As a result, using all senses to imagine a desired reality literally imprints that vision into the long-term memories and DNA (through epigenetics), thus altering one's energy and perception.

There are countless studies on sports people who have split into groups to either physically train for a game or mentally, which have shown that those who mentally train exceed (Jacqueline and Ungerlerider, 1991; Liggett and Homada, 1993). Furthermore, there is story upon story of injured people who have been told that they will never walk again or survive an incurable disease but, through the power of imagination, have gone on to live thriving lives (Chopra, 1989; Wise, 1995).

The reason, however, that there can be so many different interpretations and outcomes to the same event is often due to one's past experiences, which form foundations within the subconscious. This is summed up by Murphy (2008), who states that different people will react in different ways to the same suggestion because they have different subconscious conditioning (beliefs). When the subconscious mind is full of negative programming, it's impossible to stay in a positive frame of mind, unless this is changed at a subconscious level. All of our present habits, mannerisms and thought patterns are the result of past subconscious programming from a variety of sources. This programming can either propel us into success or plummet us down to rock bottom.

Although there are many ways of tackling these inner demons, such as counselling, Neurolinguistic Programming (NLP) and hypnosis, plant medicine in the form of psychedelics is a route typically taken by rainforest shaman. Of the many plant medicines that are still put into practice to this day, Ayahuasca, a DMT brew, is the most popular within the mainstream. This purge-prompting concoction is repeatedly reported to aid the process of physical, psychological and spiritual healing by allowing the consumer to reach altered states of consciousness, whereby the subconscious mind and various 'spirits/ aliens' are able to be heard by the conscious.

Drug- Induced States of Consciousness

McKenna's (1992) book, *Food of the Gods*, although touches base with almost all known consciousness-altering compounds (such as LSD) seems to particularly favour the use of tryptamines. The tryptamine hallucinogens, especially DMT, psilocin and psilocybin, are found throughout the higher plant families. Psilocin and psilocybin occur predominately in mushrooms, and DMT in most living things, even within the human body. Psilocybin specifically activates the areas of the brain concerned with processing signals and communication. In this way, the body is able to more freely express itself, which McKenna (1992) speculates to have opened the doors for language in our early evolution. McKenna (1992) further supports this claim by explaining how a common occurrence with psilocybin is spontaneous poetry and other vocal activity, such as speaking different languages, as a result of increased neural firing and sensory hallucination.

The English word 'hallucination' derives from the Latin verb 'hallucinari', meaning 'to wander in the mind'. Hallucinogenic experiences, often generated by consumption of external compounds, tend to occur as a result of altered brain waves. Interestingly, a recent study by Timmermann et al (2019) found that, whilst exogenously consumed DMT shares psilocybin and LSD's psychoactive traits, it does something very different to the user's brain. The researchers have likened human brainwaves of DMT to those of a dream-state (theta) and claimed that further research into this could yield important insights into the relationship between brain activity and consciousness. A previous study by Griffiths et al (2017) even showed that the psychological benefits of these mystical experiences were further enhanced when meditation was also practised.

The Matrix

'Matrix' is a term used to describe something within something else, or from which something else originates. To most people, the word usually spikes the thought of intelligent machines, long black coats and awesome martial arts. Although the movie *The Matrix* is deemed fiction, the more one delves into the science of consciousness and psychedelics, the more such films resonate as truth. An aspect of this ideology which is increasing in advocation over recent years is that of the Universal Time Matrix; or dimension timelines.

The Universal Time Matrix is said to be a mathematical program in which the consciousness expresses time and matter. Like an avatar can up-level in a game simulation, so is one said to be able to upgrade and shift into the higher dimensions of consciousness within this human form. The lower dimensions of being are 1D and 2D consciousness, which are limited to the lower, vegetation level of awareness. For humans, the main timelines are 3D, 4D and 5D.

3D Consciousness – The Material State

Here, a person feels like a separate individual from others and identifies themselves by physical things, such as their appearance. Fulfilment is found in making money and increasing social status as everything is viewed as either good or bad. A person whose consciousness is limited within the 3D will probably deem themselves as a 'realist' and be happy to follow the roles within 'survival of the fittest'. Although this may seem like a *lower* state of consciousness, part of the ascension process is being able to let others wake up in their own time. The fact that you have chosen to delve into this book is a pretty good sign that you are in the 4D state, but it is important to remember that this doesn't make you a *higher* being. One of the most difficult challenges to overcome when awakening is to let others be. Trying to anchor them into a timeline that they are not yet ready for on their soul journey will just cause friction. Be aware of all that is happening and be the guide if others want it. But if they do not, let them be. They need to take this journey.

4D – The Dream State

Within 4D consciousness, a person is beginning to awaken to the idea of there being more to life than material things. Thoughts become more powerful and one begins to shift away from perceived reality. There is a strong desire to find purpose in life and seek deeper meanings to existence. Those of 4D consciousness are beginning to develop their intuition and likely feel called to experiment with psychedelics as a means of attempting to answer their questions. At the very least, they are seeing synchronicities as their frequency changes. This is where most of us are. It's a lovely place to be as we can observe all worlds and still be grateful for all of the learning and lessons along the way.

5D- The Awakened State

Although people tend to shift between these three primary states of human consciousness, once a person is predominately in the 5D, it is very difficult to slip back into 3D because their body is so full of love and light. Once awareness has shifted into 5D, there is no more individuality; we are all one and we are all connected. Life becomes an adventure for growth and there no longer are such perceptions as 'good' and 'bad'. Instead, a 5D human will have a higher awareness and see that there is a higher purpose to all things. Life becomes full of lessons, with an understanding that this human experience is for spiritual growth and joy. Love, compassion and gratitude become a person's true sovereignty. Even death is a choice within this realm and beyond.

5D is also considered the dimension of light and information due to the fact that, here, a soul within a human avatar is able to access information from source energy and connect with others telepathically. Unsurprisingly, it is within the 5D world that one is said to be able to access information from other light beings and parallel worlds, such as extra-terrestrials and fairies. Personally, I believe that DMT allows us to take a peak into this state of consciousness by increasing the levels of inner light within our physical body, but more on that later.

As we move through the year of 2020, more and more people are going to awaken to their true divine power as they develop their *2020 vision* and begin to *see* more clearly. There are a lot of prophetic writings regarding the spiritual significance of the year 2020 which is beyond the scope of this book alone. The YouTube channel of Magenta Pixie is particularly effective at explaining these philosophies. Interestingly, Magenta Pixie states that we are able to manifest the timeline we want. It's like the Law of Attraction but on a more powerful scale beyond materialism. As humans themselves are energy generators, when enough of the collective consciousness fractalises into 5D awareness, the whole of Gaia will also shift. It is in this way that many spiritual gurus believe we can literally change the course of time and manifest the timeline we want. That is, regardless of whatever fear mongering is displayed over the news and media, we must each meditate and pray for unity and the best outcome for the planet, working for the highest good. Just simply sending out thoughts of happiness and relief at regular intervals into the Universal Time Matrix can alter the emotional frequency of the collective and move a person further into a 5D timeline.

Beyond 5D and into 6D and 7D, it is said that energy can teleport and even time travel. Within these states, time is not linear and distance cannot be measured. Consciousness, here, is part of the non-physical; the spirit realm. Only pure, unconditional love and unity can be felt. There is no judgement, no fear and no pain. Consciousness at this level can choose to come back down into the physical dimensions in order to FEEL the array of emotions that humans can elicit. This is why a human cannot go through life always in peace and seeking eternal happiness. It just doesn't exist within this realm of awareness. If your soul incarnated within human form, it wanted to feel these emotions. So the next time you wake up feeling irritable, don't blame yourself and get angrier that you are unable to snap out of it. Instead, embrace it, recognise it and love it, knowing that it, too, will pass.

Moving into 8D, 9D and 10D, it is believed that our energy is able to return to Source, merge with other soul groups and even travel to distant galaxies and incarnate within these. Finally, 11D and 12D consciousness are said to be of true GOD frequency. However, this frequency is so high that it is extremely difficult for human consciousness to even begin to comprehend it. Hence the need for stories and symbols as an attempt to make such abstract concepts more accessible.

In sum, as a soul moves through the dimensions of consciousness, they build up their spiritual sovereignty; or *treasures in heaven*, as the Bible states. The sacred secretion is a way of allowing access into this 5D realm by way of biochemically producing the spirit molecule: *DMT*. This substance puts the physical body in a state of ease and healing, as well as raising the corresponding spiritual vibration. By preserving the sacred secretion and increasing our connection with both our inner light and outer connectedness, we can actively shift our consciousness into the 5D.

Researcher John Chavez hypothesises that DMT (a psychedelic compound discussed in Chapter 12) and serotonin are equals but for different aspects of this matrix reality. By seeing serotonin as the daytime modulator (like a butterfly) and DMT as the night time consciousness modulator (like a moth), both compounds can be seen as reality regulators, depending on the time of day (and the effectiveness of the pineal gland). In this way, DMT can be seen as a portal to other realms of consciousness or a key that opens the stargates to dream school.

Humans are intrigued by dreams for a reason, and it is speculated that the release of DMT at night once allowed awakened humans to attend other realms during their sleep and learn lessons which they could bring back with them into this physical reality during the day in order to navigate along their chosen life path (like pausing a video game to check the manual). By doing this, we are able to identify and heal trauma and past life karma whilst gaining the knowledge and DNA awakening (AKA light codes- discussed in Chapter 5) that would enable us to get the most out of this physical existence.

Therefore, sleep is not only physically regenerating but is also spiritually enlightening. Unfortunately, materialism and a collective anchoring into the 3D caused a loss of ability to decode and remember such dreams. This seems particularly evident when one refers back to earlier parts of this chapter where shifts in brain wave oscillations throughout childhood were contemplated. On a positive note, the mass awakening of human consciousness is supporting the manifestation of a shift in the Earth's frequency as it, too, anchors into the 5D. As the Earth and its beings facilitate within a give-and-take reciprocal relationship, we are also remembering our potential and awakening to this new level of consciousness.

Summary

'State of consciousness' is used to describe the level of one's awareness within the physical world. Alterations in brain waves can provide a person with the ability to perceive different frequencies. It is for this reason that people often describe moments of enlightenment during meditation, sleep and breathwork. As a result of chemical precursors in a range of Gaia-grown foods, the things one ingests can affect the chemical composition of the body. Unsurprisingly, the foods consumed have a direct impact on brain waves and states of consciousness, thus connectedness and spiritual experience. Consequently, dietary choices can be seen as paramount to the successful preservation of the Christos, which is where we turn out attention to next.

Top Recommendations

Website: www.drmichaelvan.com and www.foreverconscious.com

Book: Why We Sleep by Matthew Walker

Article: Hamil, J., Hallack, J. and Baker, G. 2019. Ayahuaska: Psychological and Physiologic Effects, Pharmacology and Potential Uses in Addiction and Mental Illness. 17(2):pp.108-128. *Current Neuropharmacology.*

Podcast: The Science Of Optimal Human Performance by Dr Michal Van

Video: Dr Mercola's Tips on Getting a Good Night's Sleep, available on YouTube (and the Mercola channel, in general)

For information on the 3D to 5D consciousness shift, I would recommend looking into the work of Lorie Ladd and Magenta Pixie, both of whom are in contact with other higher dimensional light beings.

Bibliography and References

Banks et al. 2017. Telomere length and salivary DNA methylation after 48 hours of sleep deprivation. *Journal of Sleep Research.* 26(S1): p.11.

Campbell, D. 2001. *The Mozart Effect: Tapping the power of music to heal the body, strengthen the mind and unlock creative spirit.* William Morrow And Company.

Chopra, D. 1989. *Quantum healing: exploring the frontiers of mind/ body medicine.* Bantam.

Dispenza, J. 2017. *Becoming Supernatural.* Hay House.

Dobbs, D. 2005. Zen Gamma. Available online at: www.scientificamerican.com

Geyer, C. 2019. Telomeres: Are they the Fountain of Youth, or markers for the benefits of living well? *Journal on Active Aging.* 18(2):p.26-32.

Gottschall, J. 2012. *The storytelling animal: how stories make us human.* Mariner Books.

Griffiths, R. et al. 2017. Psilocybin-occasioned mystical-type experience in combination with meditation and other spiritual practices produces enduring positive changes in psychological functioning and in trait measures of prosocial attitudes and behaviors. *32(1):pp.49-69.* Journal of Psychopharmacology.

Hamil, J., Hallack, J. and Baker, G. 2019. Ayahuaska: Psychological and Physiologic Effects, Pharmacology and Potential Uses in Addiction and Mental Illness. 17(2):pp.108-128. *Current Neuropharmacology.*

Horowitz, L. 2011. *The book of 528: prosperity key of love.* Tetrahedron Publishing Group.

Hunter, C. 2010. *The art of hypnosis.* Crown House Publishing.

Jacqueline, M. and Ungerlerider, S. 1991. *Mental practice among Olympic athletes.* Golding First.

Jung, C. 1960. *The Structure and Dynamics of the Psyche.* 2nd Ed. Routledge.

Jung, C. 1969. *On The Nature Of The Psyche.* Ark Paperbacks.

Jung, C. 1974. *Dreams.* Princeton University Press.

Kolb, B., Whishaw, I. ad Teskey, G. 2016. *An Introduction to Brain and Behavior.* 5th Ed. Macmillan Education.

Liggett, D. and Homada, S. 1993. Enhancing visualization of gymnasts. *The American Journal Of Clinical Hypnosis.* 35(3):p.190-197.

Marieb, E. and Hoehn, K. 2013. *Human Anatomy and Physiology.* 9th Ed. Pearson Education.

Mayor, S. 2009. Unravelling the Secrets of Aging. *British Medical Journal.* 338:a3024.

Murphy, J. 2008. *The power of your subconscious mind.* BN

Penagos, Hector, Carmen Varela, and Matthew A Wilson. Oscillations, Neural Computations and Learning during Wake and Sleep. 44:pp.193-201. *Current Opinion in Neurobiology.*

Rabinowitch, T. 2013. Long term musical group interaction has a positive influence on empathy in children. *Psychology Of Music.* 41(4):p.484-498.

Tanaaz. *Understanding the 3 States of Consciousness: 3D, 4D and 5D.* Available online at: <www.foreverconscious.com>

Timmermann, C., et al. 2019. Neural Correlates of the DMT Experience Assessed with Multivariate EEG. *9:a16324.* Nature.

Walker, M. 2018. *Why We Sleep.* Penguin, London.

Williams, M. and Penman, D. 2011. *Mindfulness: Finding peace in a frantic world.* Piatkus.

Wise, A. 1995. *The high performance mind: mastering brainwaves for insight, healing and creativity.* GP Putnam's Sons.

Van, M. 2019. Deep Sleep Optimization (parts one to five). Available online at: <https://www.drmichaelvan.com/category/sleep-optimization/>

Chapter 4
Nutrition:

To Eat or Not To Eat

We are happy, sleepy, alert, depressed and even aroused based on what we eat. Therefore, one of the biggest controversies surrounding the preservation of the sacred secretion is what to put into the body! Considering that about 80% of the proteins in CSF are derived from the blood, which has a direct link to the nutritional value of the foods we consume, our dietary choices are paramount. This is especially important as what we put into our body, both physically and emotionally, tells our brain what the world is like and how it should respond. Interestingly, in Greek mythology, Hygeia (the goddess of health) is depicted holding a bowl, from which she feeds a serpent (the significance of which is discussed in Chapter 8). Nowadays, the symbol of Hygeia's Bowl is a sign of medical learning, which is rather sad considering how few doctors advocate diet change over medicalisation.

The gut is commonly referred to as the body's second brain due to the vast connections it has to the first brain, informing this about the environment and how it needs to respond. Predominately, communication between these two organs use the endocrine system (hormones), nervous system (neurotransmitters) and the immune system (cytokines). In short, digestion is the process of breaking down food into nutrients that can be used by cells, tissues and organs within the body. In order to use the nutrients from our food properly, the digestive system breaks these down and directs them to the areas they are needed via, for example, the lipid cycle. Unhealthy eating habits, such as eating too much food or highly-processed meats, causes impaired digestion and can have a damaging effect on the balance of the body.

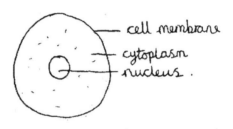

FIGURE 4 – The Cell

Cell membranes are the brain of the cell, which are primarily made of fats; the cytoplasm, though, is full of intracellular fluid which contains a range of organelles and proteins. It is for these reasons that a whole, balanced diet is always recommended. But what does that look like?

Mitochondria and Free Radicals

Mitochondria are tiny organelles contained within nearly all cells which account for around 10% of your body weight. One of their many essential roles includes producing energy by combining nutrients from what you eat with oxygen from the air you breathe (a process referred to as 'oxidative phosphorylation'). The energy molecules the mitochondria produce are called adenosine triphosphate (or ATP, for short). Mitochondria produce energy using the electron transport chain (a series of chemical reactions, basically). These reactions use electrons liberated from food you eat and protons contained within the cycle to produce energy and keep the process rolling. At the end of the chain, electrons react with oxygen to form water.

From this chain, a percentage of electrons tend to leak out and form what is called 'reactive oxygen species' (ROS). ROS molecules contain oxygen atoms with impaired electrons, making them unstable. These highly reactive atoms form potentially destructive free radicals. Free radicals react with other molecules in what are known as *oxidation reaction* in order to neutralise their unstable electrical charge. Like trying to get a horde of squirrels to share one nut, this rapidly expanding number of free radicals collects within the cell and degrades mitochondrial membranes, causing them to disintegrate. This also damages DNA by disrupting its replication, altering structure and interfering with cell maintenance activities. As mitochondria are also involved within apoptosis (programmed cell death) as well as autophagy and mitophagy, which clear out unhealthy cells, it is important to absorb anti-oxidants (through diet and grounding) to stabilise these free radicals. That said, most free radicals are accumulated from the environment by EMF exposure and toxic dietary choices, such as processed foods. Hence, minimising the consumption of these is essential.

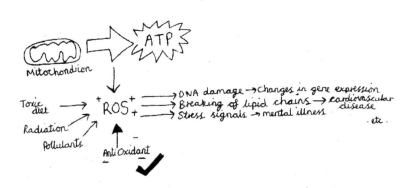

FIGURE 5 – ROS Chaos

These free radicals can cause further damage within the lipid cycle. Using the lipid cycle, cells are able to order the nutrients they need. First, the intestines coat the nutrient particles into lipoproteins. These circulate in the blood until fished out by a cell who has sent a signal out for it. However, free radicals can damage these by making the lipoproteins unreadable. These then float in the blood until, eventually, clogging the arteries. So no, fat does not clog your arteries; processed free-radical- rich fats do. According to Mercola (2017), the heart has more than 5000 mitochondria per cell, making it the most energy dense tissue in the body. This is particularly interesting considering that the heart is the centre of the human electro-magnetic field and was highly valued by the Ancient Egyptians. Mitochondria are also the foundation of the midi-chlorians which allowed Jedi's to feel the force. So which diet is best for our force-feeling powerhouses?

Ketogenic

The ketogenic diet is a high fat, moderate protein and low carbohydrate diet which prompts the production of a fuel known as ketones, which produce far fewer ROS and secondary free radicals compared to carbohydrate and sugar fuels. Ketones is the title given to 3 water-soluble compounds that are synthesised from the breakdown of fatty acids in the liver. These ketones are a source of energy in themselves and are the preferred fuel source of the brain and heart due to these organs requiring so much energy to function.

This promotion of 'fat for fuel' has taken its time in becoming mainstream as a result of a half-century long global fear of fat, which began in the 1950s when Ancel Keys went to Europe in search of the cause of heart disease. From all of the countries he reviewed, Keys cherry-picked 7 of them and generated the claim that saturated fats lead to heart disease (without any recognition of other factors such as processed foods and sugar consumption). Although no scientific data has ever proven Keys' theory, the claim made it mainstream and has contributed to the very sick nation we have today. In fact, saturated fats have been shown to provide the building blocks for cell membranes and hormones and is the optimal fuel for brain function and mitochondrial health.

Now, I know that arguments against meat consumption include cows creating methane, thus contributing to global warming, but what most of us have not been told is that it is the mass farming of cows that are fed soya and corn that is contributing to CO2 build up. In fact, carbon in cows is neutralised by the grass they consume. Therefore, pasture-raised, grass-fed and grass-finished cows likely do not contribute much to global warming due to the carbon being consumed alongside the grass neutralising methane within their digestive tract. What's more, the soya and grains fed to farmed cows is often grown unsustainably, contributing to vast acres of rainforest land being destroyed and increased pesticide levels in our atmosphere. Hence, it is the production of conventional meat that is one of the biggest contributors to global warming, not the animals themselves.

As it states within Proverbs 12:10, *"A righteous man regards the life of his animal."* Ergo, if one makes the decision to consume animal products, then considerations must be made regarding the morality of that animal's life. Miserable, abused animals pumped with toxic foods and hormones will not optimise your health and spirit. After all, we all know how much more upsetting it tends to be when watching a movie and an animal dies compared with another human. And that's because we are the keepers of the animals; their guardians. So when they die unnecessarily, it's like a failure within ourselves for not doing more to keep them safe. With that in mind, you wouldn't stand for seeing someone abuse an animal in the street, so it's important not to be a hypocrite and encourage the same abuse behind the scenes. Ignorance is not bliss, it's karmatic. Should you choose to consume animal products, or should your physical body require the nutrients of such, try to do so with as much compassion as you can.

Although far more challenging, keto can be achieved on a plant-based diet. My personal favourite fats include coconut oil (which raises good cholesterol and boosts brain function, to name a couple of the dozens of benefits), olive oil (an anti-oxidant power house that offers bone and heart protection as well as being anti-inflammatory and antiaging) and avocados (nutritionally rich and proven to be one of the safest commercial crops to consume non-organic).

Furthermore, as cancer cells are believed to thrive on carbohydrates and sugar, the keto-diet literally starves these unwanted cells. However, it is the right types of fat that are essential. Most saturated fats are fine-they're typically just fat molecules saturated with hydrogen atoms, making them less likely to become oxidised and form free radicals. Trans fats (such as margarine), though, which many food companies camouflage as saturated fats on their packaging, are in fact *plastic* fats. When your cells rebuild themselves out of these, they're literally suffocating in cellophane-like matter. So some common sense is required here when recognising the difference between whole- foods and processed '*foods*'.

Note, though, that although the conventional keto-diet states low vegetable intake, Dr Josh Axe (2019) advocates a keto diet high in green veggies in order to keep the body at a normal pH and to ensure sustainable consumption of macro- and micro-nutrients.

Atkins

The Atkins diet pushed its way through the 'fat-is-bad' gossip and came out of the other side still fighting strong (and burning pounds). This is a weight-loss programme devised by Robert Atkins which is a high-fat, high-protein, low-carb approach similar to the Ketogenic diet. The main difference is that Atkins promotes high-protein whereas Keto only suggests moderate protein (due to the fact that the human body, when low on sugar, tends to convert protein into sugar). Another key difference is that the original Atkins plan encouraged the consumption of vegetable oils, whereas the ketogenic has apparently always been built upon the promotion of healthy fats.

Both diets share very similar benefits, with the effectiveness being dependent on your personal body-type, which will be discussed later. However, Carolyne Dean (2017) does claims that magnesium is required to digest a high protein diet as more stomach acid is needed to digest protein, and the body uses magnesium to create more stomach acid. So a supplement should be considered if the diet does not accommodate for this.

The largest argument against the Ketogenic and Atkins diet is that they typically involve the consumption of large quantities of meat in order to keep fat and protein high, which is different to the plant-based diet most of our 'cousins' (apes, etc) consume. However, according to Richard Wrangham (2010), the use of fire to cook our food, particularly meat, is the reason behind human intelligence and our evolution away from tree-dwellers. Wrangham claims that the timing of our ancestors beginning to use fire to cook correlates with the evolutionary adaptations of our digestive system and increased brain capacity, caused by the increased availability of nutrients in food, easier digestion and more energy available for brain use, hence becoming smarter. Wrangham promotes an omnivore diet due to the fact that hunters would not have always been successful in catching meat, in which case it would have been the gathered fruits and vegetables which fed them that day. As the foods consumed by our ancestors would have been completely location and season dependent, there would have naturally been spells of no meat availability.

Vegan

Within the Bible, *Daniel 1:12* shows that Daniel and his friends, who lived on a vegetarian diet, were fitter that those who ate meat. Morally, vegans and vegetarians tend to report feeling happier and more connected by not eating animals, claiming to eat 'life' rather than 'death'. Veganism, in particular, is becoming increasingly popular due to concerns over animal welfare and planet Earth. It is a plant-based diet that is void of any animal products. Due to being high in fruit and vegetables, this diet tends to be vitamin rich and high in anti-oxidants, which prevents free radical damage, thus lowering risk of age-related problems such as high blood pressure and heart disease. Interestingly, a study by Pimentel and Pimentel (2003) even concluded that a plant-based diet was more sustainable for the environment than a meat-based one. In addition, when transitioning from a previously toxic lifestyle as a result of processed foods or commercial meat, a vegan diet can lower inflammation, reduce the risk of heart disease and obesity, increase

107

fibre intake and protect against diabetes (Satija et al, 2017; Tuso, Stoll and William, 2015; Mishra et al, 2013).

It should be noted, though, that a key problem with vegan diets is that they tend to be high in carbs and sugar. This can be detrimental because when you eat carbs and sugar your pancreas secretes insulin. The more insulin you have in your blood, the more signals your body gets to store fat. What's more, research tends to argue that the lack of essential fatty acids, such as fish oils, which are typical of a standard vegan diet, can contribute to cognitive impairment and depression. Additionally, many vegans often opt for soya-based products as substitutes for meat, but the vast majority of soya products are GMO and heavy in aluminium, which is directly linked to an array of degenerative diseases, typically of the brain, as well as contributing to mass rainforest deforestation.

From this, I do not want it to come across as though I'm pro-meat eating. In fact, I made the choice some years ago to become vegan myself, so that is definitely not the case. Instead, it is for this reason that I have more of an understanding of the research surrounding this dietary choice as it was of personal interest to me on my journey. Therefore, I felt that I needed to make it clear that I am no angry-vegan trying to push a plant-based diet onto anybody, as is akin to the current stigmatism. If there is one thing I have learned from all of my research and personal experience, it is that however good one person can feel on a particular diet, genetically, there is no one-diet-fits all, and some body types are just not adapted to veganism, just like some aren't to meat eating or dairy.

We are all unique, and that is a beautiful thing. If you feel so inclined to try giving up meat but you're not sure which diet choice will work for you, there are a number of other variations to the standard vegan diet that can be adopted within modern society. These include raw-vegan (only raw, uncooked vegan foods are eaten), pescatarian (vegetarians who eat fish), ovo-vegetarians (vegans that eat eggs), lacto-vegetarians (in contrast to ovo-vegetarians, lacto-vegetarians consume dairy but not eggs) and so on. Fruitarian (eating only fruit) is the most guilt-free diet when sourced locally and organically as the fruit seems to be the only form of food that actually *wants* to be eaten. That said, one cannot ignore the fact that fruits are extremely high in sugars, so long-term consumption is not optimal or sustainable.

When consuming plants as the vast majority of humans do, one must consider the increasing data on the damage done by oxalates. According to Norton (2019), an oxalate is a tiny molecule that is acidic and toxic. These typically bind to calcium and form crystals, such as kidney stones. However, these can also bind to more dangerous substances, such as mercury, which form less soluble salts that accumulate and get trapped in body tissues. Norton explains that oxalates are produced in plants and, as the human body has no way of breaking these down, cannot be metabolised by humans so must be excreted. Unfortunately, oxalates are particularly high in our most loved veggies, such as carrots, kale and sweet potatoes. That said, the probiotic Bifidobacteria possesses an oxalate-reducing enzyme when cofactored with magnesium.

Foods abundant in Bifidobacterium include yoghurt, kefir and fermented foods such as pickles and sauerkraut. However, Bifidobacterium is highly sensitive to glyphosate (the active ingredient in Roundup and other herbicides and insecticides commonly sprayed on non-organic crops). Therefore, an organic diet (even better, foods grown in your own greenhouse) is essential in reducing glyphosate consumption so that our bodies are better adapted to riding oxalates. Norton also advocates a seasonal diet to prevent the over-consumption of the same oxalates. In this way, the body is able to detox throughout the year.

Similar to concerns over oxalates are warnings about plant lectins. The Plant Paradox is a book written by Dr Steven Gundry. As a result of his decades of clinical work, Gundry (2017) claims that plants have developed natural defences against the bugs that would otherwise eat them, which can harm humans, also, when consumed at high doses. These mechanisms of defence are referred to as 'lectins'. Gundry's (2017) work shows a number of detrimental effects that may manifest due to eating plants high in lectins, such as fat storage, leaky gut and inflammation. To solve the issue of lectins, the use of a pressure-cooker, sprouting grains and/ or a Paleo diet are recommended because these break down the anti-nutrients.

If you are fortunate enough to have enough land/ garden to grow your own vegetables, then I believe these issues can also be solved energetically.

Vegetables grown in their masses as part of modern agriculture, even organic, are often crammed together in soil that is depleted or mixed with artificial nutrients and tended to by people growing them for profit only. Naturally, these plants are going to have higher stress levels, generating their own fight-or-flight-style response, which results in higher levels of anti-nutrients such as lectins, just like an animal or human would be more irritable/ snappy in stressful situations. When growing my own fruits and vegetables in the garden, I communicate with the plants, developing a reciprocal relationship with them whereby I nurture them minerals, love, protection (I spend most summer mornings removing slugs and snails!) and fill them with confidence that their seeds will be harvested and spread, supported in the same way. In return, I ask for an energy-exchange of nutrition (without the anti-nutrients) so that I can continue to support their lineage. I feel very strongly that this really works and is exactly how it should be. Some studies to support this theory include one by the Royal Agricultural Society (2009), which concluded that plants grow faster and better when humans talk to them, especially women. Other research includes that reported by Oskin (2013), showing that plants can hear, as well as the National Institute of Agricultural Biotechnology in South Korea (Vanderlinden, 2020), which concluded that plant growth was stimulated by music. An experiment by school children across the United Arab Emirates even showed how exposing plants to negative vibrations in the form of insults etc (Jolly, 2018)

The frequency of human intention during the rearing process of animals has a similar effect. Whether a human's intent is from greed or love, makes a profound difference to the vibration of the meat. The same is true for sea animals farmed in poor, unnatural environments. 'Sustainable' is not the same as **ethical**!

Palaeolithic Diet

The Palaeolithic (Paleo) diet, often nicknamed the Caveman diet, claims to foster a life-style similar to that of our ancestors that we are genetically similar to. Generally, this consists of a diet without grains, dairy, processed foods, sugar or alcohol. Any seeds, legumes or nuts that are consumed would usually be sprouted in water for a few days, as unsprouted seeds can hold onto a lot of nutrients, so are inaccessible to the gut. The argument for the paleo diet is that cereals, particularly those high in gluten, were absent on the ancient hunter and gatherer menu. Hence, as humans have apparently only been consuming cereals for around 10,000 years, it is believed that the DNA and gut microbes of humans have not had enough time to adapt to this quick and vast change in diet. That said, it is necessary to remember that the modern world and the toxins which accompany it is very different to the ancient one, so many of our plants are deficient themselves, anyway, and many of them have been hybridised by farmers over the years- even the organic kind! Most bananas, mushrooms and garlic are even hybrid! So it's probably best to go with your intuition and eat what feels nourishing and life-force giving.

Alkaline- Electric

The philosophy around the Alkaline diet is based on the body's pH (potential Hydrogen). This is a measurement of the amount of acid and base in our bodies, with 0 representing the most acidic, 7 being neutral and 14 most alkaline. Jerry Tennant (2010) states that pH is simply another way of measuring voltage. As the body is an electrical instrument that runs on electro-magnetic information via the transportation of electrons, this is not surprising. All of the chemical reactions in the body depend on voltage being at transferable levels (corresponding with a balance pH). When the physical human body is too acidic, it cannot function effectively. As every farmer knows, you cannot get high yields from a field with acidic soil and, as everything in the universe is made from the same basic elements, our bodies are no different. The Alkaline diet promotes exactly that: an alkaline body as a result of consuming alkaline foods.

Acid-forming foods include high-protein foods, such as meat, fish, eggs, most legumes and even peas, as well as most grains and alcohol. Alkaline-forming foods, though, include the majority of fruits and vegetables, nuts, seeds and spices. According to Jillian Levy (2018), the benefits of having a balance pH include:

- Protection from heart disease
- Prevention of kidney stones
- Anti-inflammatory properties
- A more balanced blood-sugar ratio, so reduced chance of diabetes

113

- Stronger bones
- Reduction in muscle wasting
- Better vitamin absorption

Recently, Dr Sebi has taken the limelight on the advocation of the Alkaline diet. Dr Sebi (born Alfredo Bowman) was an African herbalist, biochemist and researcher from Honduras who promoted effective traditional therapy for his patients, reportedly including Michael Jackson. Dr Sebi claimed that there were six fundamental food groups: live, raw, dead, hybrid, genetically modified and drugs. Dr Sebi's encouraged diet used only two: live and raw (although it should be noted that a lot of emerging research concludes that learning to cook our food contributed to our vast increase in intelligence as it enabled accessibility to more nutrients and improved digestion, so a long-term raw diet may not be appropriate for modern humans- see the work of Wrangman for more information). According to Dr Sebi, these foods were "electric" and so correspond to the natural electrical properties of the human body. This ideology corresponds with that of Jerry Tennant, who promotes the understanding of the electrical connection between the human body and diet.

Veggies such as wheatgrass, celery and seaweeds like spirulina and chlorella help keep the body's pH at a healthy level. That said, it is necessary for the stomach to be acidic so that foods can be broken down into amino acids. This is because the blood runs at a pH of 7.35-7.45, which Jerry Tennant (2010) claims to be the same as -20 to -25 millivolts (mV). The stomach, however, must be at a pH of 2 (or +28mV). To maintain this acidic environment, the stomach uses chemical reactions consisting of iodine, zinc, vitamin B1 and sodium bicarbonate, dropping these in and out of the bloodstream as required. Due to the fact that excessive alkalinity in the stomach reduces stomach acid, caution should be taken on an alkaline only diet, especially as this process of producing more stomach acid requires more magnesium, which would need to be pulled away from elsewhere in the body if the diet is not supportive. In addition, as much of the magnesium that should be in plants is heavily depleted in modern agriculture, a supplement should probably be considered. Otherwise, simply work towards balance, whether that be through Yin- Yang, Male- Female, Light- Dark, Sun- Moon... Acid- Alkaline.

With the alkaline diet still in mind, a lesser known fact that should be noted is that when we over-eat, if there is more food than the stomach can deal with, the excess sits and ferments. Overeating producing free radicals as the mitochondria are forced to release more activated oxygen, preventing detox and repair and increasing the acidity levels within the body. This is usually preventable by not eating 3 hours before bed.

Interestingly, deep breathing also keeps our blood alkaline. All too often, we are breathing much too shallow as we become preoccupied with other information surrounding us, which in turn makes our blood more acidic. This is another point which compliments the usefulness of meditation, as being mindful whilst eating allows our breathing to become more rhythmic and natural. By oxygenising our blood in this way, we remove excess carbon dioxide (CO_2), which creates the perfect environment for effective digestion (and DMT production).

In sum so far, although a more alkaline body is effective for optimising health, it is important to be aware that the stomach must be acidic in order for food to digest properly. As a result, an all-alkaline diet, such as that promoted by Dr Sebi, is fine in the short-term to detox but must be thoroughly studied before becoming a long-term commitment. This is especially true in those who have any health predispositions which may inhibit bile production or those with GERD, for example.

The Rainbow Diet

Dr Cousens and Liberman (1991) recommend the Rainbow Diet. This is based on research by Dr Cousens, demonstrating that a food's colour vibrates at the same frequency as the correspondingly coloured chakra. The Rainbow Diet suggested is vegetarian and follows the order of the rainbow, so red, orange and yellow in the morning (maybe a fruit bowl), yellow, green and blue for lunch (like a salad) and green, blue, indigo and violet for dinner (such as veggies). He also claims that white foods can be eaten at any time as they are full-spectrum. I personally don't get along with this diet as regular consumption of high-sugar foods is like an unpredictable energy-rollercoaster for me, but it's worth considering if your body is not that way inclined (plus it sounds real pretty to be able to say you're on "the rainbow diet").

The Biblical Diet

Throughout the Bible, references are made to the medicinal properties of foods and herbs. Therefore, the art of eating righteously can be seen as a spiritual act. For example, Paul in Romans 14:2-6 states: *"Let not him who eats despise him who does not eat, and let not him who does not eat judge him who eats; for God has received him… He who eats, eats to the Lord, for he gives God thanks; and he who does not eat, to the Lord he does not eat, and gives God thanks."*

Specifically, the Bible seems to advocate 'trees and plants whose edible yield is bearing seeds or is seed' (Genesis 1:29) and 'plants of the field' (Genesis 3:18), although only grains that are sprouted (Ezekiel 4:9). So fruits, vegetables, legumes, nuts and seeds, in addition to 'any animal that has a divided hoof and that chews the cud' (Leviticus 11:3), which includes cattle, buffalo, sheep, goat and deer, but does not include rabbit, pig or camel. As for seafood, the Bible states that 'you may eat any that have fins and scales', such as fish. The Bible also states that birds such as chicken and duck are fine (Leviticus 11:13-19), as are locusts, katydid, crickets and grasshoppers (Leviticus 11:20-23).

According to the words of God to Moses (Leviticus 11:46), any of the animals and insects not mentioned are 'unclean' and are prohibited, even to touch them once dead, or else you, too, will become 'unclean' until evening. By unclean, God is speaking energetically. It is written within the Essene Gospel of Peace, however, that this dietary commandment was given to the followers of Moses as they were not yet physically able to cope with the diet that the Lord actually wanted them to consume.

The Essene Diet

The Essenes are detailed more in Chapter 17, but here is just a short description of the diet apparently advocated by this group.

According to the Essene Gospel of Peace Book 1, Jesus advocated a raw lacto-vegetarian diet. That is, raw vegan plus raw milk. The text also states that different foods should not be mixed as it is too much for the digestive system and puts it out of ease. Instead, it is said that no more than 2 or 3 different foods should occupy any meal. These foods should be local (or at least as local as possible) and the consumer should not over- indulge as this also makes the blood toxic. Fasting is also heavily advocated within the ancient Essene texts.

As the Essene writings are one of the most referenced with regard to the ancient practice of preserving the sacred oil, one could argue that this is the desired diet for those seeking enlightenment on this path. However, it should be noted that these texts are not only based on modern translations of an ancient Hebrew/ Aramaic language, but much of the writings are missing or ruined. Hence, this too should be taken with a pinch of salt when considering which food-choices are best for you.

Fasting

The digestion process requires a lot of energy. During the days of preservation in particular, the body needs to put as much energy as it can spare into increasing the vibrational potency of the stored CSF and remaining in the parasympathetic state (rest and repair). Therefore, seeing as oxygen goes where needed, when eating more energy is put into the digestion process, whereas when in sympathetic (fight or flight), focus goes to arms and legs. It is for this reason that a loss of appetite is common in those with depression and why stomach aches are common after meals when one is feeling stressed.

Mitochondria, as the powerhouses of our cells, take in nutrients and break them down to create energy. According to Lee Know (2018), the theoretical life span of a human is 120 years. So how did Biblical prophets live for hundreds and hundreds of years? Know (2018) claims that a calorie-restricting diet (about 40% of usual consumption) extends the theoretical life span of all animals, including humans, as a shortage of fuel means less free radicals. Thus, with the strong advocation of fasting within the diet, the correlation here is easy to spot. However, Know (2018) does point out that calorie restriction is very different from famine and starvation due to the consumption of nutrient-dense foods. Therefore, calorie restricting diets and fasting are only beneficial if the food that *is* eaten is nutritional enough to support the function of the body.

Interestingly, fasting is a ritual that is an integral part of nearly every religious tradition. It is seen as a purification process that cleanses the body. According to Mercola (2017), the benefits of fasting include: stabilising blood sugars and levels of insulin, resting the gut, producing ketones, improving metabolism, clearing out damaged cells (autophagy), reducing overall hunger (giving you more control of your hanger) and removing excess body fat (including around the organs), as well as slowing the aging process and improving brain function.

That said, being hungry can pump adrenaline and put you on high alert for food, so must be a part of a weaning process. Scott Anderson (2017) states that low calorie diets, although reportedly lengthen life, are miserable for the long haul. Instead, Anderson (2017) advocates intermittent fasting (part-time fasting), which he claims has similar effects. I personally practice intermittent fasting (14-18 hour fasts, which includes sleep) most days to give my digestive system a break.

The Diet Of YOU

With so many diets and controversies surrounding nutrition, it can often feel pressurising to follow one strictly. One thing is for certain, though: variety and cycling is key. The world cycles in seasons according to its natural spin around the Sun, so it's obvious that we should, too. Even the ancients used seasonal dietary cycling to strengthen their survival, eating whatever was available on the land (AKA, provided by the gods). This process also prevents a build up of the same toxins and vitamins, which resonates with the natural rhythm of life whereby there are stages of highs and lows within all things.

From all of this, it can be deduced that what foods you consume is up to you, just accept responsibility for whatever part you play for both your own well-being and that of other living things, including Gaia. For example, standard veganism could be seen as a less environmentally damaging diet to follow and the Ketogenic may feel like the most physiologically appropriate. Yet, the destruction being done to the planet by pesticides and deforestation in order to grow soya (including that which is fed to commercially raised livestock) will be far more damaging physically and globally than a conscientious omnivore one. Dr Zach Bush is currently initiating a sustainable farming regime titled *Farmer's Footprint*, which optimises the relationship between farmer and produce in order to make crops as nourishing as they always were and should be. He exclaims that if farmers and consumers do not predominately switch to such practices within the next 30 years, then we may reach the point of no-return for maintaining life on this beautiful planet. Please see Zachbush.com for more details on this. Better yet, start growing your own foods and encouraging others to do the same. And if you are able to work with some local, like-minded people to generate your own micro-farm, then contact Zach Bush personally for more information as he is incredibly passionate about this natural way of living.

In addition to the above, one must remember that our environment now is extremely different to what it was in the past. As a species, we are exposed to frequencies never before reported on the planet, and each part of the world is potentially exposed to differing levels of all of these. For instance, there are researchers currently stating that Vitamin A is a toxin to the body and so should be avoided, even claiming that blue-light from screens is only damaging if there is Vitamin A in the system (see work by Dr Garrett Smith for more information). However, this does beg the question as to whether Vitamin A is and always has been toxic for the human body, or if the environment we are living in at the moment reacts with the molecule in a way that makes it toxic. Personally, I believe in too much of a good thing, and that it is the constant exposure to toxins that force our bodies out of sync with natural detox cycles, such as fasting when food was scarce in the winter.

Furthermore, each and every one of us has a unique genetic imprint which responds to the environment. The most predominant way that our DNA responds to the environment is based on nutritional intake. For me, a vegan diet feels good. I have more energy, less brain fog and feel more connected to the world around me. I do not consume soya products and only eat organic foods as local as I can get them and home-grown as much as possible (this reduces my contribution to the death of an immense number of animals, such as rabbits, during the mass farming of vegetables). Although Dave Asprey (2019) would probably argue that these positive-seeming results were because my body is full of adrenaline and 'starving', I'm a strong believer in epigenetics and do not believe there in a one-diet-fits-all approach.

At the end of the day, as long as you have done your research and make the right adjustments where needed to prevent as much deficiency as you can whilst minimalising toxification, your body is your own and only you know what makes you feel alive. And in my opinion, anyone who tries to put you down about your dietary choices without a valid analysis of your own unique genetic predispositions hasn't got any ground for the debate.

In short, we are all epigenetically predisposed to a particular diet and, as food is the primary way that we interact with our environment, the nutrients, hormones and proteins we consume all play a part in the regulation and expression of these genes and can even reverse undesirable epigenetic changes that the body may have succumb to in the past. Moreover, much of our biology resides within the quantum realm (discussed in Chapters 6 and 7) which includes communication between our cells and energy production by our mitochondria. Therefore, as there are no absolute truths in the quantum world (only possibilities), the best diet for each human will be the same. Let me repeat that for emphasis:

There is no absolute truth; only possibilities.

So listen to your body; it usually knows best.

The Microbiome

Our body is home to vast civilisations called microbes. These live on our skin, in our gut, in our eyes, and so on. Each person's ecosystem of microbes is completely unique and are constantly sending messages to each other and the rest of the body, primarily to the brain via the vagus nerve. Predominately, the gut microbes make key neurotransmitters such as serotonin, they also support the synthesis of vitamins, hence why a natural, gut-healthy diet is essential.

By feeding your beneficial gut bacteria plenty of fibre, they also produce compounds that help regulate the immune system and improve brain health. In order to keep our body in balance with the perceived environment, these microbes effect our cravings. For example, a sugar-dominant microbiota produce signals that will send cravings of sugar to the brain. Yet, your microbiota changes continuously in response to what you eat, so there is no such thing as a person with a 'sweet-tooth'; this just means you have eaten your way to a sugar-dominating biome; and you can eat your way out of it, too!

An interesting note to make here is that a baby consumes some of the mother's natural biome during the birthing process and via the consumption of breast milk. Yet, there is a type of sugar within breast milk referred to as Human Milk Oligosaccharides (or HMOs) which is indigestible. Recent research, though, shows that this sugar, in fact, feeds the beneficial bacteria within the infant's gut, notably the Bifidobacterium (which can break down plant toxins). As this particular sugar is only found in human breast milk, some believe that harvesting this could become the next big superfood! If so, it would be interesting to witness how these 'milking-women' are treated in comparison to most modern cattle.

Food Vibration

Centuries previously, most people grew their own food or depended on local farmers. Nowadays, though, the use of synthetic herbicides such as glyphosate have decimated soil microbes and their ability to mineralise the soil, deeming these unable to support the growth of nutritionally dense crops. Moreover, Mercola (2017) states that glyphosate depletes the body of minerals and interferes with ATP (energy) production. As processed foods are also depleted of minerals and electrons, the body would have to accommodate by supplying more oxygen molecules, which creates more free radicals. When one actually takes the time to consider such things, it seems obvious why health is deteriorating in Western society. According to Saint Germain, the perfect diet is LIGHT.

Saint Germain states that within all foods is the essence of solar light, which your body breaks down into energy. Each person's perfect diet will vary depending on the light resonance of their own organism and incarnated spirit. He therefore recommended that you test various food substances to see how you feel, remembering that your body is a temple and you must drive out the false sellers (fake food) and the thieves (free radicals) as Jesus did [Genesis 1:29]. It is also for this reason that local foods are better for health, as the solar essence will be more resonant with your own biorhythms due to exposure to the same lengths of the light spectrum. Foods that are said to be more conductive include raw honey, coconut water/ milk, Celtic salt, fruit juice and foods high in magnesium. Refined sugar, on the contrary, is an anti-conductor.

Supplements to Consider

Herbs and spices are the natural supplements provided by Mother Earth. As our entire being is an amalgamation of vast civilisations of organisms, a varied diet with a range of supplements is essential. Although the term 'supplement' can be stigmatised for assuming that a healthy body cannot be sustained through 'whole-foods', it's important to note that the world we live in now is very different to the world we evolved on hundreds-of-thousands of years ago. There are more pollutants, toxins and electromagnetic interreferences that have never been seen on this planet before (discovered to-date). So yes, we may have survived on a particular staple food source 2000 years ago, but we are surrounded by a lot more stress and degenerative factors now that make such a diet incapable of fully supporting our modern health. Therefore, the consumption of supplements may be considered necessary in the preservation of our healthier genetics whilst the rest of the population catches up.

For me, the following supplements are paramount:

Fulvic Minerals - Fulvic minerals are composed from the deepest layers of soil. They are the ultimate foundation for all functions of the body. Even vitamins cannot be broken down and used without minerals being present first. Consuming these not only detox the body of glyphosate, but these essential minerals also maintain the body's pH (voltage) levels.

Iodine - An essential micro-nutrient which every cell in the body requires for adequate functioning. According to Lynne Farrow (2013), iodine possesses antibiotic, antiparasitic, antifungal and antiviral properties, and can even displace metals from the body (such as aluminium). Furthermore, around 60% of iodine in the human body is stored in the thyroid glands, hence iodine is required to support optimal hormone production. Historically, seaweed and quality grey sea salt were major providers of iodine. Nowadays, modern food habits mean that most people are iodine deficient. Icelandic sea kelp can often counteract this.

Magnesium - Magnesium used to be abundant in our soil and corresponding food supply. Worms and bacteria in the soil would break down minerals that would be absorbed by the plant, ready for us to eat. Thanks to pesticides killing these essential organisms off, however, the majority of people are now significantly deficient as there are less minerals available in the soil for the plants to uptake. Furthermore, fluoride binds to magnesium, so consumption of contaminated tap water depletes what stores our bodies do have even further. Combine these points with the fact that EMFs (discussed in Chapter 2) deplete your magnesium stores and the heart requires optimal amounts of magnesium to function, and you have a very sick society with high rates of heart disease and cancer!

Magnesium is essential for health as there can be over 1000 mitochondria in each human cell which each generate ATP within the 8-step- Kreb's cycle. As a result, six out of the eight of these steps requires magnesium. Thus, low magnesium means low energy levels. Moreover, telomeres (which keep us biologically young) are also prevented from deteriorating with magnesium. Additionally, magnesium is a direct regulator of ion channels and even guards the ion channels that allow calcium to enter and exit the cells, so is necessary for voltage maintenance. According to Carolyn Dean (2017), magnesium also supports oxygen uptake, electrolyte balance, energy production and removing toxic substances and heavy metals, such as aluminium and mercury, as well as necessary for DNA and RNA production.

There are a lot of different types of magnesium supplements which have reportedly varying effects. DrAxe.com has some excellent blogs to support this decision, if necessary.

Chlorella - Chlorella is a green, single-celled, fresh-water algae approximately two billion years old. As one of the longest surviving living-organisms on the planet, it has the genetic predispositions to cope with vast environmental changes and stressors, which can be metabolised by our own bodies. Consequently, chlorella holds many beneficial effects, such as improved immune support, accelerated healing of wounds and ulcers, protection against toxic pollutants, normalised digestion and bowel function, stimulation of tissue growth and repair, reduced aging, protection against radiation, growth of friendly gut bacteria, reduction of poisons from the blood and intestines, improved body odour, normal blood cell formation, reduced fatigue, normal functioning of the nervous system and even encourages the excretion of toxic metals such as mercury.

Chlorella is also rich in iodine, vitamin B12 and protein (especially important for vegans). The best supplements are organic with a broken cell-wall to aid absorption, preferably sourced from a low-pollutant country, such as Taiwan.

Pine Pollen - Pine pollen is the pollen from pine trees. It has over 200 bioactive, natural nutrients, minerals and vitamins which are completely absorbable by the body. Pine pollen is particularly supportive of the endocrine system, upon the glands of which is where our chakras rest. An entire book could be written on the benefits of a healthy endocrine system, but a few examples include improved mood, more energy and a better relationship with the environment. What's more, this miracle pollen aids the excretion of excess oestrogens, which the human body can accumulate detrimental levels of within today's plastic-filled, commercial-dairy consuming, pesticide and herbicide- riddled environment. Pine pollen can even be harvested for free from your local environment at the appropriate time of the year.

Vitamin E - Vitamin E supports pituitary function by protecting it from damage and the effects of aging. It is also an anti-oxidant so supports the normal functioning of the rest of the body, too. Good sources are avocados and olive oil.

Fats - Not really a supplement, but healthy fats are essential for optimal brain function, especially for the pineal. Therefore, regular intake of high fat foods such as coconuts, cacao beans/ butter, olives, macadamia nuts, sprouted sunflower seeds and avocados are encouraged.

Melatonin - Melatonin is not only a precursor to the spirit molecule DMT, but it also protects mitochondrial DNA (which turns food into energy). Melatonin-Rich foods include: Tart cherry juice (researched by Dr Reiter); walnuts (these contain tryptophan, which is converted into serotonin when ingested and then melatonin at night); ginger root; tomatoes; flaxseeds (for tryptophan, as well as calcium and vitamin B6 which is required to turn tryptophan into serotonin); magnesium (which calms and helps to deactivate adrenaline); leafy greens; and cayenne pepper (this is also good for opening airways for deeper breathing).

Other supplements proposed by David Wolfe (2009) include: goji berries for longevity, heart health, adrenal, pituitary and pineal gland optimisation and increased alkalinity; cacao for its richness in antioxidants and magnesium as well as tryptophan and tryptamine; maca root for strength and stamina, stabilisation of the nervous system and endocrine system; and coconuts for improving digestion, stabilising blood sugars, regulating hormone production and feeding the brain and body using its preferred energy source: fat.

Water

Water is the principle constituent of the human body and is essential to all life. Gerald Pollack is most renowned for this theory of the fourth phase of water. That is, that water does not only exist in the states of liquid, solid and gas, but is also able to form a liquid-crystal type state. Dr Pollack discovered the fourth sate of water, termed 'EZ water', which is the gel-like structure we have in our cells. According to Pollack (2013), this fourth phase of water stores energy similar to a battery. Consequently, this substance is electron-rich, alkaline and supports mitochondrial function. Dr Pollack also found that light and vibration effected this substance and could create more of it. Therefore, the more EZ water we have in our bodies, the better our cells function. This is especially so when one considered that the upcoming 5G internet roll-out is a water de-structuring device, and humans are mostly water.

In addition to the work of Pollack, Dr Zach Bush also strongly states that hydration does not mean drinking lots of water; it is a measurement of how much water is *inside* the cells. The intracellular fluid of our cells are in this fourth phase, and it is the mitochondria that allow cells to become hydrated as they use this EZ fluid within their energy-production line. Therefore, Bush exerts that mitochondria function and hydration are *the same thing*. As mitochondria are key players in our creation of a physical light body (discussed in Chapter 6), optimal hydration can be seen as paramount to the ascension process.

Machines can be purchased which structure water, but chia seeds and flax seeds soaked in water also produce this gel-structure which can then be consumed orally. Placing water in a glass bottle and leaving it outside for 12 hours has also been shown to ionise water into this fourth phase, as the solar energy excites the water molecules and encourages this structuring. That said, the vast majority of experts advocate using your own body as a water structuring device by getting outside in natural light yourself, especially at sunrise and sunset when the frequencies of light are at their most optimal for health.

Intriguingly, water is known to hold a memory and respond to vibrations in the environment. Therefore, it is good practice to get into the habit of blessing water (preferably filtered or, even better, sourced from a natural spring) before drinking in order to release any trauma from its molecular structure and increase its ability to resonate with your own energy field.

Pollack himself encourages the consumption of a range of different types of water in order to ensure optimal health and hydration. At the time of writing, I do not live near any natural springs, so rely on my water distiller to remove toxins from the tap water, which I think vary between solarising, structuring in a machine or, more commonly, mineralising with Celtic grey salt or fulvic minerals, after blessing it with thanks and love.

As well as drinking water, one should also consider the quality of their bathing water. Historically, humans would have bathed in high vibrational, mineral-rich springs and absorbed minerals and electrolytes (such as magnesium) abundantly through their skin. It is for this reason that a regular soak in a salty bath (I personally love Epsom salts and Dead Sea salts) is recommended. You can also contact your local health spa and see if they offer *float tank* sessions, whereby you are left in conditions similar to the womb (dark and nourishing) in a bath that has such high magnesium levels that you float! Many people report reaching higher states of consciousness within these, too, which is likely due to the high vibration of the physical body.

In addition to the above, water is also a lubricant/ solvent. It allows densities to dissolve in it. It is for this reason that we release (densities, shadows, toxins, stress, pain, babies, etc) easier in water because energies dissolve quickly within this state of matter. As we continuously prepare our bodies as part of the ascension process, by allowing these densities to dissolve quickly, we can take in more light. Furthermore, water is a powerful transceiver and conductor of quantum information (see Chapter 6). Thus, water assists ascension by allowing energies to clear, transmute and/ or alchemise.

Summary

It can be seen that the diversity of the planet isn't unique to species and kingdoms of life but is vast even down to the unique ecosystems within ourselves. From my own exploration and testimonials from others, I feel safe in saying that, for now, there is no proven dietary guidelines for preserving the secretion and enhancing longevity. And as the chemical reactions within the body alter depending on what nutrients are put in, it is important for dietary choices to be a lifestyle choice so that perceptions during these days are actual felt differences, not just the body reacting to a different environment. Personally, I would place thought-patterns and light (see Chapter 6) as the most paramount factors towards mental well-being and Chrism preservation. But I also repeatedly emphasise that what works for one person will not work for another as a result of physical genetics and spiritual blueprint.

Thus, finding what foods work for you is a journey you must take alone. Try different strategies, supplements and sources, note those which make you feel good (physically and mentally) and those that don't. Foods are a gift from Gaia, that should provide us with energy and focus. If your diet doesn't, then it probably isn't the right one for you. Genetic testing is one way to go as you can see exactly where your roots are, physically, and where any genetic predispositions and limitations are- which is a good start for anyone who can afford these.

Always remember: *"Whether you eat, drink or whatever you do, do all for the glory of God." (Corinthians 10:31)* and as God is within us all, consume a diet that makes you feel healthy and energised, both physically and morally.

Recommendations

Website: Extreme Health Academy

Book: Healing Is Voltage by Jerry Tennant.

Article: Samsel, A. and Seneff, S. 2015. Glyphosate pathways to modern disease 3: Manganese, neurological disease and associated pathologies. 6:45. *Surgical Neurology International.*

Podcast: Extreme Health Radio

Video: Jennifer Dechaine. *Epigenetics: You Are What You Eat* [YouTube]. TEDx Talks. 4 March 2015.

.

Bibliography and References

Anderson, S. with Cryan, J. and Dinan, T. 2017. *The Psychobiotic Revolution.* National Geographic.

Asprey, D. Biohacker: How To Become The Ultimate Super Human [podcast]. *London Real.* 6 October 2019.

Axe, J. 2019. *Keto Diet.* Orion Spring.

Barnard, N. Your Body In Balance: Will a Vegan Diet Improve Your Health? [podcast]. *London Real.* 27 October 2019.

Bikman, B. Physiological Effects of the Ketogenic Diet [podcast]. *Take Control of Your Health.* 14 April 2019.

Carey, N. 2012. *The Epigenetics Revolution.* Icon Books.

Colleen, A. 2016. *10% Human: How Your Body's Microbes Hold The Key To Health and Happiness.* William Collins.

Cowan, T. Dr Mercola Interviews Dr Cowan on the New Biology of Water [podcast]. *Take Control of Your Health.* 13 October 2019.

Dean, C. 2017. *The Magnesium Miracle.* Ballantine Books.

DiNicolantonio, J. Importance of Dietary Fats [podcast]. *Take Control of Your Health.* 13 November 2019.

DK. 2017. *How The Body Works.* Penguin Random House.

Farrow, L. 2013. *The Iodine Crisis.* Devon Press.

Gundry, S. 2017. *The Plant Paradox.* Harper Wave.

Gundry, S. Healthy Aging Begins and Ends in the Gut [podcast]. *Bulletproof Radio.* 27 June 2019.

Jolly, B. 2018. *Students insult plants in unique anti-bullying experiment.* New York Post

Know, L. 2018. *Mitochondria and the Future of Medicine.* Independently Published.

Land, S. Dr Mercola Interviews Siim Land on Metabolic Autophagy [podcast]. *Take Control of Your Health.* 15 September 2019.

Lee, W. and Rosenbaum, M. 1987. *Chlorella: The Sun-Powered Supernutrient and its Beneficial Properties.* Keats Publishing.

Levy, J. 2018. *4 Steps to Achieve Proper pH Balance.* Available online at: <www.draxe.com>

Lewis, D. 2015. *Saint Germain on Advanced Alchemy.* Meru Press.

Liberman, J. 1991. *Light: The Medicine of the Future.* Bear and Company.

Mercola, J. 2017. *Fat For Fuel.* Hay House.

Mercola, J. Eat Like a Carnivore [podcast]. *Take Control of Your Health.* 7 July 2019.

Mishra et al. 2013. A multicellular randomized control trial of a plant-based nutrition program to reduce body weight and cardiovascular risk in the corporate setting. 67(7):p.718-724. *European Journal of Clinical Nutrition.*

Mousa, Haider Abdul-Lateef. 2016. Health Effects of Alkaline Diet and Water, Reduction of Digestive-tract Bacterial Load, and Earthing. *Alternative Therapies in Health & Medicine.* 22:p.24-34.

Norton, S. n.d. *What is oxalate and how can it impact your health?* [online]. Available at: <www.sallyknorton.com>

Norton, S. Dr Mercola Interviews Sally K Norton on Oxalate Toxicity. *Take Control of Your Health.* 10 November 2019.

Oskin, B. 2013. *Sound Garden: Can plants actually talk and hear?* Livescience.com

Pimentel, D. and Pimentel, M. 2003. Sustainability of meat-based and plant-based diets and the environment.78:s660-663. *American Journal of Clinical Nutrition.*

Pollack, G. 2013. *The Fourth Phase of Water.* Ebner and Sons Publishers.

Royal Agricultural Society. 2009. **In.** Vanderlinden, C. 2020. *Talking to plants can help them grow faster.* Spruce.com

Saladino, P. Kick Veggies to the Curb and Go Full Carnivore [podcast]. *Bulletproof Radio.* 27 August 2019.

Satija, A. et al. 2017. Healthful and unhealthful plan-based diets and the risk of coronary heart disease in US adults. 70(4):pp.423-425. *Journal of American Coll Cardiol.*

Shananhan, C. 2016. *Deep Nutrition.* Flatiron Books.

Tennant, J. 2010. *Healing Is Voltage.* 3rd ed. Independently Published.

Tuso, P. 2015. A plant-based diet, atherogenesis and coronary artery disease prevention. 19(1):pp.62-67. *The Permanente Journal.*

Vanderlinden, C. 2020. *Talking to plants can help them grow faster.* Spruce.com

Wolfe, D. 2009. *Superfoods.* North Atlantic Books.

Wrangman, R. 2010. *Catching Fire: How Cooking Made Us Human.* Profile Books LTD.

Yurdagül Zopf, Dejan Reljic, & Walburga Dieterich. 2018. Dietary Effects on Microbiota—New Trends with Gluten-Free or Paleo Diet. *Medical Sciences.* 6(4):p.92.

Chapter 5

Cosmos:

Old MacDonald Had a Heavenly Farm

When Father Sun descends in the West and darkness engulfs the Earth, the twinkles of the night sky naturally intrigue the consciousness. As these would continuously shift and wander across the background of darkness throughout the year, stories for both entertainment and recall purposes unfolded. What's more, as a branch of physics referred to as Quantum Mechanics is continuously proving that every single atom in the universe is intimately connected via a phenomenon referred to as entanglement, it is of no surprise that celestial orbs near and far influence each of us and our planet at constantly varying levels throughout our lives. Some of the basic, ancestral knowledge of these cosmic bodies in relation to the sacred secretion are explained within this chapter, but more explicit links are made in Part 2. For now, we will start with giving credit where it is due to the giver of all life on this conscious, living organism we call both a planet and home.

The Sun

Our Sun was formed from the supernova of another star, which allowed for heavier elements to form zinc, copper, iodine and cobalt (all of which our bodies require). The Sun is the largest object in our sky and is the source of light, heat and life. It, along with the layers of the Earth's atmosphere, creates the perfect condition for conscious life. In particular, the ionosphere is an abundant layer of electrons, ionised atoms and molecules that stretches approximately 30 miles above the surface of the Earth, about 600 miles up [see FIGURES 2 and 30]. According to NASA (2013), this region is affected by solar conditions and is the celestial power station that makes radio communication possible. The Earth's crust is also a conductor, hence why the Sun's electrical energy is termed 'father energy', as it gives its light/ life force for others to conceive/ germinate/ birth life with.

Adoration for the Sun, as the father of life and consciousness, has been evidenced on cave walls since as far back as 14,000 B.C. The great plasmic ball even allows us to exchange information using its photons (light energy) and is at the core of modern time keeping. The ancients knew of this connection between the Earth, the Sun and other celestial bodies, hence constructed monuments to enhance this, such as pyramids and stone circles. Many historic roads also track the annual movements of the Sun, possibly preparing for certain ceremonies. Consequently, stories of the Sun's presence in the sky and effect on the planet have accumulated all over the globe. Some of the best-known examples include:

- Ra/ Re, the Sun-God of Egypt who created the world. Re cried one day, and humans were made from his tears. Ra travels each day across the sky in his boat, then would pass through the underworld at night.

- Helios, a Greek solar deity, who drove his fiery chariot across the sky during the day, before getting a boat over the sea back to the start just to begin the journey across the sky again.

- Belenus of the Celtic culture who also rode across the sky in his horse-drawn chariot.

- The Native Americans saw the Sun and Moon gods as forbidden lovers, which is why the Moon disappears when the Sun comes about.

- The Magi who visited the baby Jesus followed the star from the East (the Sun rises in the East each day).

- The lion, due to its mane appearing like a shining Sun, is a frequent personification of the Sun, such with the Egyptian solar deity and daughter of Ra, Sekhmet.

Sun worship also played an important role in early Paganism. Manly Hall even speculates a connection between Paganism and Atlantis due to similarities in the way both civilisations are said to have expressed their gratitude to the Sun.

The Bible stories are multi-layered (explained in Chapter 15), which means that, due to being written by a collective group of individuals with varying professions and experiences over elongated periods of time, each story is accountable for a number of varied interpretations. This is admitted within the Bible, as Jesus said that he was a serpent (energy), bread (knowledge), light (the Sun), the door (note for later that 'claustrum' means *door*) and the good shepherd (Aries), to name a few.

One of the more obvious layers is one of cosmic/ astrological origin. Within this layer of interpretation, Jesus/ Yeshua/ Christ was the SUN, not the SON. Like the Sun, Jesus was referred to as 'the light of the world'. He is also regularly drawn with a 'halo' which appears suspiciously similar to the Sun, too. In this way, the story of Jesus is a tale of the Sun moving through the star constellations and how the energies of this affect us on Earth. It is a story of the stars and the connection between us and the heavens: "As above, so below." Furthermore, great Solar lords such as Ra, Horus, Mithras and Jesus are all symbols for the inner Christ and were all born from immaculate conception on December 25th and died at age 33. Hence it can be seen that the story of the Son is not unique to Christianity but is in fact a tale retold all over the world throughout millennia. The fact that such a story has prevailed for so long indicates that an element of truth within it must resonate with the unconscious at some level.

Although a solar year only takes 365 days (the length of time it takes the Earth to orbit around the Sun), it takes 2160 years for the zodiac constellations to appear to shift across the background of the Sun (caused by the Earth's natural shift). Therefore, it takes 25,920 years for the Sun to do a full lap of the zodiac. This is referred to as a 'Great Year' and is documented as an astronomical 'Age'. At this moment in time, the Sun has left Pisces and is shifting into Aquarius. Ergo, it is said that we are entering the 'Age of Aquarius', the sign of Man and the carrier of water. This has an obvious impact on the energies of life on Earth due to the dominating influx of stellar frequencies. For example, in the Old Testament we can see the documentation of change in energy from the Age of Taurus to the Age of Aries, whereas the New Testament shows a transition from Aries to Pisces. Finally, Revelations presents a prophecy of the signs for the end of the Age of Pisces and moving into the Age of Aquarius (this is detailed more thoroughly later, in Chapter 16). Randall Carlson also speculates that it is a time of preparation for the next cosmic chaos, likely from meteor impact.

Second to the Sun, the next most adorned cosmic body is the Moon. From Earth, the Sun and Moon appear about the same size because, although the Sun is 400x bigger, the Moon is 400x closer, synchronising their powerful energies into perfect resonance. Surprisingly, the Earth's orbit around the Sun is egg-shaped, as is the orbit of the Moon around the Earth. Hence, with the Earth being part of both eggs from the Sun and Moon, one can see how the ideology of the Sun as father and Moon as mother came about. Additionally, as the Moon *receives* light from the Sun, this cosmic body is aligned with feminine frequencies, like a woman who *receives* light/ life force from a man in order to conceive a child. It is for this reason that many of the ancient mythologies tell tales of gods as great adulterers, as they gave their *light* to a number of other *bodies*, such as planets and their moons.

The Moon

There is a theory, based on analyses of lunar rocks, that the Moon and Earth were once one, like a mother bearing a child. Although these bodies were separated by an unknown phenomenon, the Moon can still be seen with the naked eye, watching over and supporting life on Earth. In fact, research by Dr Maggie Aderin-Pocock suggests that most ancient calendars were actually lunar-based, the oldest of which (discovered to-date) is believed to be over 30,000 years old. Even the British Celts commenced their 'month' on the 6th day after a new moon and celebrated new year on the 6th day after the first new moon following the spring equinox.

There are 8 phases of the Moon cycle, depending on its position between the Earth and Sun. For instance, during a New Moon, the Moon is sitting between the Earth and Sun, so appears invisible. On the contrary, when the Moon sits on the opposite side of the Earth from the Sun, it is able to fully reflect the Sun's light, making it appear full. The position of the Moon not only affects its appearance, but also its energetic impression on Earth. As the Earth rotates, the part closest to the Moon is pulled by the Moon's gravity, causing tides.

During a Full Moon, this gravitational pull is about 7% greater. On land we normally do not feel or notice this, but it is still happening all of the time. This is where the term 'lunatic' originated from, as the effects of the Full Moon were said to increase excitement within the body, thus causing a sky-rocket in crime rates and hospitalisation. As the Moon is extremely magnetic, its influence on our also magnetic Earth and us as beings full of iron and magnetite is undoubtable. One factor is that the Moon slows the speed at which the Earth spins.

According to Thomas Burgoyne, the Moon is the universal mother and emits female energy. Burgoyne states that when the Moon is in the presence of other cosmic bodies, such as star constellations, its influx becomes more potent and the magnetic frequency transmitted is intensified. This supports the theory of the sacred secretion as it explains how the magnetic properties of the Moon (which is visible to the Earth based on its ability to reflect photons of light from the Sun) increases the energetic effects of the phase of the zodiac which it resides within at that moment in time.

The Zodiac

Evidenced by the abundant of examples, from stained glass images at Chartres Cathedral in France, to the astronomical clock in Prague and the stone henges of England, the zodiac has clearly inspired our ancestors for millennia. By creating images from these star constellations to make them easier to identify and to document their energetic influence on the planet, systems of recording could be used.

Within the modern era, the dominating forms of astrology include the Tropical and the Sidereal. As it stands, there's roughly a 24 degree difference between the tropical and sidereal zodiac systems, which has caused some controversy for astrologers as this has led to a 2.5 day difference in the astrological timing of the Moon's energy said to be residing within a particular constellation on the belt, and when it can physically be seen with the naked eye to be there. This is probably the biggest debate within the sacred secretion preserving community, and one which has yet to be put to rest.

Let's get a brief overview of each.

The Sidereal Zodiac System

Sidereal literally means 'in relation to the stars' so is built upon the foundation of the background of stars, based upon where the actual constellation can be seen right now from Earth. As the Earth has a natural wobble on its axis (as a result of the pull of the Moon's gravity, but also believed to be accelerated by climate change) the appearance of the star background slowly shifts. Thus, the stars and zodiac themselves have not moved, but appear to as the Earth moves. This system measures time based on the apparent movement of the physical star constellations.

The Tropical Zodiac System

The Tropical Zodiac, however, is founded upon the zodiac belt. Followers of this system start the astronomical year as the day of the Spring Equinox being the first day of Aries. From here, the 30 degree precession of each angle of the zodiac belt can be followed in order to progress through each sign. This is the system that online Lunar Calendars tend to put forward and measures time based on the seasons and equinoxes/ solstices.

So which one should be followed when preserving the sacred secretion?

The truth is, no one can be sure. George Carey (2013) classically claimed that "[the anti-Christ world] make the moon enter a sign of the zodiac two and one-half days before it does enter it and thus pertuate the lie…". This corresponds with the two systems, whereby the popular Tropical system has the Moon enter a sign 2.5 days before it physically does, as evident within the Sidereal system. Yet, if the belt of the zodiac has never physically moved and is following the same system used by the ancients who documented the birth of the sacred oil, then one could argue that perhaps Carey was mistaken.

According to Ptolemy, an ancient Greek astronomer who lived in Alexandria, Egypt, and refined the Tropical zodiac from the Egyptians, the Tropical system was indeed designed in order to coordinate the stars so that we always had a means to stay aligned with the cosmos, regardless of what is visible as a result of the planet's wobble (precession). During the second century AD in which Ptolemy completed this work, he knew of the precession cycle and understood the Sidereal system, but still followed the Tropical Zodiac, aligned to the equinoxes and solstices rather than the actual stars. Apparently, this version of astrology sought to understand human behaviour through the influence of the cosmos, rather than being a way of communicating with the wider universe, like the Sidereal. In this way, the Tropical Zodiac is used as a coordinate system, by which the zodiac is aligned to the energy of the travelling Sun, rather than the visible constellations. This allowed the zodiac to be evenly distributed and calibrated around Earth's relationship with its giver of life: the Sun. For instance, during each of the solstices, the Sun is at the exact latitude of one of the tropics

(Summer Solstice in the Northern Hemisphere aligns with the latitude of the Tropic of Cancer, which is when the Sun 'enters' the zodiac sign of Cancer). So the Tropical system synchronises with the Earth's energy centres/ nervous system; the lines of latitude and longitude (meridians) that relate to its crystal core/ heart.

Basically, during the equinoxes and solstices, energy influx from the Sun peaks and the Earth's meridians vibrate higher in correspondence. It is during these energy exchanges that the Tropical system aligns with corresponding star constellations. In this way, the Tropical system can be seen as more aligned to intuition, spiritual knowing and energies, thus has a more *feminine* frequency, whereas the Sidereal focuses on what can be proven and seen physically, which is a more *masculine* vibration. This is similar to ancient Celtic traditions, whereby the visible front-side of the body was seen as the masculine and the mysterious back-side was considered the feminine.

Therefore, as the Bible is a way of communicating the knowledge of this ancient practice into the modern era, it could be deduced that the Tropical system is the one designed to be followed in order to prepare for the spiritual seed and was designed specifically so that the future had a governing point. This point could be further argued by the fact that Ptolemy provided such practice during his studies in Alexandria, Egypt, which we know housed the largest library of the ancient world. It has even reported to have contained the works of such great thinkers as Homer, Plato, Socrates and even the original writings of Hermes. It contained documents from all over the world and many scholars reportedly even chose to live within the library. Unfortunately, the

Great Library of Alexandria disappeared by the 5th century AD, likely as a result of centuries of Roman and Christian control. Consequently, whether Ptolemy was divinely influences by the collection of ancient scrolls when refining Tropical astrology to preserve such knowledge which was being corrupted, or whether he himself was influenced by the Romans in order to deceive the masses, we can't know for sure.

Another point to consider is that the Bible states that the first month is that in which Passover is celebrated. Nowadays, we know Passover to term the literal passing-over of the sacrificial lamb: Aries. Exodus 12 states that the lamb is to be slaughtered. Astrologically, this seems to depict the passing of Aries across the equatorial cross, hinting towards a Tropical Zodiac. The same extract, however, also exclaims that any uneaten lamb must be burned the next day, which seems more in-line with the Sidereal as the Sun passes Aries. So one cannot be completely sure.

Personally, I feel inclined towards the Tropical System as it is the most aligned to the actual felt-frequencies of Mother Earth and Gaia's energy grid, which we are profoundly resonant with, and I feel the effects of the sacred secretion more during these days. Nevertheless, following both systems when preserving the sacred secretion (for at least the 5 days that would account for both, just to be sure) is recommended, especially as I have heard testimonies from people who have felt the effects of the preservation in the days that followed the Tropical timings, aligned with the Sidereal.

As mentioned, each of the 12 houses of the zodiac contain about 30 degrees of space each, measured by degrees of right ascension (time). These consists of:

ARIES- The Ram, also commonly depicted as a Lamb. Aries begins the astronomical new year during the Spring Equinox as Aries 'Passes Over' the equinoctial cross. Hence, the slaying of the lamb. The Bible, then, is not advocating the killing of baby sheep but is merely describing a cosmic vision. Thus, Aries is the scapegoat; the lamb of God who took away the sins of the world (in order to start fresh in the new cosmic year).

TAURUS- The Bull, also commonly depicted as an Ox. Within Ancient Egypt evidence of star worship during the Age of Taurus is evidenced by a Sacred Cattle Cult, whereby cows and bulls were idolised. Biblical stories such as those of Moses scorning his people for worshipping the Golden Calf is a sign of the shift between the Age of Taurus to that of Aries.

GEMINI- The Twins, commonly symbolised as emerging from eggs. This sign is also sometimes depicted as a peacock. In Greek mythology this constellation is behind the story of the twin brothers Castor and Pollux, one immortal and one mortal; depicting our spiritual and physical selves.

CANCER- The Crab, also historically depicted as a Donkey or Scarab Beetle. There is also the symbol of the crab upon the breast of the statue of Isis (mother of Horus in ancient Egyptian mythology). If one considers the point that this sign is also related to the donkey and it is

149

during this month that we celebrate the Summer Solstice, then the story of a donkey carrying the pregnant mother towards the birth of the SON/SUN as well as that of a donkey carrying Christ into Jerusalem on Palm Sunday makes much symbolic sense.

LEO- The Lion. Also believed to be the Age of which the great Sphinx and Pyramids of Egypt were built. In fact, the Sphinx faces the Eastward emerging stars on the Spring Equinox, thus watching the rising 'Age of' constellation progressing throughout each Great Year. At this moment in time, the Sphinx stares at the space between Pisces and Aquarius as the planet shifts between these ages of man.

VIRGO- The Virgin, or Woman. In mythology around the globe, the 'sun-god' is always born of a 'Virgin' at midnight on December 25th, which is the time that the constellation Virgo is seen shining above the horizon in the East. This sign is also symbolic of the divine feminine energy.

LIBRA- The Scales, or Balance. On the 21st of September, at the time of the Autumn Equinox, the length of day and night are equal in Libra's scales. This is the only constellation that is not of a living thing.

SCORPIO- The Scorpion, also commonly symbolised by the ancients as a Serpent, Eagle or Phoenix. It is also the symbol of concealed spiritual mystery. This can be seen as the fall of Man from balance and equilibrium (Libra) by deceit (Scorpio). These interpretations show how man can leave behind the animal nature of the scorpion by embodying serpent wisdom in order to reach the peak of freedom as the eagle and reach full enlightenment as the reborn Phoenix.

SAGITTARIUS- The Archer, or beast. It is also symbolised as an Ibis or Swan. This represents the dual nature of life; of both hunter and facilitator to life and maintenance on Earth.

CAPRICORN- The Goat, or Deer. Capricorn symbolises 'sin' and is the scapegoat of the Israelites. The Christmas story has it that even Jesus was born in the stable of the goat, in order that he may conquer the remaining signs of winter (death) and thus save mankind (be reborn in the Spring).

AQUARIUS- The Water Bearer, also commonly symbolised by the ancients as a Man. Within the New Testament, Jesus is said to have told his disciples that they should "follow the man carrying a pitcher of water" in order to find Christ to symbolise the increase in spiritual consciousness as humans shift into the Age of Aquarius.

PISCES- The Fishes. This represents confirmation and baptism of water, as well as the great flood because when the Sun passes through this sign the rainy season commences.

In more recent years, it has come to light again that there is, in fact, a thirteenth constellation within the zodiac belt. **OPHIUCHUS**, also known as Serpentarius, resides between Scorpio and Sagittarius and is the sign of the Serpent-Bearer. Consider for a moment the fact that, in original Aramaic texts, Jesus was referred to as a 'naggar'. It is commonly believed that this was mistranslated as *carpenter* from 'nanger'. In actual fact, nagger (naga) means *serpent*. If true, then the constellational equivalent of Jesus could have been that of Ophiuchus; the sign of both man and serpent who is 'returning' as more people are now talking about this constellation. This zodiac system is often referred to as the **Galactic System**.

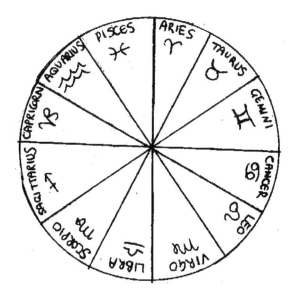

FIGURE 6 – The Zodiac Belt

Reverend Dr Red believes that the Age of Serpentarius and the Age of Aquarius are happening simultaneously. If one considers both signs hand-in-hand, then the idea of a water-carrier and a snake-tamer show relation to much of the literature surrounding the astronomical Christ. Yet, he also claims that each human must choose their path, even suggesting that this is what the Mayans were proposing when their calendar ended in 2012. Here, the choice will be between the 12-zodiac Age of Aquarius or the 13-zodiac Age of Serpentarius. As Jesus within the Bible clearly states that we are to follow *the man carrying a pitcher of water*, I am inclined to believe that it is the former in which we should maintain focus on. That said, a deep-dive into the subject is not one that I have yet taken at the time of publication.

Nonetheless, the idea of a person having to choose which Age they wish to follow between these signs is not one that is evidenced anywhere else that I could find. However, it does seem to correlate with the current train-of-thought in which mass awakening is shifting consciousness between the 3D, 4D and 5D frequencies of awareness (see Chapter 3). A theory which seems to resonate with this is that the Sidereal System is our physical journey, the Tropical is our energetic and the Galactic is our shadow self (karma from past lives and ancestral trauma). For example, my birthday is February 5th. Therefore, my Tropical is Aquarius, my Sidereal is Capricorn and my Galactic is Capricorn. So my energetic/ soul purpose is in-line with the Aquarian characteristics (humanitarian, emotional expression, intellectual advancement) and my physical and shadow missions are related to Capricorn (all work but no play, patience). Figure 7 is a brief breakdown of each of the zodiac signs based on each system.

Re-focusing on the original 12 signs, these zodiac signs can also be split into their corresponding elements based on personality: Fire (Aries, Leo and Sagittarius), Water (Cancer, Scorpio and Pisces), Air (Gemini, Aquarius and Libra) and Earth (Taurus, Virgo and Capricorn). The stars that make up each of these constellations could very well be the centre of other solar systems too far away for us to yet interact with.

Constellation	Tropical	Sidereal	Galactic
Aries	March 21 – April 20	April 15 – May 15	April 19 – May 13
Taurus	April 21 – May 21	May 16 – June 15	May 14 – June 19
Gemini	May 22 – June 23	June 16 – July 15	June 20 – July 20
Cancer	June 24 – July 23	July 16 – August 15	July 21 – August 9
Leo	July 24 – August 23	August 16 – September 15	August 10 – September 15
Virgo	August 24 – September 22	September 16 – October 15	September 16 – October 30
Libra	September 23 – October 23	October 16 – November 15	October 31 – November 22
Scorpio	October 24 – November 22	November 16 – December 15	November 23 – November 29
Ophiuchus			November 30 – December 17
Sagittarius	November 23 – December 21	December 16 – January 14	December 18 – January 18
Capricorn	December 22 – January 19	January 15 – February 14	January 19 – February 15
Aquarius	January 20 – February 18	February 15 – March 14	February 16 – March 11
Pisces	February 19 – March 20	March 15 – April 14	March 12 – April 18

FIGURE 7 – Zodiac Signs

Orion and Sirius

Fascinatingly, Adrian Gilbert (2000) discovered that the vast pyramids of Egypt correlate with the star constellation Orion. Gilbert speculates that this was to preserve knowledge of the astronomical impact for future generations. When one considers that it is the constellation Orion (a literal 'man in the sky') that can be seen rising in the East ahead of the Great Sphinx on summer solstice, the structure could have been foretelling the emergence of a new age; where man (us) and lion (Sphinx) meet again to understand the stars. Thus, it is in this generation now that we are re-awakening, as foretold by the fathers of alchemy- the Ancient Egyptians. In this way, it can be seen that the pyramids of Egypt in relation to the Nile (the Earth version of the Milky Way) appear as a view of the heavens, frozen in time.

The Planets

Within our solar system there are (debatably) 8 other planets. The impact of these on the Earth is dependent on their own place of orbit around the Sun, which naturally led to mythical stories that were passed down through the generations, much like those of the zodiac. The psychoanalysis Carl Jung (1960) classically reported that the movement of the planets impacts nature and the human psyche by reacting with the Earth's *anima telluris* (animal magnetism). As the cosmos shift, so does our perception and personality, opening the path to deeper understanding if we pursue it. According to Jennifer Gehl (2019) the alignment of these planets contribute to the solar system's own

Kundalini energy. Thus, if us as the living consciousness of Gaia can express, harvest and release this energy, we can provide this healing serpent energy to Gaia. Typically, the characteristics of these planets comprise of:

Mercury - The name Mercury derives from the winged-messenger of the Roman gods (presumed to be adopted from the Greeks). As Mercury orbits the Sun so quickly, it receives a lot of energy from the other planets through it, hence being the 'messenger'. According to Thomas Burgoyne (2013) this is the planet of intelligence and science. As it is the messenger god, it can be meditated on in order to improve communication skills. Crystals that vibrate with Mercury include agate and aventurine. It is also associated with the throat chakra and rules the signs Gemini and Virgo.

Venus - From the Roman goddess of love and beauty; a fitting name for the brightest planet observable with the naked eye. Venus teaches love, contentment and peace. Venus influences the signs Taurus and Libra and is associated with the sacral chakra (the womb space).

Earth - Our own planet is the only one not named after a Roman god, but it is associated with the Greek Goddess Gaea (Gaia), who is also believed to be the mother of Uranus. Personally, I believe that the Earth has a crystal core which is able to store infinite masses of information.

Mars - Named after the Roman god of war, most probably due to its blood-red colour. It is also considered the planet of passion and determination. Mars rules the sign Aries and the root chakra.

156

Jupiter - The Roman king of the gods and the largest planet in our solar system. Thomas Burgoyne (2013) claims Jupiter's influence is cheerful and generous. It also produces energy of psychic awareness and philosophy. Jupiter rules the sign Sagittarius and the crown chakra.

Saturn – Correlated with the Roman god of agriculture and harvest. It is also associated with karma. According to Santos Bonacci and Kelly Marie- Kerr (2019), the mythical Satan is based on the planet Saturn. This comparison of Saturn's energy to Satanic energy is due to the belief that it drives ego, anger and materialistic vibes, from a time when this frequency ruled the world by being the dominant planet in the sky. Saturn influences the sign Capricorn and the third eye chakra.

Uranus - Given its name from the deity of the heavens and father of Saturn. Yet, it is the planet of rebellion, freedom and revolution. Uranus rules the sign Aquarius and the heart chakra.

Neptune - From the god of the sea, probably from its blue colour. It is also the planet of dreams and enhanced spiritual awareness. Neptune influences the sign Pisces and the solar plexus chakra. (This can spark particular interest when considering that Pisces is the sign of Jesus and the solar plexus is said to be our inner sun.)

Pluto - Although no longer officially classified as a 'planet', Pluto is named after the god of the underworld (most likely due to being the furthest- and coldest- body from the Sun). Thus, Pluto is the planet of rebirth and adaptability. Pluto influences the sign Scorpio.

[NOTE: Cancer is ruled by the Moon and Leo is ruled by the Sun]

Sedna – A distant planet in our system that made a solar return this year [2019] after 11,000 years. Its frequency is related to water, emotional understanding and unique creative expression. Now that its vibration has returned to our area of energetic-harvest, Sedna- expert, Jennifer Gehl (2019), claims this is a time of nurturing and healing of past trauma. By healing ourselves, we can heal the planet. Like a teacher whose words you only hear when of a certain age of comprehension, Sedna's wisdom (frequency) is now influencing each of us and manifesting in a variety of imaginative ways, just as the nature of water can appear in a wide range of forms. These manifested interpretations of the same frequency can be likened to the colours of the light spectrum that, when seen in reverse, all emerge from the one source: pure [white] light. So we are all healing at the point in history, in whichever way best resonates with our own soul and inner light.

Chiron – Another distant planet whose orbit lies between Saturn and Uranus. Chiron-master, Barbara Clow (2013), states that Chiron- energy relates to connection with spirit. It is due to this increased connection that Clow titles Chiron the "rainbow bridge" as it bridges the energies of outer and inner planets (much akin to the heart chakra of the chakra system). Like Sedna, Chiron energy is a wound-healer, here to support the healing of the collective consciousness of our planet.

These planets are not only the physical counterpart to a variety of mythological characters and personalities from folklore, but they each play their part in our planet's consciousness and ascension process.

Summary

It is clear, then, that we are not a lowly planet orbiting a larger plasmic body, but we are in fact part of a larger village of celestial orbs, all affecting and supporting each other energetically. Adrian Gilbert (2000) even likens the planets of our solar system to the Kabbalistic Tree of Life (see FIGURE 12). The exact impact that each of these bodies has on us individually is as unique as a fingerprint as a result of our biorhythms. Each human, then, can be equated to a photographic snapshop of space-time based on energetic vibration at the time of birth. With regards to the sacred secretion, the most dominating of these cosmic energies are those in our immediate atmosphere, influencing us via direct and indirect photons of light from the Sun.

Recommendations

Website: www.gaia.com

Book: The Light Of Egypt by Thomas Burgoyne.

Article: Na, S. et al. 2016. Changes In The Earth's Spin Rotation Due To The Atmospheric Effects And Reduction In Glaciers. *Journal of Astronomy And Space Sciences*. 33(4):pp.295-304

Podcast: The Kundalini, The Christ and the Sacred Secretion. Kelly Marie-Kerr on The TruthSeekah Podcast, August 2019.

Video: Sadhguru, 2018, How Does The Solar System Affect Our Life? [YouTube]

Bibliography and References

Aderin-Pocock, M. 2018. *Book of the Moon.* Penguin House.

Bauval, R. and Hancock, G. 1996. *Keeper of Genesis.* Heinemann.

Boland, Y. 2016. *Moonology.* Hay House.

Burgoyne, T.2013. *The Light Of Egypt, Volume 1 and 2.* Martino Publishing.

Carey, G. 2013. *God-Man: The word made flesh.* Martino Publishing.

Clow, B. 2013. *Astrology and the rising of Kundalini.* Bear& Company.

Gaia, 2015. *How To Align With Planetary Energies.* Available online at: <www.gaia.com>

Gehl, J. 2019. *The return of planet Sedna.* Healing Arts Press.

Gilbert, A. 2000. *Signs in the Sky.* Bantam Press.

Hanuise, C. et al. 2006. From The Sun To The Earth: Impact Of The 27-28 May 2003 Solar Events On The Magnetosphere, Ionosphere and Thermosphere. *Annales Geophysicae.* 24(1):pp.129-151

Hayes, M. 2004. *The Hermetic Code in DNA.* Black Spring Press.

Jung, C.1960. *The Structure and Dynamics of the Psyche.* Routledge and Keagan Paul.

Kerr, K. 2018. *The God Design.* Seek Vision.

Mendillo, M. et al. 2018. Comparative Ionospheres: Terrestrial and Giant Planets. *Icarus.* 303:pp.34-46.

Na, S. et al. 2016. Changes In The Earth's Spin Rotation Due To The Atmospheric Effects And Reduction In Glaciers. *Journal of Astronomy And Space Sciences.* 33(4):pp.295-304

Sidorova, A. 2018. *Planets and Subtle Body: How Planet Energies Are Related To Chakras.* Available online at: www.exemplore.com

160

Stacey, F. and Hodgkinson, J. 2013. *The Earth As A Cradle For Life.* World Scientific.

Wheatley, M. 2014. *Divining Ancient Sites.* Celestial Songs Press.

Chapter 6

Light:

and the Half-Sun Prince

The photon is the force carrying particle behind all electromagnetic interactions. John St Julien Baba Wanyama is commonly heard within his YouTube videos on syncretism referring to the photon as an 'angle of light', deeming them the true player behind the phrase 'angel of light'. Once this is comprehended, it is no longer difficult to understand why the ancients were often said to have been visited by God's 'angels', as these may well have simply been the term used to mean 'vision' (which tended to appear during meditative and sleeping states of consciousness).

Sunlight is made up of many different wavelengths of light. The known forms of these are: cosmic rays; gamma rays; x-rays; far ultraviolet; mid and near ultraviolet (ultra violet literally meaning 'above violet'); violet; indigo; blue; green; yellow; orange; red; shortwave infrared (infrared meaning 'below red'); infrared; radio waves; and electric waves. The fact that we can only see the coloured parts of the spectrum within our current field of vision proves that there is far more to the world than a human can see. We can, however, sense these and respond to them, like getting a suntan and synthesising Vitamin D.

The power of light is referenced throughout the Bible, evidencing its relevance and perceived power throughout history. From religious literary sources, some of the most renowned references to light include:

- **"Let there be light" [Genesis 1:3]** – In the beginning, the first thing God creates is light. Therefore, light is the foundation of all life.
- **"The light of the body is in the eye. If, therefore, thine eye be single, the whole body shall be full of light." [Matthew 6:22]** – Here, it is commonly believed that the 'single eye' is referring to the pineal gland/ optic thalamus. Consequently, when one is able to see past the materialism reported to the brain via the physical eyes and, instead, listen to the sights from the pineal-eye, inner light is emitted.
- **"God is light; in him there is no darkness at all" [John 1:5]**
- **"I have come into the world as light so that no one who believes in me need remain in the dark" [John 12:46]**
- God sitting on his throne in heaven, encircled by the colours of the rainbow, the **"seven lamps of fire" [Revelations 4:5]** – These lamps of fire are, in fact, the chakra system. If God's throne is surrounded by the chakras, then it can be inferred that our body is indeed the throne of God.
- The Koran also has a chapter entitled 'Light': **"Allah is the light of the heavens and the Earth... light upon light, Allah guideth unto his light whom he will"** – Thus, Allah is God,

God is the light of the Earth, the light of the Earth is the Sun, the Son is God in physical form on Earth, and the Christ Oil is the physical Son. Allah, in this way, uses his 'light' to guide.

- In Egypt, Pharaoh's names often ended in the suffix **-re** or **-ra** ("Sun") to indicate their divine status. As Ancient Egypt is renowned for its advocation of spiritual advancement, the pharaohs' names can be translated as meaning 'light' or 'enlightened'. They may have even had this enlightenment enhanced by the energy-rich dark rooms of the pyramids.

An entire book could be written on the references to light in ancient literature, but the above are just a few that are relevant to the sacred secretion at this current point of remembering within this practice. From this, it can be seen that there is particular reference to inner light. The remainder of this chapter will seek to detail some of the current philosophies around the meaning and purpose of inner light.

The Photoelectric Effect

Einstein received his 1921 Noble Prize in Physics for his documentation of the Photoelectric Effect. This concluded that light behaves like a wave in some circumstances (like in the slit experiments) and particles in others (through photoelectric properties- such as when reflecting off of metal). Today, the wave-particle duality of light is accepted. Thus, many metals emit electrons when light shines upon them, and light affects the movement of electric charges. Interestingly, de Brogile suggested that all atoms- not just light- act as both particles and waves. Such phenomena seems to be effected by consciousness. That is, that human thought and presence can affect the action of particles, supporting the old saying: "Where attention goes, energy flows."

It is intriguing to note that scientist Robert Becker (1985) showed that this photoelectric effect was also evident within the body and had profound healing effects, even providing the necessary foundations for potential limb and organ regrowth. Similarly, Jerry Tennant proclaims that muscles elicit a piezoelectric effect when they move/ when we exercise, acting as rechargeable battery systems and deeming us literal *beings of light*. This would explain why we feel dull when we don't move as we are not honouring the needs of our *light body*. This is also the same force at work when the Moon reflects light energy from the Sun and stars to Earth.

Bioluminescence

Bioluminescence is the production and emission of light by a living organism, deriving its name from a hybrid word, from the Greek *bio* for "living" and the Latin *lumen* for "light". Bioluminescence is a naturally occurring form of chemiluminescence where energy is released by a chemical reaction in the form of light. Fireflies, anglerfish, and other creatures produce light in this way through the chemicals luciferin (a pigment) and luciferase (an enzyme). Luciferin reacts with oxygen to create light and luciferase acts as a catalyst to speed up the reaction, which can also be mediated by calcium ions or ATP. Basically, oxygen can be used to produce visible light. The pineal is designed to emit inner light and is affected by external sources of light. This in turn influences the communication between other cells within the body via 'messengers of light'. It is in the same way that the human organism can produce inner light, which has been evidenced in recent years by the fact that the pineal has been shown to produce luciferin (see Chapter 14).

Biophotons

Biophotons are photons of light produced by a biological system, such as a cell, the emissions of which are a type of luminescence. German biophysicist, Fritz-Albert Popp, showed that light is released from the DNA within cells. He called these biophotons and claimed that this light can repair damaged cells, in a phenomenon known as 'photo-repair' (much like Jesus [light] healing the sick [cells]). Sayer Ji (2013) summarises the purpose of biophotons within his article: *The Human Body Emits, Communicates with, and is Made From Light*. Sayer states that our cells and DNA use biophotons to store information and even speculates that these outputs are governed by solar and lunar forces. Due to the fact that the famous double-slit experiment (whereby one photon can be in multiple places at once but, when observed, only chooses one course of action) shows that electromagnetic energy is linked to the consciousness observing it, it is not surprising that such energy is also manipulatable through intention, such as meditation and visualisation.

To sum, this evidence suggests that the human form is able to change and emit DNA frequencies via light energy. Similarly, DNA expression can be adapted based on external energy influx, such as Moon phases. Furthermore, research by Murphy et al (1993) demonstrated that the DNA helix is able to attract and modulate photons and electrons, proving the DNA's ability to intelligently interact with the electromagnetic field. Thus, when considering that our light energy is our sovereignty as we can store, exchange and emit these in varying quantities, the purpose of money as an energy exchange can be seen as of good when conducted with pure gratitude and honouring, but of evil when giving/ taking from a place of power and greed.

In addition, biophotons are used by the cells of many living organisms to communicate, which facilitates energy/information transfer that is several orders of magnitude faster than chemical diffusion. Even when we go down to the molecular level of our genome, DNA can be identified to be a source of biophoton emissions. Popp et al (1984) even proposes that DNA is so biophoton dependent that is has *"excimer laser-like properties"*, enabling it to exist in a stable state far from thermal equilibrium. Technically speaking, a biophoton is quantum light of non-thermal origin in the visible and ultraviolet spectrum emitted from a biological system. For us non-scientists, this simply means that DNA uses light as a form of communication, both internally and externally and that this method of communication is exponentially faster than any other.

Consider this: a single photon can store the genetic signature of DNA and the blackhole zero-point portal in our galaxy (our cosmic womb) all

167

in one place at the same time, hence is able to remotely transfer super charged DNA via the photon belt's cosmic web (so we can transfer DNA light codes within the collective consciousness of Earth *and* of other solar systems). As Gaia anchored into 5D consciousness (explained later in this chapter) in recent decades, her photonic light is forcing Earth's sentient beings (that includes us!) to ascend alongside her, like our own mitochondria. This process is sped up as more human beings not only take in these energies and generate these photons of light within themselves, but by encouraging and enabling this energy exchange with others within the collective consciousness.

According to Chang (2017), the Sun and Moon affect biophoton emissions through gravitational influences, synchronising to rhythms associated with the lunisolar tide. Therefore, when the Moon enters our star sign, the release of biophotons (inner quantum light) is affected and influences communication within our genome (genetics).

Light Codes

The term *light codes* is increasing within the mainstream and is typically referring to the activations given to humans in order to upregulate their previously dormant genetics, also referred to as encryptions. Basically, a person receives light codes, which cause biophoton release that leads to a specific DNA activation/ expression. This trigger could be as simple as a word or tone. The current theory of DNA leads us to believe that our genetics are hereditary and can only be adapted epigenetically by physical means. Practitioners who use the phrase 'light codes', though, are aware of the non-physical ways in which potential can be accessed.

Light codes can be understood as energy, biophotons, light patterns, colours, sounds, shapes, sacred geometries and so on. Even the food we eat and the water we drink hold these DNA altering codes. This is why crystal elixirs and solarising/ lunarising water (discussed in Chapter 20) can be so effective during the awakening process. Light codes are also accessible through communications with other worldly beings, including ancestors and other galactic modalities or energies from parallel worlds, such as fairies (earth spirits) and merfolk (water energy), via meditation or mindful communication. Here, a person is able to energetically tap into a frequency that causes a biophoton response and subsequent DNA activation.

Humans can even activate their light codes by simply viewing the drawn light language depicted by enlightened gurus, many of which also physically speak light language, which can awaken potentials by simply being heard. Yoga and dancing are also acts of physical activity which massage the unlocking of particular codes. One that I have always felt particular connection with is the use of hand gestures, much akin to the use of hands as channels in practices such as Reiki, which influences the expression of the body's energy (including these DNA light codes). This is particularly interesting when considering the huge increase in popularity of a kind of *hand-dancing* phenomena performed by children and teenagers, similar to the more classical *hand jiving*.

Many children seem naturally inclined towards the expression of light language in such physical ways.

Here is a short light code transmission that I received during a meditative state whilst channelling the frequency for a successful receiving of the sacred secretion seed:

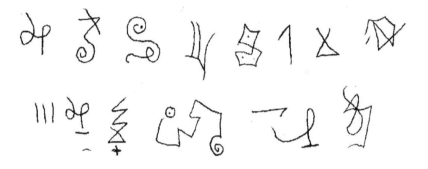

FIGURE 8 – LIGHT CODE

Clearly, all roads lead to the same place of enlightenment. As light beings, we are remembering how to navigate this matrix of realities, seeking help when ready to do so. As like-attracts-like, when a person is ready to shift their level of consciousness, they will attract the necessary light codes that will assist this transition. Then, as higher frequencies of light are embodied, even higher levels can be held. This is ascension and the meaning behind one's "*light* body". Life within this physical realm, then, could be seen as a game, whereby our DNA consists of all of the potentials and options that we can take as we navigate towards completion.

In short, the vibrational input from the external environment changes the electromagnetic frequency of one's own physical body and causes a cascade of reactions through the transportation of biophotons, which activates and upregulates parts of the DNA. In this way, these light codes can be seen as literal *downloads* from universe, similar to those imbedded as part of the Matrix movies.

As mentioned previously, the planet Earth is said to have anchored into 5D consciousness itself and, as a result, we are given the opportunity to access more abundance of light codes which support our journey alongside this macrocosmic entity. And as more and more humans upregulate their own energy in resonance, the planet can continue to ascend even higher, into 6D and beyond. We are all doing our part by simply existing and enjoying the ride.

So, light codes are frequencies which modulate our DNA and can upgrade our physical vehicle into higher states of awareness, including into the 5D consciousness. DMT and other psychedelics offer a glimpse into such parallel worlds of existence, which can begin the process of unravelling the encryptions on one's current strands of DNA. The sacred secretion is a way of upregulating inner light and accessing forms of these light codes which are connected to the cosmos. When one is able to activate and embody enough light, a person is said to develop crystalline DNA and present a literal *light* body, which emits higher vibrating energy which can also empower others who seek it. Those who feel called into such practice in order to support the collective often call themselves *light workers*.

Light workers recognise themselves as the physical manifestation of pure light and consciousness and seek to use this to guide others. They are actively on the spiritual path and are able to anchor into the higher dimensions of spirit in order to bring the Earth into greater levels of harmony and connectedness. Similar to a light worker is that of a *starseed*. These phrases often overlap and a person can be both; a starseed simply feels more connection to the cosmos. As DNA/ light codes are able to travel vast distances across space and time, starseeds can even hold encrypted DNA from other galaxies.

Jude Currivan, author of *The Cosmic Hologram*, collectively calls all of these beings 'way-showers'. Currivan describes way-showers as expressions of consciousness here to wake the rest of the world up to the fact that we are part of the cosmos. Thus, they literally *show the way* to awakening. I personally prefer the term *way-showers* as it represents all aspects of earthly consciousness, whether of terrestrial or extra-terrestrial influence, and it does not differentiate into *groups*. Instead, we are all equal. The fact that there are increasing numbers of way-showers incarnating on Earth is a phenomenon previously explored by Doreen Virtue.

According to Doreen Virtue (2009), prayers from the beings of Earth during the world wars were heard and help was sent in the form of light workers, which she refers to as *Indigo Children*. These began the revolution of waking up for humanity. In and around the 1990s, a further influx of help is said to have incarnated into physical form as *Crystal Children*. These were the starseeds who wanted to witness and support the mass awakening of Earth. At the moment, Doreen claims that *Rainbow Children* are being born, who are brand new souls who have chosen to begin their spiritual journey on Earth as 'like attracts like' and we, as a planet, are emitting these higher frequencies of love and happiness.

Whether Doreen's interpretation resonates with you or not, the fact remains that our DNA is full of encryptions which can be activated and modulated via light codes. Such philosophies are even more evident when considering the structure of the brain.

Neuromelanin

Melanin is a chemical that attracts light, is bioelectrical and is able to shift energy from one state to another. Fascinatingly, within the brain is a dark pigmented material called neuromelanin. This is highly sensitive to light and movement and has a high iron content that makes it especially sensitive to changes in the magnetic field. According to Edward Bynum (2012), as we look up the evolutionary ladder, brain melanin (AKA neuromelanin) increases. Bynum claims that neuromelanin is highly sensitive to light and magnetism and has luminous bio-conductivity properties; thus deeming light as the fifth-dimensional force. The part of the brainstem withholding the neuromelanin is called substantia nigra (Latin for 'black substance') and forms part of the basal ganglia, which, interestingly, looks like the sign of Aries (a pair of horns).

Importantly, the substantia nigra is responsible for the regulation of dopamine, a neurotransmitter responsible for emotional responses, specifically motivation and pleasure-seeking. According to Bynum (2012), when the Sacred Serpent (AKA the sacred secretion) enters the 4th ventricle (a fluid-filled space in the brain), the entire region begins to vibrate. This could be viewed as an 'earthquake', just like the one that is said to have shook the world as Yeshua/ Jesus Christ died on the cross.

The presence of neuromelanin is further evidence of the fundamental link between brain function and light. The question is: If melanin can convert light into heat, could it not also transform UV radiation into other biologically/metabolically useful forms of energy? This may not seem so farfetched when one considers that even gamma radiation, which is highly toxic to most forms of life, is a source of sustenance for certain types of fungi and bacteria.

Light as Physical Energy

Dr Pollack (2013) states that the Sun's electromagnetic energy builds potential in water as it becomes charged by photons. Pollack suggests that, similarly, solar energy may build energy in our human bodies due to the fact that cells grow faster with warmth, plus light builds energy in water. As humans are mostly water, it could be argued that photosynthesis is not unique to plants, and that laying out in the Sun like a primrose may in fact be just what the [naturopathic] doctor ordered for us humans, too! With this in mind, let's briefly consider the role of the mitochondria again.

The mitochondria within our cells use a cascade of chemical reactions to produce energy, which is very complex but, basically, glucose goes in and ATP (energy) comes out. As one glucose molecule can be converted into 38 ATP molecules, this is a pretty fair deal! (Although 1 fat molecule generates 129 ATP molecules, which evidences the body's preference towards fat energy over sugar.) Interestingly, through this system a human can produce (per gram) 10,000 times more energy than the Sun every second. I may be off the mark, but, to me, it seems perfectly reasonable to propose that the claim within the Biblical Revelations that vast numbers of humans with higher consciousness (reached by 'going within' to connect to God) have the ability to empower the Earth and heavens without the requirement of the Sun and Moon, seems plausible.

Within the frequency of the Age of Aquarius, this could be symbolised metaphorically as humans being the waters of the Earth, which are given power and excited by the Sun, causing an increase in vibration (like water evaporating up into the clouds). Once the collective is strong enough (when full saturation of the cloud has been met), the structure and dimensions shift and pour down in order to give full life to Gaia and the other creatures in which we were put in charge to care for (in the form of rain; physically accessible matter).

With such an important role in the functioning of every part of the body, these living organelles called mitochondria are truly the essence of life. Interestingly, mitochondria even emit biophotons, which further enhance communication in the body via light. According to Magenta Pixie (2019), when one becomes awakened spiritually, that process of enlightenment is in fact simply a charging of the mitochondria. Pixie claims that, as the batteries of the human body, channelling energy within the body (e.g. through raising the Kundalini or preserving the sacred secretion) gives mitochondria a higher charge, which can then activate dormant DNA and cause light body transformations, including upregulating the individual and collective consciousness into the 5D.

In sum so far, light is a gift from our Father Sun, which provides energy and healing to all parts of the body. Thus, light is literally the 'food of the Gods'. In plants and animals, bioluminescence is believed to be a form of communication. As such, ancient humans may have used inner light in the same way, communicating with each other both physically and spiritually, possibly even telepathically. Unfortunately, many modern technologies block and prevent the expansion of such luminescence.

Blue Light

Blue light is a wavelength of visible light within the electromagnetic spectrum which, when it hits our eyes, signals to the brain that it is daytime, so melatonin production should be halted. Naturally, the red sunset, then darkness at night, stimulate the pineal gland to start producing melatonin again, thus calming the brain and sending the body into sleep. However, with so much artificial light nowadays emitting this blue part of the spectrum (through such means as TV and phone screens), the brain is not able to read this signal, leading to the poor-quality sleep detailed in Chapter 3. Putting orange screen shades on electronics and wearing blue-light-blocking glasses in the evening are some simple ways of supporting hormone regulation, which we can see is intrinsically related to the light spectrum.

Sun Gazing

Sungazing is the act of staring at the Sun at the time of rise and set in order to absorb the light frequencies responsible to optimal health and circadian function. Although this is gaining popularity in the modern era, even the Ancient Egyptians and Aztecs are said to have practised sungazing. Some people, such as Indian Guru: Hira Ratan Manek, claim to have not eaten since beginning the practice of sungazing, stating that they *eat the sun.* The benefits of sungazing include increased melatonin production and circadian rest (optimal for pineal health), increased energy production and reduces stress (due to the alignment of hormone production), improved eyesight and immune system, steady weight loss/ gain in order to reach your body's *preferred* weight, and, apparently, a bigger pineal gland!

So how do you do it? At sunrise and sunset, when the Sun is closest to Earth, stand barefoot on the earth (if possible) and look directly at the sun for 10 seconds, increasing by an additional 10 seconds every day that you complete this practice until, according to Sungazing.com, you reach the safety-peak of 44 minutes. From personal practice, my REM sleep time (discussed in Chapter 3) almost doubled once I started sungazing, so I consequently believe that there is also a link between taking in these red- sun frequencies and spiritual development/ DMT production.

177

Summary

Our entire being is governed by light. Light gives us energy in the form of food growth and vitamin synthesis, as well as providing us with the ability to navigate via our physical and spiritual senses. In the modern age, bio-hacks are required in order to maintain light equilibrium, such as through blue-light blocking glasses and increased infra-red light. Moreover, not only does light give us life, but our own microcosmic bodies are also able to emit photons in the same way in order to establish energetic connection and to give energy back to source also, in a give-and-take fashion, much akin to the relationship we ourselves have to our own inner microbiome. Thus, non-physical energies cause physical reactions within the body, which then release further non-physical energy, in a beautiful cycle of life (or light!). These light codes can be activated in a number of ways, such as by meditating on various symbols within sacred geometry, which we will delve into next.

As more light code transmissions are received and utilised, the DNA begins to convert into what is termed *crystalline DNA*. Crystalline DNA is DNA of a higher light quotient/ frequency that is resonant with quartz (including Gaia's crystal core). This allows for increase access between dimensions and for quantum shifts, deeming a person capable of bilocation, telepathy, telekinesis and other forms of 'psychic' abilities. The physical body will also feel lighter and more radiant due to more biophotons and mitochondria. So, when we talk of crystalline DNA, we talk of higher vibrating DNA; when we talk of the light body, we mean a physical vessel that is able to hold a higher quotient of light. They are both interrelated. Ascension, then is the process of increasing your body's light quotient. When our bodies are vibrating higher, we can even conceive and birth other beings that can hold higher frequencies, who may even remember their past lives and have 'powers'. It's like upgrading to a new vehicle or changing your character's armour on a game in order to reach higher levels and succeed in missions. The sacred secretion, then, can be seen as a cheat code for this game.

Recommendations

Website: www.weare1inspirit.com

Book: The Body Electric by Robert Becker

Article: Popp, F. et al. 1984. Biophoton emission. New evidence for coherence and DNA as source. Cell Biophysics. 6(1):pp.33-52.

Podcast: Extreme Health Radio

Video: Dr Jack Kruse – Blue Light Toxicity, Mitigating 5G & Mitochondrial Health [YouTube]. 7 August 2018. *Extremehealthradio*

Bibliography and References

Aberts, B., Hopkins, K., Jonson, A., Morgan, D., Raff, M., Roberts, K. and Walter, P. 2019. *Essential Cell Biology.* 5th Ed. WW Norton and Company.

Adaes, S. 2019. Mitochondria: 10 ways to boost the powerhouse of your cells. [online] Available at: <draxe.com>

Al-Khalili, J. 2012. Quantum: A Guide for The Perplexed. Orion Books.

Becker, R. and Seldon, G. 1985. The Body Electric. Harper Collins Publishers.

Bynum, E. 2012. Dark Light Consciousness. Inner Traditions.

Dispenza, J. 2017. Becoming Supernatural. Hay House.

Hayes, M. 2004. The Hermetic Code in DNA. Black Spring Press.

Hugo J Niggli, H. et al. 2005. Laser-ultraviolet-A-induced ultraweak photon emission in mammalian cells. J *Biomed Opt.* 10(2):024006.

Ji, S. 2013. The Human Body Emits, Communicates with, and is Made From Light. *GreenMedInfo LLC.* Available online at: <www.greenmedinfo.health>

Kedia, S. 2020. *Sun Gazing: How to Sun Gaze and Sun Gazing benefits.* Themindfool.com

Know, L. 2018. *Mitochondria and the Future of Medicine.* Green Publishing.

Kobayashi, M., Kikuchi, D. and Okamura, H. 2009. Imaging of ultraweak spontaneous photon emission from human body displaying diurnal rhythm. PLoS One. 4(7):e6256.

Lane, N. 2005. *Power, Sex, Suicide.* Oxford.

Lewis, D. 2015. *Saint Germain on Advanced Alchemy.* Meru Press.

Liberman, J. 1991. *Light: Medicine of the Future.* Bear and Company.

Mercola, J. 2018. *Feasting on Sunshine.* Mercola.com

Montagnier, L. et al. DNA Waves and Water. Available online at: <http://www.rexresearch.com/montagnier/montagnier.htm>

Murphy, C. et al. 1993. Long-Range Photoinduced Electron Transfer Through a DNA Helix. Science. 262(5136)

Niggli, H. 1993. Artificial sunlight irradiation induces ultraweak photon emission in human skin fibroblasts. J *Photochem Photobiol* B. 18(2-3):pp.281

Peake, A. 2013. *The Infinite Mindfield.* Watkins Publishing LTD.

Pixie, M. 2019. *The black box programme and the rose gold flame as antidote.* Independently Published.

Popp, F. et al. 1984. Biophoton emission. New evidence for coherence and DNA as source. *Cell Biophys.* 6(1):pp.33-52.

Schwabl, H. and Klima, H. 2005. Spontaneous Ultraweak Photo Emission From Biological Systems and the Endogenous Light Field. Forsch Komplementarmed Klass Naturheikd. 12(2):pp.84-49.

Shambhallah. 2018. *Sungazing 101.* Sun-gazing.net

Virtue, D. 2009. *The Crystal Children.* Hay House UK.

Wallace, D. 2009. Mitochondria, bioenergetics and the epigenome in eukaryotic and human evolution. 74:pp.383-393. *Harb Symp Quant Biol.*

Chapter 7

Laws of Nature:

And the Cosmic Hallows

In 2006, Stephen Hawkings suggested that all that has, will and could happen is encoded in a huge information field. Jude Currivan (2016) supports this by evidencing that information is quantized because this is the most effective means of communication, including the recording, storing, processing and retrieving of information, both locally and nonlocally. These quantum bits (qubits) are reported to be the informational building blocks embedded within the probability factor of physics. Hawking and Hertog (2006) proposed that the universe started in a superposition of all possible outcomes and that, with each action taken by us, wave functions (states) collapse to create that conscious reality. Therefore, all possibilities are available to us in this present moment, it is only when we observe and alter our energy field with an emotional output that a particular path manifests. The electron reactions in nature that make this possible are collectively referred to as the 'laws' or 'principles' of nature, which are seen as the 'consciousness' of the planet. Ecologist James Lovelock coined the name of the Greek

182

goddess Gaia to describe the scientific principle in which nature has its own self-regulating systems and mechanisms, deeming the planet a living organism. It is for this reason that the term 'Gaia' is used throughout this text when referring to the Earth. It is these laws of nature that ensure all organisms, including Gaia, follow cyclical paths and patterns. Often, these patterns can be seen visually as shapes.

Sacred Geometry

The universe is governed by number frequencies. When a snapshot is taken of these vibrations, a visual representation manifests in the form of shapes. Even the human form can be likened to a snapshot of all of the frequencies from the surrounding influential bodies that come together to create a perfect form: the human being. Sacred Geometry is the title given to the collection of shapes and patterns that repeatedly appear in varying sizes throughout the natural world. From these lines and waves, everything in the world manifests and, consequently, follows the same rules and cycles. In this way, the entire universe is a geometric design projecting in both macro and micro forms, as if created with intelligent intention. These patterns and ratios are also evident in music, light and even cosmology.

On a numerical level, these shapes resonate at 3, 6 and 9 (Hopkins, 2017), which could explain the reasoning behind Nikola Tesla's famous saying: "If you only knew the magnificence of the 3, 6 and 9, then you would have the key to the universe." The human body itself, when stretched out, forms a perfect circle (360= 3+6+0= 9) and, according to

Leonard Horowitz (2011), even the emotion of love has a frequency of 528 hertz (5+2+8=15=1+5=6). Additionally, the chakras of the body also follow the same repeated, symmetrical rules of sacred geometry, each increasing in complexity the further up the body in which the energy resides. Each of the 3D shapes related to a chakra can be seen within the Fruit of Life (see FIGURE 11) These geometric shapes are even referred to as *geometric* keys, thought to be able to work as light codes to trigger memories both physically and spiritually. With a natural attraction to flowers and the doodling of shapes, sacred geometry seems to be etched into the human psyche at the foundational level.

FIGURE 9 – The Seed of Life

Geometric thought-forms even allow you to key into the creative process, which is why so many people practice meditating on specific shapes. The most notable of these includes the Seed of Life (7 circles). The appearance of the Seed of Life also shows striking resemblance to that of at atom (the building block of all energy and matter) as well as the zygote multiplying into a blastocyst (following conception).

The most renowned shape in sacred geometry is that of the Flower of Life. The Flower of Life is like a 2D overlapping of circles which, as the name suggests, appears similar to a flower. Within this, varying dots can be connected which result in the manifestations of every other shape, including 3D representations. David Hopkins (2017) has had some exceptional experiences when focusing on this geometric form, which he claims can even allow one to birth their desired reality. Basically, a person meditates on this image and observes what emits from it. Interestingly, the Flower of Life typically contains 13 circles (one in the middle and twelve surrounding it), which follows the 12+1 pattern we see throughout the physical world, not least in the zodiac (12 constellations + 1 Sun) and the Bible (12 disciples + 1 Christ), which, together, form the one; the whole.

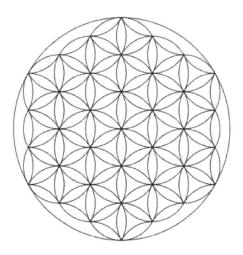

FIGURE 10 – The Flower of Life

From the Flower of Life, one can create the Fruit of Life (much like the *seed* which grew into a *flower* in order to merge male and female energy together via pollination so that the child, the *fruit*, can spread the vibration and continue God's work). The Fruit of Life appears as a six-point star (like the Star of David) and is created from 13 circles (the 12+1, again). Within the Fruit of Life, one can depict Metatron's Cube.

Metatron was the biblical prophet Enoch before God ascended him to heaven. Thus, he is between divine god and human, helping all of creation to maintain balance between the physical and the spiritual. In sacred geometry, Archangel Metatron, the angel of life who oversees the flow of earthly energies through his mystical cube (which contains all of the geometric shapes and patterns of God's creation), oversees the Tree of Life in Kabbalah.

Interestingly, his cube is depicted as the crown of this, paralleled to the literal angel or star on top of the tree, as is accustom to Christmas tradition. This is evidence towards the belief of the Christmas festival being linked to the sacred secretion and our corresponding return to God the father. Such philosophies hold even stronger truths when one considers that it is Metatron, the angel on top of the tree, who sends creative energy from the heavens down to the base of the tree, which Archangel Sandalphon (Metatron's spiritual brother), using Shekinah (the female part of God's energy) reflects that power back up the tree again in order to ensure a constant flow between God, angels and people. (If this doesn't make sense yet, read it again at the end of Part 1.)

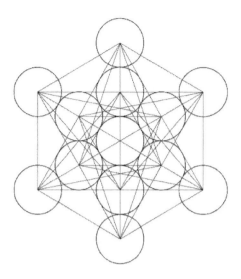

FIGURE 11 – Metatron's Cube

Now, what is particularly interesting about the Kabbalah Tree of Life is its relation to our own solar and chakra systems ('As above, so below'). Within this, it can be seen how the archangels of God relate to our closest cosmic bodies and the chakra system. From FIGURE 12, the flow of energy can be seen from the lighter lining, from the zodiac and in a zig-zag fashion (like a lightning bolt or serpent) down to the body-Earth. Hence, we can see how the energy from the zodiac passes through the solar system until it reaches the Earth, and how this relates to the energy centres of the physical body, as well as the Archangels of God .

Of all the study I have taken into Sacred Geometry, Randall Carlson by far has enlightened me the most. His explanations are so thorough, understandable and compelling that anyone can make sense of this phenomena. Carlson's research (see Bilbliography) shows that the sacred geometry of the ancients communicates some key numerical terms, notably 25920. We know that there is around 25,920 years in a Great Year (how long it takes the Sun to do a full lap of the zodiac), which can be split into 12 Great Months (one for each sign) and 4 Great Seasons. It is these 4 Great Seasons which, historically, tend to cause the most upheaval for Earth. These seasons, symbolised in ancient mythology as the Bull, Lion, Eagle and Man, dictate when chaos is due to hit the planet. Randall refers to these as the 'pulse of global change' and they often manifest as meteor impact, ice ages, flooding, etc, and lead to mass extinctions. Thus, just as each chakra resonates with a specific geometric shape connected to varying energetic forces such as star constellations, which manifests physically in the form of glands, hormones and moods, the Earth also has its own biorhythms within the universe. As we are part of this collective being called Gaia, our own frequency also waxes and wanes in resonance.

As mentioned previously, Gaia recently anchored into 5D density, and those of us who develop the 'light body' will be able to hold the frequencies high enough to ascend with her. The physical, 3D human body is carbon-based, hence *the number of man* being 666 (based on the atomic structure of Carbon 12, which has 6 protons, 6 neutrons and 6 electrons). According to Chang (2019), in order to survive the higher frequencies (including 5G technology), the human form needs to develop a crystalline body, also known as the *light body*. The crystalline form differs from the carbon as the cells of the body acquire more silica/ quartz potential. Quartz crystals are the batteries of the stone family. They are energy transmuters (like the pineal gland) and are even used in computers and watches to this day. Humans with a crystalline body develop the ability to control frequency and reach higher levels of light due to increased biophoton exchange.

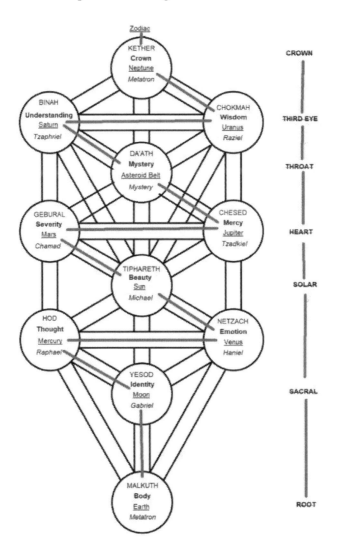

FIGURE 12 – The Tree of Life

Ways of structuring the body into this crystalline form include sun-gazing, drinking structured water, meditating with and wearing crystals, and, of course, preserving the sacred secretion, to name a few. But more on that, later. For now, here are some other key sacred geometric terms worth knowing:

Fractals - Dimensions that appear the same at different levels, like a pattern that the laws of nature repeat at varying scales. Some examples of fractals are snail shells, broccoli, leaves and even the fact that both the Earth and humans are about 70% liquid. Similarly, the microcosm (human being) can be seen as a fractal of the macrocosm (universal energy). Thus, phenomena observed in the heavens directly manifests inside each person, too, in resonance with the laws of nature. According to Jude Currivan, fractals are the clearest evidence of the universe's holographic nature. That is, that all things are an expression of information; of the One source expressing itself within aspects of consciousness. Currivan states that scientists take decades (even millennia) to prove what seers, sages and shaman have always known intuitively. Her vast studies of physics have led to her conclusion that DNA acts like a computer, capable of downloading information from the cosmos. This is because expressing information in the form of quantum bits is proven the most effective means of conscious and universal communication. Humans, as microcosmic gods, are fractals of source energy. By raising and preserving the sacred secretion, a crystalline human returns to the Christos Fractal Family; the fractal of Christ consciousness. In this way, we can be seen a literal God-seeds.

Another example is a rhomboid calcite crystal. If this is dropped, it will chip off into smaller rhomboid shapes. This is because the stone is a perfect fractal. The small make up the hole and vice versa; the whole exists within the whole.

The Fibonacci Constant, also known as the Golden Spiral or Golden Ratio - A mathematical formula that manifests everywhere in nature. The Fibonacci Constant is found by systematically adding the previous two numbers (e.g. 1+1=**2**, 1+2=**3**, 2+3=**5**, 3+5=**8**, 5+8=**13**, 13+8=**21**, etc.) It is often depicted as a spiral to demonstrate the symmetry of all life on Earth. Within the human body, the Fibonacci Constant is evident not only within the DNA helix, but, if you follow the golden ratio along the circumference of the brain, the spiral will end at the exact point of the pineal. Consequently, it is evident that the pineal is, in fact, the central seat (or throne) of the entire being. Interestingly, the human face as well as the human body also follow the golden ratio- as demonstrated by the work of Ernst Neufert and Le Corbusier. So, again, it appears that the human form is indeed a product of intelligent design. Other examples of the golden ratio at work in nature include the seed heads of flowers, vegetables such as cauliflower, shells, galaxies, DNA molecules and, of course, the pinecone (signified in Chapter 11). Fascinatingly, the Sphinx lies at the golden ratio of the Giza Plateau.

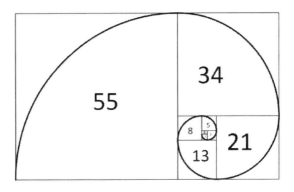

FIGURE 13 – The Golden Ratio

Although similar, the Fibonacci sequence is a sequence whereas fractals are geometric objects.

This short passage in no way exhausts the vast information available on Sacred Geometry. It is a field of extreme interest to me and one I will continue to study into the future as it feels fundamental to a deeper understanding of the birthing process of all life, including the spiritual seed, within this planet of clear intelligent design. The fact that the entire universe follows such specific rules is evidence for the 'as above, so below' theory. Intriguingly, further evidence of the interconnected ties between the macro and microcosms of the universe is within the straight ley lines of the globe. See, the geomagnetic and electromagnetic fields around and within the Earth create a grid system, which the ancients believed to be the planet's nervous system. This phenomenon was used by the ancients to provide power to such holy monuments as cathedrals and stone circles.

Ley Lines

The Earth's magnetic field is generated via the dynamo theory; that is, that the electric currents in the liquid outer core generate the magnetic field. This happens because the liquid outer core has an abundance of free electrons that form a current due to the pulsating magnetic field, which is why we get electrons when grounding. Solar flares, cosmic rays and other terrestrial phenomenon then further effect this. From these there are specific 'meridians' (also called 'nadis' or 'leys') which emit distinctive geometric patterns. These are said to be the nervous system of the Earth and thus are, energetically, very powerful. Maria Wheatley (2014) claims that these frequencies are beneficial to living organisms, although some may be more beneficial to certain creatures over others. As a result, the ancients would often mark these powerful energies using circular structures, which further energised the area as the frequencies become concentrated.

Wheatley (2014) also believes that the ley system is an astrological clock. This could be explained by the Earth's position (and the place of the ley lines in correspondence) to the solar influx, which would interfere with the geomagnetism of these natural power lines. Therefore, certain times of the year would increase the power of certain leys. Stone circles and monuments placed on these powerlines could then harvest these increased energies at particular intervals, leading to the formation of annual festivals and celebrations, such as the solstices and equinoxes. What's more, it is even believed that the energy of these power lines can be harvested to produce a free, everlasting flow of energy, like those dreamed by Tesla.

This natural earth energy regulates DNA and the cells of our body. Each second, 810,000 cells are being replaced, re-built by the food we eat but having their communication effected by the energy fields around us. Certain Hertz frequencies even trigger cell rejuvenation. Therefore, where one lives and sleeps with respect to these power lines will have obvious effects on the organism, as well as how much interference there is between a person (microcosm) and the Earth-home (macrocosm). It is for this reason that Grounding (described in Chapter 2) is strongly advocated, by way of ensuring connection between a person and the planet. So consciousness is simply an awareness of existence, whereas enlightenment is self-realisation. Awakening, then, implies waking up to your true nature and your unique connection to the larger macrocosm.

The Hermetic Principles

Richard Feynman once famously said, "If you think you understand quantum mechanics, you don't understand quantum mechanics". As a result of this incomprehensible quantum world, laws of nature have manifested that can teach the resulting outcome of these correspondences. In Ancient Egyptian times, these rules of the Earth were more readily referred to as the 'Hermetic Principles'.

Hermes was a great master who passed on his wisdom to the Egyptians. Following his death, he was crowned as a god and renamed Thoth. When Hermes teachings were written down, they were encoded within alchemical and astrological metaphors so that only those who were permitted to use it, for the greater good, would be taught to understand it. Rather aptly, the students of the Hermetic teachings were referred to as the Hermetists- the original alchemists, astrologers and psychologists. The text encoding these principles is the Kybalion, which clearly states that: "When the ears of the student are ready to hear, then cometh the lips to fill them with wisdom". Therefore, as Hermes renounced, only those who are ready to understand, will. Interestingly, the Ancient Greeks also had Hermes as a messenger of the gods, whose symbol was the caduceus: two snakes wrapped around a rod with the top unfolding into wings (the importance of which is described in the next chapter).

From this, it could be deduced that Hermes, the teacher and messenger of Godly powers, manifested to conscious beings around the world in order to spread his knowledge of the laws of nature.

The seven key Hermetic principles are:

1) The Principle of Mentalism ("All is mind" and we are all part of one, larger, living mind.)

2) The Principle of Correspondence ("As above, so below; As below, so above" as there is always correspondence between the principles and planes of being.)

3) The Principle of Vibration ("Everything moves; Nothing rests; Everything vibrates" and from this manifests all things.)

4) The Principle of Polarity ("Everything is dual... Everything has its pair of opposites", from male to female, positive to negative, Judas to Jesus, dark to light, and all are necessary for balance.)

5) The Principle of Rhythm ("Everything flows", all action has a reaction and everything follows cycles.)

6) The Principle of Cause and Effect ("Every cause has its effect; Every effect has its cause" meaning that there is no such thing as chance or coincidence.)

7) The Principle of Gender ("Everything has masculine and feminine; Gender manifests on all planes" and all creation is possible with this principle.)

In short, these principles show that nothing is permanent but, instead, always becoming or changing. What's more, they are believed to be in full operation on all planes, whether physical, mental or spiritual, thus can be seen as a gateway of communication between these. From this, the Egyptians developed the ideology that spiritual evolution is connected to the heavens. That is, that life and consciousness has the potential to evolve, through the systematic application of the principles of the Hermetic Code, into higher states of being.

Because we evolved on this planet, our bodies are made up of the elements of the Earth, which react to the immediate environment. As a result, Michael Hayes (2004) claims that the Hermetic Code is the blueprint for all existence and is echoed in the structure of our DNA. Hayes states that DNA was preordained by nature itself and so is geometrically aligned to these laws. For example, 8 is the number of full notes in the major musical scale and the number of gods in the early myths concerning creation as well as the number of days within Easter week (from Palm Sunday to the Sunday of resurrection) and the number of minutes it takes for the Sun's light to reach Earth. Multiplying 8 by itself equals 64, which is the number of RNA triplet-codon combinations comprising the genetic code. Thus, it can be seen that the human organism is genetically designed in the same way as Gaia, by following these Hermetic principles and codes.

These initial 7 principles then lead to the 11 corresponding laws of nature, which Bob Proctor (2016) details as:

1) The Law of Thinking: No other power or force in the universe is as powerful or quick as human thought. The thoughts you repeatedly think (e.g. I'm stupid, I'm ugly, I have no money, I never get sick, I'm popular) imbed in your subconscious mind. Hence, whatever your dominant thoughts are, you become.

2) The Law of Supply: All of the energy and knowledge that ever was and will be is 100% present all of the time. It cannot be created or destroyed, only changed in state. There is an infinite supply of energy from the infinite source of the universe to supply all of our needs.

3) The Law of Attraction: The vibration that we are in attracts harmonious vibrations; you will always gravitate towards that which you give your attention to. We are all magnetic creatures and good things happen when we expect them to; whatever you believe must come true. It's law.

4) The Law of Receiving: What you have in life is a reflection of what you have been giving. You must give to receive. If you want love, you must give love. If you want abundance, you must think abundant thoughts. And, when we give, we

make room to receive more, like giving away an old cooker to make room for a newer, better one.

5) The Law of Increase: In short, gratitude! Everybody works better and harder when they are praised. All living things, including humans, learn best from positive praise; universal energy is no different. Be grateful for all of the good that you have in life, even if it is simply that you woke up this morning, so that the universal energy knows what to give you more of. But be careful as this works both ways! Avoid giving time to negative thoughts.

6) The Law of Compensation: Into your hands will be placed the exact results of your thoughts; you will receive that which you earn. Whether it is a controlling desire or a dominant aspiration, the universal energy will give you exactly what you ask for, as long as you provide a service (positive or negative) to get it. Get better everyday at what you do.

7) The Law of Non-Resistance: Whatever you resist persists. Humans must learn to react, not respond. Don't accept anybody else's negativity or anger. Just let it go. Don't fix an emotion to a negative experience.

8) The Law of Forgiveness: We cannot change the past. Forgive yourself and forgive others; their forgiveness will follow. Disease is due to negative thoughts. Form the habit of not holding on to anything. Do not carry bad thoughts. Forgiveness causes growth.

9) The Law of Sacrifice: No one becomes great by accident. We have infinite potential and must discipline our thoughts and

actions in a way that will reflect our desires. We must be willing to give up a bad habit in order to create new, positive habits (e.g. giving up fast food dinners for a healthier heart).

10) The Law of Obedience: Humans must obey nature's laws. Like the farmers who must learn when the season is right to sow their seeds, humans must become nature's servant by understanding the laws. Life was meant to be easy; follow your gut instinct.

11) The Law of Success: The laws deny us nothing. The powers inherit in us are infinite. Advancement in all things is the laws' great purpose All processes of nature are successful; night always follows day. What you believe, you receive.

From these, the most renowned is the Law of Attraction. For many, this usually triggers thoughts of trying to manifest a new car or job. When enough charge is accumulated, it collapses the wave function and energy can become matter. However, the Law of Attraction works on all levels. It is because of this natural energy that we are entangled to karmic bonds and may have particular shadow work triggered for release at a specific age. This is in order to bring genetic trauma to the surface to be transmuted and released when we are in a situation capable of doing so. This is important in order to clear the shadows and prevent them from being passed further down the ancestry line. Cosmic influences at the moment are also triggering the vast majority of us to work through these energies now as part of Gaia's own purging and ascension.

That said, the go-to-argument against the Laws of the universe functioning in this way tend to fall into the bracket of "opposites attract- just look at some magnets". However, Dr Pollack, an international leader in science and engineering, claims in his book *The Fourth Phase of Water'* (2013) that the like-charges themselves don't attract; the attraction is mediated by the unlike charges that gather in between, which draw the like-charges towards one another until the attraction is balanced. Pollack exerts that the old-dated ideology of "opposites attract" has led to unnecessarily complex interpretations and supports his claim that like-likes-like. Take the nature of clouds, for example, where the like-likes-like mechanism holds the droplets together. Pollack also uses the example of the origin of life, stating that life probably started with the dispersal of substance that then condensed into entities that used the like-likes-like phenomena to self-assemble into cells, pre-cells, and so on, deeming this like-attracts-like mechanism of intelligent design.

As water is such vast and necessary component of Earth's habitable environment and is also one of the predominate elements of the human body, its structure and purpose clearly contribute to the intelligent design of the human form.

The God- Body

The elements of the human body are predominately deduced from oxygen, carbon and hydrogen. Seeing as the Double-Slit experiment has also been successful with such atoms (Arndt and Zeilinger, 2002) and Al-Khalili (2012) claims that the genetic coding properties of DNA molecules are based on bonds between pairs of these, it could be inferred that, if quantum coherence between these can be maintained, the whole DNA can evolve in a superposition. In the same way, Penrose and Hameroff (1996) propose that the microtubules within the brain (hollow cylindrical structures in neurons which are commonly referred to as the 'organisers' of the body due to their ability to communicate and organise neighbouring cells) have just the right properties for a superposition to exist within the mind. This theory is referred to as the 'Orchestrated Objective Reduction'. What's more, the Sum- Over-Histories explanation of the double-slit experiment proposes that the atom explores all possible paths simultaneously, but the way the paths cancel depends on what options are made available.

What all of this means on a basic level is that the human body is perfectly designed to abide by and make use of the natural laws.

Hence, if a person can physically observe an outcome mentally and put themselves out there to make the available paths evident, then one could physically alter their future. An article by Avery Thompson (2016) even details how a recent double-slit experiment (titled the 'delayed choice experiment') showed that photons sent through the slits one at a time still interfered with one another, concluding that observing a photon can change events that have already happened. Could this be evidence towards time not being real and eventual time-travelling? I think so!

The quantum-weirdness doesn't stop with the double-slit experiment, either. Sackett et al (2000), Sherson, Julsgaard and Polzik (2005) and

Lee et al (2011) have all shown that entanglement (two atoms influencing each other faster than the speed of light) is possible on the macro-scale, too. They proved this by entangling larger quantities of atoms, up to gases and even diamonds. Interestingly, Grinberg et al (1994) had previously even used brain wave samples to show entanglement between humans who were at vast distances from one another. These experiments could prove how our collective consciousness is able to influence the thoughts and actions of others whom we have interacted (entangled) with during our lives. Dr Becker (1985), who is renowned for his knowledge of electromagnetism and their effects on the body, claimed that the electromagnetic field of the universe is so tightly intertwined that even using a toaster now can affect atoms within the furthest galaxy.

Jahn and Dunne claim that psychokinesis is an ability anyone can learn to use because consciousness itself is a form of wave-particle phenomenon (energy manipulation). This is further evident through the 'acoustic levitation' phenomenon, whereby the properties of sound (vibration) are used to reduce gravity and lift physical mass, including solids and liquids (Falde, 2019). Basically, even sound vibration effects the bonding between physical matter. This could even explain how the pyramids were built. According to Abul Hasan Ali Al-Masudi, papyrus was imprinted with 'magical' sacred geometric symbols on each side of the pyramid stone, which was guided along a fenced path that had metal poles on each side to increase the sound vibration and corresponding levitation effects. Ergo, with psychokinesis being seen as a complimentary exchange of 'resonance' between the thinker and the object by means of collapsing the wave packets of quantum systems outside the brain, this phenomenon could in fact be very possible.

If our personal energy field is able to interact with the energy fields of others, which is at a much smaller scale, it seems clear that these energies would also affect much stronger fields on a Gaia-scale, whether that be by responding to solar-lunar influxes or producing synchronicities. The various atmospheric layers surrounding the Earth provide the perfect context for these electromagnetic communications to be received. By finding ways of maintaining connection to these energies, we put ourselves in a position of openness in order to receive messages and guidance from other conscious, cosmic bodies.

Synchronicities and Repeated Numbers

When our vibration is electronically in-sync with the universal electro-magnetic field, it can alter space-time and we become aware of these alterations through intuitive feelings, ideas, visions, dreams or signs. Signs include anything significant we see or hear in response to our thoughts and are often referred to as 'synchronicities'. I remember very clearly driving my car to work one morning when, all of a sudden, I became aware of the licence plate on the car in front, which read as the brand name I was using during my visualising. As this was so unusual, this confirmed for me that the path I was taking in my life was the right one for me at the time. When you become consciously aware of a sign but are unsure of the meaning behind it, ask your subconscious mind what the sign is telling you to be directed along the right path. Einstein even once quoted that: "Synchronicity is God's way of remaining anonymous".

Other common physical signs include feathers, overhearing conversations, loud noises to bring you back to the present, animals showing themselves and songs that either get stuck in your head for no reason or lyrics that cause a rush of emotion within us, as well as, most commonly, repeated number patterns. Repeated numbers are among the primary method that the universe uses to communicate because, as sacred geometry and fractals show us, all is connected mathematically, like a perfect recipe book. One of the ways these number patterns are revealed to us is through seeing the same time. Humans are a species who govern their whole lives around time- when to get up, how long to fast for, when to leave work, etc. It is paramount to our physical and social existence in this day and age, so it seems an obvious and fool-proof way for Gaia to communicate with us. Times that are reportedly noticed the most include 11:11 (11 is a sacred number, a master number) and patterns of 3 (also a key number that represents trinity, the whole).

Carl Jung, a colleague of the famous psychoanalysis Signmund Freud, was a psychologist intrigued by synchronicities, claiming that such occurrences are a result of psychic factors. Jung (1960) also linked his synchronicity research to the sacred marriage of the Sun and the Moon. He claimed that the astrological and alchemical connection between these influences the human psyche through disturbances in the Earth's magnetic field. Jung supports the idea of humans being the microcosm, created from the Godly macrocosm that is the universe and claims that synchronicities occur when the laws of the soul resonate with the cosmic alignment of the body. Thus, when the soul is on the right path in this dimension of space-time, or when a particular event is looming which the soul's purpose requires attendance of, divine synchronicities present themselves.

In brief, there are electromagnetic fields all around every single one of us right now, we just need a machine to tune in and access them to make them perceivable to your senses. Within the human body, that machine is the brain. Furthermore, if the quantum world shows that time does not exist and that quantum rules are manipulatable within macro-organisms, then one could also assume that knowledge and spirits are also accessible within such an invisible realm, if one could only get onto the same brain wave- length in order to 'hear' these.

Summary

This chapter is hard-going to comprehend, but it hopefully demonstrated how strongly all within the universe is connected and manipulatable and how the human body is a product of intentional, intelligent design. In conclusion, then, there are natural laws that govern all life in the universe. These laws are fundamental and must be followed, with no exceptions, whether that be by a tiny butterfly or an entire galaxy. Thus, even the slightest activity (physical or mental) influences the rest of the universe. And, vice versa, why changes in cosmic energy effects the internal workings of the body. By strengthening the collective consciousness through connecting with one another and sharing experiences, even telepathically, we can not only cleanse ourselves through the uptake of Gaia's energy, but we can also provide power to the planet by giving up our own healing thoughts and frequencies.

Top Recommendations

Website: www.popularmechanics.com and www.sacedgeometryinternational.com

Book: PEMF by Bryant Myers

Article: Hameroff, S. and Penrose, R. 1996. Consciousness Events As Orchestrated Spacetime Selections. *Journal of Consciousness Studies.* 3(1):pp.36-53.

Podcast: 'Earth Ancient' and 'Destiny' with Cliff Dunning.

Video: Bob Proctor: The 11 Forgotten Laws, available of YouTube in full.

Bibliography and References

Al- Khalili, J. 2012. *Quantum: A Guide For The Perplexed.* Orion Books.

Becker, R. and Seldon, G. 1985. *The Body Electric.* Harper Collins Publishers.

Bynum, E. 2012. *Dark Light Consciousness.* Inner Traditions.

Carlson, R. 2017. *Catastrophes of Ancient Earth.* [podcast] Earth Ancients. 17 August 2017.

Carlson, R. 2018. *New Evidece of Catastrophic Global Floods.* [podcast] Earth Ancients. 11 August 2018

Carlson, R. 2019. *Cataclysms, The Holy Grail and The Holes in The Human Story.* [podcast] The Higherside Chats.

Church, D. 2018. *Mind To Matter.* Hay House.

Dispenza, J. 2017. *Becoming Supernatural.* Hay House.

Falde, N. 2019. *Acoustic Levitation: Floating on a Wave of Sound.* Available online at: <www.ancient-origins.net>

Furlong, D. 2003. *Working With Earth Energies.* Piatkus.

Grinberg et al. 1994. The Einstein-Podolsky-Rosen Paradox In The Brain: The Transformed Potential.

Hameroff, S. and Penrose, R. 1996. Consciousness Events As Orchestrated Spacetime Selections. *Journal of Consciousness Studies.* 3(1):pp.36-53.

Hayes, M. 2004. *The Hermetic Code In DNA.* Black Spring Press.

Hopkins, D. 2017. *Sacred Geometry and the Flower of Life.* [podcast] The TruthSeekah Podcast. 1 December 2017.

Horowitz, L. 2011. *The Book of 528: Prosperity Key of Love.* Medical Veritas International Inc.

Jones, M. and Flaxman, L. 2009. *11:11 the time prompt phenomenon: the meaning behind mysterious signs, sequences and synchronicities.* New Page Books.

Jung, C. 1960. *The Structure and Dynamics of the Psyche.* Routledge & Kegan Paul.

Lee et al. 2011. Entangled Macroscopic Diamonds At Room Temperature. *Science.* 334(6060):pp.1253-1256.

Myers, B. 2013. *PEMF: The 5th Element of Health.* Balboa Press.

Narby, J. 1999. *The Cosmic Serpent.* Orion Books.

NASA. 2013. *Earth's Atmospheric Layer.*

Proctor, B. 2016. *The 11 Forgotten Laws.* [video] Available on YouTube.

Sackett, C. et al. 2000. Experimental Entanglement of Four Particles. *Nature.* 404:pp.256-259.

Sherson, J., Julsgaard, B. and Polzik, E. 2005. Distant Entanglement of Macroscopic Gas Samples. *NAII.* 189: pp.353-372.

Thompson, A. 2016. The Logic- Defying Double- Slit Experiment Is Even Weirder Than You Thought. Available online at: www,popularmechanics.com

Three Initiates. 2017. *The Kybalion.* Independently Published.

Wheatley, M. 2014. *Diving Ancient Sites.* Celestial Songs Press.

Chapter 8

Serpents:

And the Prisoner of Genesis

The word serpent derives from the Latin word 'serpens', meaning "crawling/ creeping thing". Interestingly, although a common phobia, mythical and spiritual history is full of symbolism for the serpent.

A few examples include:

- The serpent of Genesis
- The serpents emerging from the Hindu God Shiva
- The snake centred on the Egyptian Pharaoh's crown
- The Caduceus (Hermes' rod), the name of which derives from the verb *cado* meaning "to fall". Thus, the winged pole can be seen to depict the fall and rise of man. Physiologically, this relates to the CSF system (see Chapter 11)
- Buddha with Nagas
- Serpent gods of Kerala
- The seven headed (chakra energy) snake of Babylon

- The Temple of Kukulkan in Mexico, which was built with such precision that, during the equinoxes, the stair patterns and shadows combine to create the illusion of a giant serpent

- The Dogon of Mali, the Yoruba of Dahomev and the shaman of the Zulu tradition all write about coils, spirals and hidden rivers within the Earth, which bear resemblance to serpentine forms, energy and leys

- The brain stem looks like an emerging serpent from the spine

- The double helix of DNA, which appears to be the basic design for all evolutionary phenomena, also depicts two intertwining snakes

- The transverse view of the claustrum (FIGURE 27)

- In Greek mythology, Python (a great snake and the child of Gaia, born after the great flood) lived at the centre of the world guarding a cave (womb). As Gaia is the consciousness of Earth, Python could be the consciousness of man.

- Also in Greek mythology, the serpent-god Dionysos, the half-brother of Apollo (the messenger between the physical world and spiritual world) was slain by two Titans before being born again in human form

- The Mayan god, Kulkulcan, was the "feathered serpent god", who controlled the elements. The main Mayan pyramid, El Castle, was dedicated to Kulkulcan and showed the connection between the Great Serpent and the cosmos (with 365 steps, 52 panels).

- The Aztecs also adopted the "feathered serpent" god and used this to symbolise the blending of heaven and earth
- In Hindu mythology, the symbol for water is the serpent
- In Egypt, the ouroboros serpent symbolises 'all in all'
- The largest stellar constellation, Hydra, is a serpent. As is the famous Draco (or Dragon, but in fact is very serpent-like)
- The pharaoh's of Egypt used the Uraeus (an upright form of the cobra) to symbolise sovereignty, royalty and divine authority. This is consistently seen in the centre of the pharaoh's head ornament.

The serpent symbol, then, has a myriad of meanings across cultures, including death, resurrection, healing, fertility and procreation. Many have speculated the true metaphorical meaning behind the spiralled emblem, from the Hydra star constellation to the spine; the DNA helix to DMT-rich tree vines; the rivers of life to the Milky Way. Even Jesus is considered a serpent in some theories, supported by the fact that he left white robes behind in the tomb after his resurrection, just like a serpent leaving behind old skin.

The Cosmic Serpent

Celestially, the snake represents the Moon due to the fact that the Moon changes its shape throughout the course of a month, appearing to 'shed its skin'. The shape of a waxing and waning Moon can also be likened to that of a moving snake, with the full moon appearing like a spiralled, sleeping one and a new moon representing the shedding of old skin.

Similarly, the snake has also been equated to the Milky Way band observable all over the Earth, due to its long, wave-like appearance (which has also historically been linked with the Nile of Egypt). With this in mind, stories such as those relating to the celestial egg guarded by a serpent can be seen to have clear links with the sacred secretion if one considers their own spiritual seed as the egg, whose birth-right is secured by the Moon and stars above. This phenomenon has been observed throughout history, some of the most famous of which are evident as the Pyramid of Kukulcan in Mexico and the Native American Serpent Mound of Ohio.

Serpent Worship

Serpent Mounds are evident around the world to clearly depict the importance placed on this symbol by the ancients. The most renowned of these is the serpent mound of Ohio. The fact that the skeleton of a snake was found here leaves no room for doubt that this image is, in fact, representative of the celestial snake. A simple internet search of this will reveal images from various angles of the mound as well as drawings of how specialists believe the mound looked in the past. In short though, the mound looks to represent a serpentine shape consuming an egg. This 'snake' has a coiled tail and three distinctive 'hump' shapes.

With the coil pointing true North, the 'humps' correlate perfectly with the sunrise on Winter Solstice, Equinoxes and Summer Solstice. At the end is the head, pointing directly at the direction of the setting Sun on the Summer Solstice, consuming the 'egg'. Accordingly, the serpent mound can be seen as a cosmic clock, able to tell ancient civilisations the exact time and date of these key events. If one considers the ideology of the snake as the Moon and the egg as the Sun (or son), this phenomenon could indeed be foretelling how the Moon consumes the solar seed (photons) from the Sun in order to bring life to Earth.

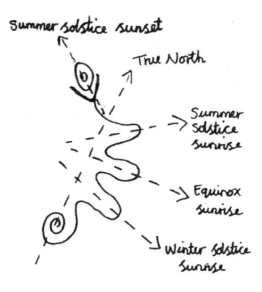

FIGURE 14 – The Serpent Mound of Ohio

Further down in Mexico, the Pyramid of Kukulcan can be found. This pyramid has been built with such precision that, twice a year during the spring and autumn equinoxes when day and night are balanced, the light and shadows generated by the Sun create the illusion of a serpent. This serpent appears from the tip of the pyramid, as if gliding in from the heavens, and crawls down the pyramid to the base and into the crowds observing. Mythically, it is said that this snake, who represents the descended form of the god Kulkulcan, returns to earth to commune with his worshippers, bless the harvest and provide good health before entering the sacred water, bathing in it and continuing its journey to the underworld. With such similarities with the tale of Christ, who descended to earth as God in human form, healed and preached and was baptised all before returning to heaven, this phenomenon could even be an early, physical representation of the New Testament Bible story, exaggerated over continents and time. If so, then the Son (Sun) could have originally been a serpent-god. This holds for some interesting considerations when one remembers that it was a snake that tempted Eve to eat the forbidden fruit.

Serpents: The Design Of The Gods

The spiralled and twisted serpentine shape is illustrated throughout the human body. With the sacrum as the tail, the spine as the body and the skull as the head, the most notable of these is that of the spinal column. Attached to the spine is a myriad of nerves and tissue, including the brain, which make up the central nervous system (CNS). As our vastly evolved nervous system is what gives us intelligence and ability over that of the animal and plant kingdoms, this could be seen as a god-like design. The serpentine shape also appears similar to the corpus collosum in the brain, a thick nerve-tract which pictorially bridges the pituitary to the pineal (female and male; physical and spiritual; balance between worlds).

The image of the serpent is particularly interesting when considering the relevance of the sacred secretion as, when the shaman of the Amazon Rainforest were asked how they knew from the thousands upon thousands of plant species within the rainforest which plants to combine to create the DMT- rich ayahuasca, the shaman stated that the plants and serpents told them how. This sounds remarkably similar to the Biblical tale of the Fall, whereby Eve was told to eat from the Tree of Knowledge by a snake, upon doing so she then 'woke up'.

Jeremy Narby (1999) believes that these snakes, which are also extremely common visions reported by those who have taken DMT, are symbols of our DNA. That is, that the serpents talking to us within these altered states are in fact our own ancestry line within our genetic inheritance which are communicating and directing us along the path to enlightenment. It is impossible not to notice that the symbol of intertwining serpents looks surprisingly similar to the DNA double helix. As DNA is like the bio-language of Earth, which hasn't changed a letter in four billion years, every living thing on the planet is made up of the same 20 amino acids (compounds in the body). Thus, molecular biology in this way confirms the unity of nature: the whole. Further similarities can be seen when comparing the structure of DNA to that of a physical ladder.

Ladders are referenced throughout religious history, from representing the seven steps that symbolise the universe within the Mysteries of Brahma, to being the passage of the soul's approach to perfection within the Mysteries Of Mithras. Within the Old Testament, Jacob even dreamt of a ladder that connected heaven and Earth, "with the angels of god ascending and descending on it" (which, as we learned from Chapter 6, likely represent biophotons). It is also the symbol of the Shaman profession. Shamanism is a practice that involves a practitioner reaching altered states of consciousness in order to channel the spirit world and bring healing. During their visions, Shamans are believed to gain knowledge from higher beings, often spirits of pure light.

The serpentine form, then, is clearly one of universal significance. Light, sound and even brain activity are depicted in this wavy structure. It is for this reason that, when attempting to decode the meaning behind the *snake* in various tales of mythology, one must read the surrounding imagery in order to get a true interpretation of the idea being presented. This way of reading is akin to many ancient languages, such as the Egyptian hieroglyphs.

Pingala and Ida Nerves

The Hindus teach of three distinct channels in the spinal system: Pingala (from the left brain which flows down the right-side of the body), Ida (from the right brain that flows down the left-side of the body) and Sushumna (which flows along the spinal cord and through the seven chakra energy centres). The Pingala is associated with the colour red, the masculine, the Sun and warmth. The Ida is associated with the colour white, the feminine, the Moon and coolness. These connect the main chakras; the lower to the higher, Earth to Heaven, creating a spiral of vertexing, circuitry energy. Within these channels flows Prana (life force energy), which follows these channels via Nadis.

Nadis are the pathways/ channels/ energy rivers of the body. Learning to balance the Prana energy within both the Ida and Pingala pathways is the first step in many spiritual practices still used today, such as Kundalini Yoga, which focuses on raising this 'serpent' energy up the body and beyond. This serpent energy, once raised, can be harvested at faster and more successful rates as time goes on, hence why the Bible states to *lay the path* for Christ.

Those who achieve awakening through Kundalini practice claim to feel an electric current running up their spine, like a serpent, towards the cerebellum of the brain, which is shaped like wings. Also, structurally, the snake is simply a head and spine which move in a wave-like motion. Consequently, the symbol for Kundalini is a pair of snakes entwining around what appears to be a staff, through each chakra energy centre, with a set of wings and a crown floating above the serpents' heads (similar to images of dragons). This image is also used in Ancient Greek mythology as the symbol for Hermes, the messenger of the Gods who could travel between the physical and non- physical realms.

Shamanic rituals use movement and sound, similar to those used within Kundalini practice, to vibrate the body in a way that promotes astral connection and spiritual experiences. Often, these rituals also include the consumption of plants, to relax the physical body and increase the 'psychedelic' experience within the mind. Shamans are masters when it comes to using the Earth's natural resources to amplify their experiences of reality and healing practices. Quartz, the most abundant mineral on the planet, is used by Shamans around the world during their rituals. This is because the atomic structure of the quartz crystal vibrates at a stable frequency, making it an excellent receptor and emitter of electromagnetic waves and frequencies of energy from the universe. Hence, quartz has the ability to release electricity and even lines the Egyptian Great Pyramid, which is believed to have been used as a giant electric power plant and for wireless communication for the ancient civilisation. Crystals are also often used during Kundalini practice as it is believed to enhance the vibration of the energy. For example, citrine absorbs negative energy and releases positive, whereas amethyst creates an energy field around the body which resonates with other dimensional energies, thus enhancing psychic ability.

Like all physical and non-physical practices, resources can be used to amplify and improve the effectiveness of the experience. But, at the end of the day, it is commitment and determination that are key to success. Kundalini is simply a spiritual practice for improving connections within the physical body. It is this ideology, of male and female energy being released from glands within the brain before travelling down the spine, meeting in the sacrum and rising again, that is repeated throughout religious and spiritual practice around the world, including that of the sacred secretion. The movements and chanting involves within Kundalini practice are also clear manifestations of the light codes discussed in Chapter 6.

Dragons

In Greek, serpent means 'drakon' (dragon). Furthermore, in the 'Dictionary Of Symbols' (1996), the dragon represents the union of two

218

opposed principles and, in the vast majority of cases, the winged serpent symbolises hidden or secret knowledge. Take the story of Adam and Eve, for example. The male and female (energies) are persuaded to feed on 'knowledge' by a snake. This 'knowledge' enabled the pair to 'see' clearer. They were then apparently thrown out of their garden by God, who had otherwise concealed the rest of reality from them. This is a story of awakening which I often compare to the modern Matrix films, as the male and female characters consciously 'unplug' from previous programming to become aware of true reality.

In Chinese alchemy (Cooper, 2016), the dragon represents the odd and yang, whereas the tiger symbolises the even and yin. There are obvious similarities here to the idolisation of lions and cats in ancient Egypt and praise given to serpents and dragons in ancient Mexico. The coming of these two creatures could be seen, then, as symbolising balance of the whole. Now, within Gnosticism, the coming together of the lion and snake is metaphorical of the union of the Sun and Moon: Male and Female. Thus, the teachings of early Christianity and Judaism (Gnosticism) can indeed be seen as an evolution of consciousness; the bringing together of the ways of Egypt and Mexico- male (yang) and female (yin). Fascinatingly, discoveries have even been made of lion-headed serpents illustrated around the world. This hybrid creature is commonly called the Chnoubis. The most interesting of these is displayed at the Kelsey Museum of Archaeology in Michigan. This talisman depicts a serpent's body holding 7 spherical eggs within its coils, with a lion's head which is surrounded by 12 rays of light. Clearly, this has an uncanny resemblance to the idea of serpent energy in the body, powered by the 7 chakras, raising to the lion (Sun/ God) head, which is further influenced by the 12 signs of the zodiac encompassing it.

In ancient Egypt, this image of Chnoubis (also known as 'the deliverer' and 'the Spirit of all Knowledge') is frequently depicted on amulets and jewellery as protection from disease and poison (just as preserving the sacred secretion can rid the body of toxicity and sin) and to regulate fertility. According to Manly Hall (1928), Christ was the personification of Chnoubis- the divine mind. Celestially, Chnoubis is said to be the guardian of the 12-angled pyramid: the dodecahedron (akin to sacred geometry). If one delves deeper into the Gnostics, even the word Nazarene (the home city of Jesus Christ), for example, can be equated to the Hebrew word 'naas' meaning 'serpent'.

FIGURE 15 – Chnoubis Examples

Serpent Wisdom

Archangel Metatron is considered the lord of serpent wisdom. Metatron (the biblical Enoch, discussed in Chapter 7) is said to have delivered to Tarot as a way of enclosing divine wisdom. Although much of this information is reported to have disappeared alongside the Great Library of Alexandria, the main imagery within the Tarot is still visible to this day. (Interestingly, Alexandria is also reported to be the original grounds in which the first versions of the Bible were translated into Greek.)

The Major Arcana of the Tarot are as follows: The Fool; The Magician; The High Priestess; The Empress; The Emperor; The Hierophant; The Lovers; The Chariot; Strength; The Hermit; The Wheel of Fortune; Justice; The Hanged Man; Death; Temperance; The Devil; The Tower; The Star; The Moon; The Sun; Judgement; The World. For one with a basic understanding of the sacred secretion, the order of the Major Arcana Tarot cards detailed above read with great similarity to that of the story of Christ- both biblically and internally.

Summary

This chapter in no way exhausts the vast information available on the sacred serpent, but does provide context for the image and, hopefully, demonstrates its perceived significance and power. When one delves further into the Biblical story of Revelations with a metaphorical-eye, even the sealed scrolls can be likened to coiled-energy that can be awakened for good or evil, just like the symbol of the snake or dragon.

To pull together the ideas presented in the chapter, though, I would like to quickly draw attention to the vast references throughout religious doctrines of the *bruising of the serpent's head*. Kersey Graves, author of *The World's Sixteen Crucified Saviours*, notes many historical links to this same idea, including: the snake of Genesis within the Christian Bible; Osiris of Egypt who 'bruised the head of a serpent after it bit his heel'; Krishna of India who has been depicted on stone monuments with his heel on the head of a serpent; in the Mexican Antiquities, the first woman created is told that she should bear a son who should bruise the serpent's head; in an ancient Etrurian story, instead of the *seed of the woman* standing upon the head of a serpent, it is the woman herself who is represented as standing with one foot on the head of a serpent. Now, note that the word *heel* actually means the bottom or lower (such as the heel of a ladder), the word *bruise* means to break up or a result from impact, and that the *head* represent the top or upper levels. When considering the idea of the serpent as a representation of a human's inner knowledge potential and energy systems, the thought of God presenting the 'punishment' that women will succumb to 'pain' during childbirth and the birthed 'seed' will *bruise* the *head of the snake* actually seems to be more of a *consequence* rather than a punishment. That is, that because the human ate the fruit (of knowledge), they now have the power to give birth to a seed (the sacred secretion) which can, at the base (of the chakra system) impact the head of the serpent (energy) and be raised into enlightenment.

In short, the serpent has an extremely distinctive body shape which can be compared with many phenomena, including moving energy (as in

Kundalini), the chakra system (a rainbow snake, or dragon, just like the multi-coloured rainbow that appears in the heavens as the result of Sun and rain), knowledge (akin to the neuron and developed nervous system), Moon phases (serpent-like, spiralling energy), time (evident from shadows that move throughout the day/ year), creation and eternity (forming a full circle with its tail in mouth), the Earth (as in mounds), psychedelics (like the vines used in ayahuasca brews), the unconscious mind (according to Carl Jung), fertility (like the sperm cell) and even DNA/ inherited potential (due to the double helix structure), to name a few of the most relevant. With all of this in mind, stories such as a snake that tempted humans into awakening by consuming the eye-opening 'fruit' lays the path for many interpretations. This is akin to the Bible, which can be understood in vast contexts due to the many literary layers applied to the morals of the stories. These layers include that of the sacred secretion and of sacred union/ sexual alchemy.

Top Recommendations

Website: www.spellsandmagic.org

Book: The Cosmic Serpent by Jeremy Narby.

Article: The Serpent as Divinity by Robert Mason. Available at: <http://www.reptilianagenda.com/research/r020600a.shtml>

Podcast: Earth Ancients with Cliff Dunning

Video: 'Jeremy Narby on Nature & Life Intelligence'. 21 February 2015. *Tree TV* [YouTube]

Bibliography and References

Cooper, J. 2016. *Chinese Alchemy.* Hodder and Stoughton.

Eden, G. 2016. *Chnoubis.* [online] Available at: < www.spellsandmagic.org>

Gehl, J. 2017. *Sacred Healing: a gift from the Gods.* Earth Ancients [podcast] 8 April 2017.

Hall, M. 1928. *Secret Teachings of All Ages.* Reprinted in 2004 by Jeremy Tarcher.

Mason,   R.   *The   Serpent   As   Divinity.*   [online]   Available   at: <http://www.reptilianagenda.com/research/r020600a.shtml>

Mexico.   *Pyramid   of   Kulkulcan   at   Chich'en   Itza.*   [online]   Available   at: <atlasobscura.com>

Narby, J. 1999. *The Cosmic Serpent.* Orion Books.

Chapter 9

Sacred Sex:

And the Chakra of Fire

Although sexual desire is considered a taboo subject in modern society, the ancients, on the other hand, knew of its sacred power, both cosmically and personally. As such, goddess cultures have inhabited the Earth for millennia. There are numerous stories throughout cultures of a female giving birth from conception of a spiritual father. For example, Isis (star) coupled with her brother Osiris (Orion). Following Osiris' death, Isis searched for his pieces in order to reassemble his body, which resulted in their child, Horus, being born, thus from a spiritual father. Interestingly, throughout historic Egypt were sculptures and depictations of erections in temples, even Tutankhamun's mummy is reported to have been fully erect at a 90 degree angle. However, Christian and Arabic invaders are said to have destroyed these during the 18th and 19th centuries, at which time religion was on the decline and churches were trying to regain power.

John Allegro, one of the original translators of the Dead Sea Scrolls and author of 'The Sacred Mushroom And The Cross', believes that sacred psychedelic mushrooms (as discussed in Chapter 1) were in actual fact thought by many ancient cultures, such as the Essenes, to be a manifestation of God himself on Earth. Allegro claims that the ancients thought of the rain as the sperm of God, which fertilised the land. The red and white (wine and bread) mushroom is said to be the son of God, consumed by those of Earth as a sacrifice in order for them to be shown the way to heaven (or parallel dimensions). The shape of the mushroom itself can be seen as similar to that of a penis, which Allegro claims intrigued the ancients enough to create penis-resembling art. In a similar way, the long, elongated mushroom holds a similar resemblance to the form of a serpent.

Unlike current religious dogma, the Taoists teach living in harmony with our natural, sexual impulses. In Tao Sexology, the energy from both partners is combined to form a miracle; a child. When having sex for pleasure, rather than to conceive, then by pulling the sexual energy up it is not wasted and the nutrients (such as vitamins, minerals and amino acids) that would otherwise have been wasted (if not trying to create a baby) are retained within the body. Therefore, when one does choose to conceive a baby, more energy can be channelled to empower a more energetic child. According to Chang (1986), this energy can even be used to determine the gender of this child.

The Sacred Side of Sex

The dictionary defines sacred as: "reverently dedicated to the same person, purpose or object... secured against violation or infringement as by reverence of sense of right". Once clarified, the idea of sacred sex seems far more achievable. Being attached and connected to other people is innate in the human psyche, and mental health conditions often develop when this connectedness is not felt or if hormonal imbalances prevent the adequate sensation of this. It is believed that one of the reasons this generation is addicted to sex and porn is due to this craving for duality. So sacred sex, then, is when time and effort is put into feeling connected with another's soul. For example, those who have had long term partners know the difference between 'just sex' and 'making love'. It is this *making love* which is sacred due to the connection felt.

In order to utilise sexual energy, it has to be made to flow up through the spinal column to the higher chakras. Eventually, this sexual energy can be channelled in order to attain higher levels of consciousness, rather than a sexual urge that controls the mind. During intercourse, the male and female (yin and yang) energies entangle and compliment each other. It is recommended by Bruce Frantzis (2012) that during such times, when energy levels are racing, that both partners focus on breathing deeply from the diaphragm and sharing energies. This energy exchange is crucial. To Daoists, sexual alchemy involves the combination of female Yin energy and male Yang energy between partners. Through the use of the sacred breath and inner fire, this energy can be channelled. If this energy is not moved up to the higher chakras, it can get stuck and lead to excessive sexual desire. In short, this leads to harmonisation between the male and female energy which can be felt rising up like a ladder (or a snake).

Different positions can activate certain acupuncture meridians, create biodynamic pressures on internal organs and glands, as well as stretch and bring better blood circulation to various parts of the body. Moreover, by clearing energy blockages during sexual meditation in this way, this powerful energy can be harvested elsewhere in the body to be used as fuel to give more energy and focused healing. As your body becomes more alive and both partners become more connected, you will start to feel and know your anatomy deeper.

Sexual meditation can be achieved with only one practising partner. Yet, when sex is immoral (not sacred), the mind's attention is taken away from being relaxed and preserving the body and seed, and instead focuses on the production of pleasure-seeking hormones such as dopamine (which is also responsible for addiction) and energies which can be passed on. So it is more powerful if both partners practise it.

According to Cassandra Lorius (2011), sacred sex involves changing the focus from going after your own pleasure to devoting yourself to your partner and supporting them in the accumulation of their sexual energy. In this way, sex is not good or bad, but a way of connecting to higher vibrations via partnered alchemy. Using meditative techniques such as focused breathing, remaining present and visualisation, an individual can detach from the lower urges that push for orgasm. By instead focusing on the present, sensory experience, rather than the end product, with a mate who is attuned to you emotionally, sacred sexual energies can be harvested.

With regards to same-sex intercourse, the same principles apply. All humans contain elements of both male and female energy, so a simple visualisation of the holy matrimony of this flow is all that is required to signal this vibration of pure love and inner fire to the great universe. Further clarification of this is evident within the works of the ancients, such as the Egyptians, whom practiced same-sex intercourse during god and goddess worship.

Sacred Union and Womb Wisdom

In ancient times, men and women would heal and open together in sacred union to facilitate the process of conscious creation and conception, this included creating a child who was perfectly crafted through love (the 'chosen' one, as their conception would have been conscious and prayed for). This is where the original terminology behind Jesus/ Yeshua being born of 'immaculate' (clean) conception and of a 'virgin' (healed womb) mother. Ancient Egypt was abundant with Womb Wisdom Mystery Schools, whereby women would be initiated as priestesses as they healed and purified their womb portals in preparation for either conscious creation (being a manifester of energy into matter for the divine) or for birthing a christed child. This supported the evolution of souls, as wombs could hold higher frequencies of light-bodied children. Being a 'virgin' also meant being *sovereign*, meaning that a woman had control over her own energy and would only have sex with a sacred union partner. Mother Mary was initiated into these schools, hence why she was able to birth Jesus Christ, as was Mary Magdalene [Note that, traditionally, a *holy hor* meant 'holy womb'- meaning an empowered woman, not a prostitute as some historic Bible interpretations would have us think!] which is why she was the favourite apostle, wife and lover of Yeshua.

Jesus/ Yeshua and Mary Magdalene were (and still are) what was known as a *Christ Couple*. The energies of Yeshua and Magdalene can be tapped into during meditation even to this day in order to call in a sacred union partnership such as this from the collective energy field. When one reads the Bible, it can be seen that Yeshua removed Magdalene's "7 demons" (her energy centres which could not heal and energise optimally until she had healed her body within a sacred union partnership) and then Mary shared with him her Holy Grail (her womb magic). More information on sacred union partnerships are abundant in *Womb Awakening* by Bertrand and Bertrand.

Anatomically, the vagus nerve is connected to the cervix of a woman, stimulating healing and raised energy following orgasm. Interestingly, melatonin is found in female vaginal fluids, so there is every possibility that DMT may be released here, too. Women also tend to feel increased sexuality and sensuality during their monthly bleed, which Bertrand and Bertrand link to all levels of magic. It is for the reasons above and more that women were the original shamanesses in many ancient cultures and sacred union with an empowered woman was much sought after by men. In Tantric traditions, male initiates into the goddess and womb mysteries were known as Lords of the Fish (which holds similarities to Jesus' title of *Fisher of Men*). According to McTaggart (2003), sacred union couples are also able to manifest (as advocated by the Law of Attraction) up to six times more powerfully.

To sum, sex is innocent and pure when conducted with a partner who is honouring of your body, and more so when both partners have done/ are doing the work to heal inherited traumas that may be stored in their bodies and energy fields. A person's sexual energy is extremely powerful and has been used as part of sex magic rituals for aeons. Another practice which aims to harvest powerful sexual energies includes that of semen retention.

Semen Retention

Semen retention is another practice that is commonly used during sacred sex. By preventing ejaculation and instead focusing on the combination of yin and yang energy from both partners combining, a 'sacred seed' can be spared from a 'spiritual father'. Preserving this seminal fluid decreases lower materialistic functioning, such as the ego. This is because losing sperm lowers the energy reserves and reduces the amount of Chi produced.

Semen retention is a practice highly profiled by many great leaders of the world, including Napoleon Hill, author of *Think and Grow Rich*. Hill believed that sexual energy should be harvested, emphasising the need to transmute sexual desire into physical energy to strengthen our connection with the divine. Hill (1937) claims that: "So strong and impelling is the desire for sexual contact that men freely run the risk of life and reputation to indulge in it. When harnessed, and redirected along other lines, this motivating force maintains all of its attributes of

231

keenness of imagination, courage, etc, which may be used as powerful creative forces."

Abstaining from sexual behaviour is also common in Shamanic practice prior to performing a ritual, as a way of directing energy. However, the body does need to clear itself out of old energy occasionally. Taoist Chang (1986) claims Age x 0.2 = frequency of ejaculation (in days) in order to optimise health. When a man is giving up his energy/ life force light, this can be gifted to a partner he loves and trusts, who can then channel this light as part of their sacred union manifesting. This is why men often feel tired after sex whereas women feel more energised.

The Sacred Seed

As the cultivation of the sacred seed (AKA. raising of the chrism and preservation of Christ consciousness) is an internal alchemy, the practice of sacred sex, as a means of sexual alchemy, can be seen as a way of using this magic to turn sexual energy into manifestation energy. Which of these your body requires during each unique preservation period (based on your current alignment and progress along your personal life path), however, can only be heard by you. Therefore, during the days of preservation, there are two clear options:

1) Abstaining from sexual desire altogether, which will both hand the control over to the parasympathetic nervous system (allowing the body to relax and heal) and heighten creative awareness (thus enhancing one's ability to receive subconscious and collective conscious messages).

232

2) Perform acts of sacred sex with an emotionally connected partner, who can increase your own energetic flow by offering you theirs. This can be with a partner who's own preservation time is not yet, meaning that all attention can be placed on enhancing the vibration of yours, or with a partner who shares your star sign, whereby effort can be placed on balancing the energies between you both.

As in all alchemy, it is fire that is the necessary component to transmute one material to another. Within human biology, this fire is love. We have all heard stories of mothers who have lifted weights far beyond human capabilities to save their children, partners who have saved each other from impossible situations, animals in nature whom have prevented the death of another, and even prisoners who, when feeling that all hope is lost, have found God and carried on.

Therefore, as long as it is sacred and concentual on all parts, I believe that listening to your inner self with regards to sexual desire is paramount. Whether that means that modern society will label you as heterosexual, homosexual, transsexual, bisexual, trisexual, quadsexual, extra-terrestrial, or whatever, it is our unique vibration and spiritual purpose on this planet that influences our internal alchemical requirements to produce and preserve the sacred seed. That said, it is important to note that children and animals do not have this sacred ability to cultivate such energy, so any sexual desires focused in such way is abuse on both the individual legally unable to consent and of your own spiritual journey. News stories headlining such abuse in churches and cathedrals in the past are in no way connected with the sacredness of this practice. These were mere hypocrites who abused their power and were not in any way linked to God or God's will. Such desires are temptations from negative past life karma or lost souls, which must be overcome by means of therapeutic intervention beyond the scope of this book alone.

But let's not ponder on such uncomfortable subjects within a book designed to promote beauty and love. Sexual intercourse between adult partners in love is a sacred act.

Self- Love

Another physical partner is not necessarily required at all. Self-love (also known as solo-sex) is another way of exploring your own sexual energy. By focusing on the exploration of breath-work, the movement of energy from the lowest chakras right through to the highest, as well as tapping into that emotion of gratitude and love, the alchemical cultivation of the seed, raising of the chrism and preserving and protection of Christ energy can be enhanced. Taoists even advocate Solo-practice first to master sexual meditation before sharing with a partner as you need to understand your individual energy and embrace this practice.

In sum, the most important ingredient in alchemically producing the sacred seed and protecting it is LOVE. Whether your spiritual body chooses to abstain from sexual pleasure, share sexual energy with another, or cultivate this energy individually during self-love, the most important aspect of sacred sex is learning to slow down, explore sensuality and connect with the universal energy field.

Porn and Sex Addiction

When speaking of immoral sex and abstinence, the true intention was not to prevent couples with energetic bonds from reaching higher states of consciousness through sexual euphoria. Instead, we were being warned against the problems that arise if these desires become our main goal. If one succumbs to sexual addiction, then their energy can never move out of the lower chakra areas as thoughts are continuously concentrated here. Likewise, watching porn, with all its taboo and fakeness, imprints an unrealistic impression on the brain. From this, the brain forms the habit of releasing dopamine when watching porn, which can leave one in a state of depression when they are not. Porn distorts a person's view of sexuality (and reality) and takes the spirit away from a focus on love and connection.

With pornographic imagery everywhere nowadays, from music videos to newspapers, even children are exposed to these unrealistic sexual references at a time when their minds are too immature to process and analyse the content logically. Consequently, generation upon generation are growing in a distorted world, with false ideologies and unreal expectations of other people. When you add social media to the mix, it's no wonder there's so many relationship breakdowns and mental health issues nowadays! Fortunately, every negative has a positive. By being aware of what takes us away from enlightenment, we open our eyes to what brings us closer.

Summary

Sexual desire is another form of energy that can be harnessed and used for the greater good of the entire organism. But, just like no diet suits all, sexual energy and desire is no different. We each have our own energetic imprint on the planet and unique path towards enlightenment. Thus, finding someone with sexual preferences that match your own, and using these to connect with one another on new levels, is the ultimate goal. In this way, we can not only heal any previous trauma by balancing energy and hormone levels, but we can lay the path for more positive experiences by engaging with, and therefore manifesting, feel-good emotions on a more giving, loving plane. (As a bonus, orgasms are far more intense and whole-body during sacred sex, too!)

As we connect with someone (or ourselves) sexually, we can accumulate these lower energies and raise them up to more spiritual centres within the body. By practising control of these lower desires, one is able to lay the path for the spiritual seed by clearing the chakra system of energy blockages and aligning the systems of the body accordingly. Genetically speaking, we are apparently attracted to those whose DNA compliments our own as a way of producing offspring of the highest potential.

When preserving the sacred secretion, it is recommended that abstinence is practised at first until one is able to fully control this sexual energy and use meditation in this way to increase the power and vibration sent through the body. This takes time and perseverance. So go at your own pace and see what works for you.

Top Recommendations

Website: https://achharia.files.wordpress.com/2017/07/taoism-chang-stephen-the-tao-of-sexology.pdf (online version of The Tao Of Sexology book)

Book: Womb Awakening by Azra and Seren Bertrand.

Article: Hernandez-Kane, K., & Mahoney, A. 2018. Sex Through a Sacred Lens: Longitudinal Effects of Sanctification of Marital Sexuality. *Journal of Family Psychology.* 32(4):pp.425-434

Podcast: Sexology by Dr. Nazanin Moali.

Video: Johnathan White's 'Sexual Kung Fu' channel.

Bibliography and References

Allegro, J. 1970. *The Sacred Mushroom and the Cross.* Hodder and Stroughton Limited, London.

Bertrand, A. and S. 2017. *Womb Awakening*. Bear and Company.

Chang, S. 1986. *The Tao Of Sexology.* Atlantic Books, London.

Chia, M. 2018. Mantak Chia- Sexual Energy. *London Real.* Available on YouTube and on the London Real podcast. 28 January 2018.

Fletcher, E. n.d. 5 Ways Meditation Can Help You Have Mind-Blowing Sex [online]. Available at: <www.mindbodygreen.com>

Franzis, B. 2012. *Taoist Sexual Meditation.* Energy Arts Inc, California.

Hackathorn, J., Ashdown, M., & Rife, B. 2016. The Sacred Bed: Sex Guilt Mediates Religiosity and Satisfaction for Unmarried People. *Sexuality & Culture.* 20(1):pp. 153-172.

Hernandez-Kane, K., & Mahoney, A. 2018. Sex Through a Sacred Lens: Longitudinal Effects of Sanctification of Marital Sexuality. *Journal of Family Psychology.* 32(4):pp.425-434.

Hill, N. 1937. *Think And Grow Rich.* Reprinted in 2015 by Mindpower Press.

Lorius, C. 2011. *The Sacred Sex Bible.* Godsfield Press, London.

McTaggart, L. 2003. *The Field.* Element.

White, J. 2019. Semen Retention: Harnessing Sexual Energy [YouTube]. Available online 12 July 2019.

Yudelove, E. 2000. *Taoist Yoga and Sexual Energy.* Llewellyn Publications.

Chapter 10
Cell Salts of the Zodiac:
The Last Supper

From headaches caused by geometric storms to the malfunctioning of electronics during Mercury retrograde, it is common knowledge that planet Earth and all living things thriving upon it are influenced by astronomical bodies. The most famous of these influences is that of star signs. It is widely believed that the star constellation which the Sun happens to be dominating at the time of birth is a predictor of personality traits, future career prospects and even romantic relationships. What isn't as well understood is exactly how these signs can influence the human body. Yes, the stars send out an electromagnetic field, but what is happening biologically?

According to researchers such as George Carey, William Schuessler, Santos Bonacci and David Card, there are 12 mineral cell salts which effect the vibration of the blood. These 12 salts are essential components of all humans, animals and plants, and are even reported to be all that remains after the human body is reduced to ashes. Each salt is readily used as part of the essential building blocks of the human body to maintain mood, cell production, organ function and so on. These cell salts, also called tissue salts, include electrolyte molecular compounds formed from calcium, potassium, magnesium, sodium, iron, phosphorus, sulphur, fluorite, chloride and silica.

An electrolyte is a substance that produces an electrically conducting solution when dissolved in a solvent, such as water. If an electrical potential is applied to such a solution, the dissolved electrolytes separate, causing a current. For the cell salts, this cosmically-influenced current provides electromagnetic power to the spiritual seed. These salts are referred to as 'inorganic' as they lack both carbon and hydrogen bonds. Other inorganic compounds include water, salt, acids and bases (alkalis).

Interestingly, each salt is particularly responsive to one of the 12 zodiac signs. That is, the vibratory nature of one star-sign effects the vibratory nature of one particular mineral cell salt. It is therefore believed that the internal levels of each of these salts is what manifests as personality as they resonate with different stellar energies, which then correspond with hormonal secretions for a felt-experience (such as mood). This can also explain why once one thing goes wrong, everything seems to go wrong, as variations in cell salt quantities effect balance, coordination, focus and connectedness.

First contact with these cell salts would have occurred within the womb. Although some of each would have passed over to the baby from the mother's stores, it would be the 9 salts of the 9 zodiac signs that the Sun passed through during foetal development that a person has the most abundance of. This is due to the fact that the unborn baby, whose cells are multiplying rapidly, would be building those cells under the influence of the current dominating Sun sign and the abundance of the corresponding cell salt. Thus, at the end of the typical 9 month gestation period, the baby would be born with stores of and the previous experience of producing 9 out of the 12 cell salts, leaving the other 3 lacking.

According to Santos Bonacci, this is what the Bible may have originally meant by "in sin did my mother give me birth", as the word 'Sin' in Hebrew means "to fall short of completion" or "lacking wisdom". (The body "lacks the wisdom" or experience of the other 3 salts, falling short of the complete zodiac circle.) As such, although intake of all 12 mineral salts are essential for cell production and energetic balance, the 3 cell salts which the body lacks are consumed more readily in order to account for this deficiency. Hence, a higher intake is required. This is evident within the Bible on numerous occasions. For example, George Carey claimed that each zodiac sign and corresponding cell salt related to a disciple of Christ (New Testament).

This ideology is also supported by Manly Palmer Hall's reference to Leonardo Da Vinci's painting of The Last Supper, whereby each disciple can be seen to represent a different zodiac sign. By paying close attention to the hand gestures of each disciple, Hall explained that the disciples begin with Aries (the start of the astrological year) and follow through to Pisces (the end of the astrological year). Thus, the following can be deduced of the corresponding disciple to each starsign: Bartholomew as Aries; James the lesser as Taurus; Andrew as Gemini; Judas as Cancer; Peter as Leo; John as Virgo; Jesus as the Sun; James as Libra; Thomas as Scorpio; Philip as Sagittarius; Matthew as Capricorn; Jude as Aquarius; and Simon as Pisces. In Da Vinci's painting, one can clearly see Judas (Cancer), who has spilled salt, sitting by Peter (Leo), Mary Magdalene (in place of John to show a clearer depiction of Virgo) and James (Libra). Christ's hands are laid out, showing the balance within him between all of the disciples (zodiac salts).

From the above, the three disciples- Peter, John and James - can be speculated as the three salts that Jesus was deficient in. This claim is strongly evident within the Bible if we do the math accurately. Within Exodus 12:2, the Lord said to Moses during Passover, "This month is to be for you the first month, the first month of your year." Passover is end of March to April, within the sign of Aries (hence the metaphorical 'lamb'). If we skip now to the New Testament of Luke 1:26, we are told that Jesus was conceived on the sixth month (six months after Passover takes us to end of September and Libra, the balance between the spiritual and physical). If we then count on nine months from this date of conception, we end up at the end of June; the Summer Solstice. Ergo, the Son (Sun) is born, evidenced by the brightest star in the sky (our solar Sun at its peak). Furthermore, if this is the case, then the mineral cell salts the Biblical Jesus would be deficient in are that of Leo (Peter), Virgo (John) and Libra (James).

It is for this reason that it was Peter, John and James that Jesus chose to accompany him during periods of great transformation. For example, in Matthew 17:1, Mark 9:2 and Luke 9:28 these three disciples accompanied Jesus up a high mountain, where he was transfigured

242

before them; *Jesus' face and clothes shone as white as light*. At which point, the three disciples become "heavy with sleep" (referring to the sleep hormone, melatonin, which converts into the spirit molecule, DMT) before witnessing Moses and Elijah appear before them and talking to Jesus (showing Jesus' new ability to tap into the collective consciousness of the universe and receive information from higher beings, including ancestral knowledge). Thus it can be seen that in the presence of the 12 mineral cell salts, with higher levels of presence from the three salts that the body is deficient in, the sacred seed can be escorted more readily to the brain (the 'high mountain') where enlightenment can be achieved and ancestors (DNA/ light codes) can be reawakened.

Whilst reading the Bible, the following passages also resonated as evidence of the advocation for cell salts:

- The three wise men bearing gifts (deficient salts)
- The three angels visited Abraham announcing that his wife was to give birth to a son [Genesis 18] (three months passed and nine to go)
- Noah had three sons who sailed with him over the waters [Genesis 6] (the three deficient salts required for completeness)
- Jacob had 12 sons, nine of which were kept in prison for 3 days until, eventually, all 12 were reunited with their father [Genesis 42-46]
- Jesus raised three people from the dead (three salts re-introduced into the body)

- In the parable of the good Samaritan, it was the third person who helped the man who was robbed [Luke 10:30] (all three deficient salts are required for salvation)

In addition to the above, classical biblical researchers Inez Perry and George Carey also claim that references to stones, rocks, minerals, salt, ash and the disciple Peter throughout the Bible are also symbolic of these 12 tissue salts.

With regards to optimising the health of the human body, a balance of all 12 salts are necessary. These also enable easier diffusion of the sacred secretion within the body's spinal fluid due to the fact that these salts are electromagnetically conductive and so make the cerebrospinal fluid *'as clear as crystal'*. In addition to requiring the complete 12 zodiac cell salts to cleanse the waters (CSF) for the seed, the body functions by means of 12 systems (respiratory, skeletal, cardiovascular, etc) and 12 cranial nerves. There are also 12 nerves from the solar (Sun) plexus, which spread its messages (like Christs' disciples). Thus, a balance of all 12 are required for optimal health. So just like Christ required 12 disciples to reach full enlightenment, Gaia needs input from the 12 constellations of the zodiac to awaken her own life forms.

The Salts of Salvation

Here is a brief overview of each of the 12 tissue salts. For more information, see the Bibliography of this chapter.

Kali Phosphate (Potassium of Phosphate) - This salt is correlated with Aries: the God-head.

Natrium Sulphate (Sulphate of Sodium) – Nat Sulph is tied to Taurean energies and the neck.

Kali Muriaticum (Potassium Chloride) – This is linked to Gemini as well as the skin and shoulders.

Calcium Fluoride (Fluoride of Lime) – This combination vibrates to the sign of Cancer and influences the heart (breast plate).

Magnesium Phosphate – Mag Phos relates to impulsiveness and the solar plexus, which corresponds with Leo.

Kali Sulphate (Sulphate of Potassium) – Kali Sulph relates to the zodiac sign Virgo and the bowels. Interestingly, 'Kali' is Vedic for *mother*. What's more, this tissue salt is abundant in the ocean, which links with the name Mary, which derives from *Mar*, meaning 'water'.

Natrium Phosphate (Sodium of Phosphate) – Here, the balancing scales of Libra manifest microcosmically as the two kidneys.

Calcium Sulphate (Sulphate of Lime) – Like the serpent related to creative energy, Scorpio here is represented as the generative organs.

Silica – Silica is another name for quartz and is the cell salt of Sagittarius, which corresponds to the thighs of the body.

Calcium Phosphate (Phosphate of Calcium) – This combination is linked with Capricorn and the knees.

Natrium Muriaticum (Sodium Chloride) – Sodium chloride, more commonly known as salt, is tied with the balance of water within the body, like the water-bearing sign of Aquarius, as well as the ankles.

Ferrum Phosphate (Phosphate of Iron) – This final tissue salt balances oxygen levels in the body and corresponds, visibly, to the feet and the sign of Pisces; like the Christ who could walk on water.

Like all things, the production of cell salts follows universal laws and cycles. An embryo is further proof that creative energy follows a path of curvature. As the foetus develops in a curved way, the following image has been put together, adapted from the original by Inez Perry, to show the relationship between each body part to the zodiac.

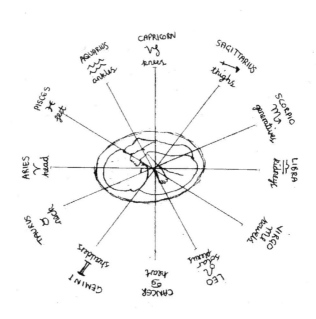

FIGURE 16 – The Cell Salts in Relation to the Human

Consuming the Twelve

The form in which any salt crystallises naturally depends on its rate of vibration. Fortunately, as the human body is a powerful alchemical laboratory, it has evolved to successfully take and rearrange elements from the environment in order to create the materials it needs to rebuild and enhance survival. The cell salts and their precursors (the atoms that can be arranged to create each salt molecule) are set free from food during the digestion process and are carried into the circulation of blood and CSF through the intestines. Hence, FIGURE 17 is a table which splits the zodiac into its 12 main signs, followed by the corresponding mineral cell salt of each and foods rich in the precursors required for the body to build these salts. It's worth noting that food supplements can also be purchased for these salts, the most popular being those produced by Dr. Schuessler and Bioplasma. Personally, I have not yet tried these so cannot advocate for or against them. I have, however, conducted research into the types of foods which more deeply condense these salts and their building blocks. These tend to be plant-based. As plants draw the salts from soil (Mother Earth), these are then readily available for use to consume. It is important to ensure that these fruits and vegetables are from organic and preferably local sources, though, as modern non-organic farming grow crops in mineral deficient soils, hence the food will be lacking in nutrients, including the cell salts. Furthermore, by also consuming foods that have been grown locally, the plants would have grown within a similar electro-magnetic field, thus will resonate more readily with our own energetic field and would not have lost as many nutrients in transit.

When looking at the table, remember to consider the exact date of birth. For example, if you were born prematurely then you may require additional salts depending on how long you were in gestation and for how long of that month. Moreover, if you were born early within a star sign, then the body would not have had sufficient time to develop this particular salt store, so may also require additional intake, also.

The atomic precursors for all these cell salt molecules are also evident within Celtic Sea Salt (grey salt). So consuming this as part of a balanced diet will also support the production of each of these compounds. With regards to the sacred secretion, we must remember the following:

- It is the blood that contains the material for every tissue of the body and supplies nutrients to every organ, including the brain and formation of new neurons
- As all blood passes through the heart, the composition of it has a direct influence on the protruding aura
- The salts effect the blood's vibration in resonance with the zodiac signs
- Salt-water is a conductor of electricity
- Salt compounds are the most concentrated solute in cerebrospinal fluid

Sign	Salt	Food
ARIES March 21-April 20	Potassium Phosphate AKA. Kali Phos.	White beans, cucumbers, almonds, spinach, hazelnuts, lentils, avocados, kale.
TAURUS April 21-May 20	Sodium Sulphate AKA. Nat Sulph.	Lentils, spinach, peppers, paprika, pumpkins, celery, leeks, spring onions.
GEMINI May 21-June 20	Potassium Chloride AKA. Kali Mur.	Cucumber, hazelnuts, lentils, spinach, sesame seeds, potatoes, carrots, apples.
CANCER June 21-July 22	Fluoride of Lime AKA. Calc Fluor.	Raw vegetables, sesame seeds, spinach, broccoli, mushrooms, squash, pineapples.
LEO July 23-August 22	Magnesium Phosphate AKA. Mag Phos.	Brazil nuts, white beans, corn, walnuts, peas, bananas, plums, limes, gooseberries.
VIRGO August 23-Sept 22	Potassium Sulphate AKA. Kali Sulph.	Hazelnuts, almonds, spinach, lentils, peas, lettuce, flax seeds, lemons.
LIBRA Sept 23-Oct 22	Sodium Phosphate AKA. Nat Phos.	Lentils, asparagus, spinach, rose hips, olives, carrots, basil, mint, peaches.
SCORPIO Oct 23-Nov 22	Calcium Sulphate AKA. Calc Sulph.	Almonds, cucumbers, lentils, cauliflower, leeks, onions, turnips, brusselsproats.
SAGITTARIUS Nov 23-Dec 21	Silica AKA. Silicea.	Cucumbers, peas, carrots, strawberries, parsley, cabbage, nettles, apricots.
CAPRICORN Dec 22-Jan 19	Lime Phosphate AKA. Calc Phos.	Almonds, cucumbers, white beans, dandelions, cherries, spinach, dates.
AQUARIUS Jan 20-Feb 19	Sodium Chlorine AKA. Nat Mur.	Reed beets, radishes, tomatoes, celery, figs, pecan nuts, oregano, sauerkraut.
PISCES Feb 20-March 20	Iron Phosphate AKA. Ferrum Phos.	Spinach, hazelnuts, sesame seeds, tomatoes, blueberries, currants, garlic.

FIGURE 17 – Cell Salt Table

Hence, by maintaining a balance of all 12 salts, the body is able to respond more harmoniously and completely to divine energy. As noted previously, these salts are also found within the cerebrospinal fluid- the liquid in which the sacred "seed" is born, strengthened, crucified and resurrected. Furthermore, as magnetism pulls apart ions and changes the chemical composition of various molecules and salt ions within water exposed to magnets (creating purer water that can be used more readily), it can be seen that the change in magnetic charge as the Moon's energy (affected by the star sign it currently resides in) would clearly impact the cerebrospinal fluid salt composition. These studies would also support the ideology behind cell salt generation as varying magnetic influences can generate changes in salt ion composition.

Therefore, as a full balance of all 12 salts is required to vitalise the cerebrospinal fluid, and as the cerebrospinal fluid is the transporter of the sacred seed, it is clear that optimum levels of each are essential for successful preservation of the Chrism.

Summary

To conclude, by consuming a diet which supports the balance of all 12 cell salts provided by Earth (the mother), the human organism is in a position of balance from the star energies of the universe (the father). These produce an electrical current within the CSF, like serpent energy empowering the spiritual egg. And if that was not enough to convince you, consider the fact that magnets work especially well in salt-water as the sodium (salt) weakens the magnetic field of the water and improves the influence of external magnets through the liquid. Now, also bear in mind that magnets can make oil rise to the top of a glass of water. Hence, with an adequate balance of the variety of zodiac cell salts, the Moon's magnetic influence on one's cerebrospinal fluid increases and the Christ [oil] can rise.

Top Recommendations

Website: www.universaltruthschool.com

Book: Carey, G. *The Zodiac and the Twelve Salts of Salvation.* Martino.

Article: 'Cell/ Tissue salts' by Santos Bonacci

Podcast: Walrad, C. *Tissue Salts in Food Sources.* Your Journey to Wellness. Published 5 July 2017.

Video: "12 Cell Salt Intro- Natural Remedies of Dr Schuessler, George Carey, Inez Perry" [YouTube] 2 December 2015

Bibliography and References

Bonacci, S. *Chemistry of the Living Tissues- The Twelve Zodiacal Cell Salts.* Available online at: <https://universaltruthschool.com/syncretism/celltissue-salts/>

Bonacci, S. Secret of Secrets: The Elixer of Life, hiding in the Bible. *MrAstrotheology.* [YouTube] 14 August 2012

Bonacci, S.Santos Bonacci talks on Cell Salt Deficiencies and Facial Diagnosis. *Circle Healing Network.* [YouTube] 15 February 2016

Card, D. 2004. *Facial Diagnosis of Cell Salt Deficiencies.* Kalindi Press.

Carey, G. 2013. *The Zodiac and the Twelve Salts of Salvation.* Martino Publishing.

Carey, G. and Perry, I. 2013. *God Man: The Word Made Flesh.* Martino Publishing.

DiNicolantonio, J. 2017. *The Salt Fix: Why The Experts Got It Wrong And How Eating More Might Save Your Life.* Piatkus.

Emm, D. *12 Cell Salts.* Three videos available on YouTube: https://www.youtube.com/watch?v=QsswcMX7nqk

Grant, B. n.d. *Magnetism and Plant Growth- How Do Magnets Help Plants Grow.* Available online at: <www.gardeningknowhow.com>

Hall, M. *Brilliant Hidden Messages- Da Vinci's "Last Supper".* Available online at: <https://sagaciousnewsnetwork.com/brilliant-hidden-messages-da-vincis-last-supper/>

Ori, J. 2017. *How Do Magnets Work in Saltwater?* Available online at: <www.sciencing.com>

Chapter 11

Anatomy:

And the Ventricle of Secrets

Before getting into too much detail about the Christ oil/ Sacred Secretion, there is some important background understanding that one must consider. The purpose of this chapter is to provide this knowledge ready for connection-making later.

Each human being began its life as a single cell, a fertilised egg. This then divided and multiplied, at which point masses of cells became differentiated and specialised for certain functions. A neuron, for example, is a cell of the nervous system that is specialised to initiate, integrate and conduct electrical signals. Such signals include igniting new electrical signals in other cells or stimulating a gland to secrete a substance. On the other hand, epithelial cells are specialised for the selective secretion and absorption of ions and organic molecules.

Anatomy refers to the structure of an organism and their parts. Each of these parts is an amalgamation of atoms.

Atoms

The units of matter that form all chemical substance are atoms. The major atoms in the human body are hydrogen, oxygen, carbon and nitrogen, which work alongside minor atoms such as magnesium, potassium, sodium, iodine and iron. Within an atom, the sub-atomic particles of positively charged protons and neutral neutrons make up the nucleus, which are orbited by negatively charged electrons. The orbital route of the electrons can hold just 2, so an atom with more electrons will house multiple layers or orbiting electrons (known as the 'shell').

Typically, atoms are electrically neutral as they contain equal numbers of negative electrons and positive protons. Sometimes, however, the atom may gain extra or lose one or more electrons; they will then acquire a net charge and become an ion (AKA electrolyte). For example, when a sodium atom (Na), which has 11 electrons, loses one so now has 10 electrons but still 11 protons, it becomes a positively charged sodium ion (Na+). On the contrary, a chlorine atom containing 17 electrons is one electron shy of a full outer shell (remember that those electrons orbit it layers of 2). Therefore, if it gains an electron it will become a negatively charged chloride ion (Cl-) as it now has 17 protons but 18 electrons. Finally, if the positively charged sodium ion (Na+) and the negatively charged chloride ion (Cl-) meet, a state of equilibrium can be met and we are left with the sodium chloride molecule (NaCl, more commonly known as salt). This is the predominant solute in extracellular fluid (fluid outside of the cell, including blood plasma and cerebrospinal fluid).

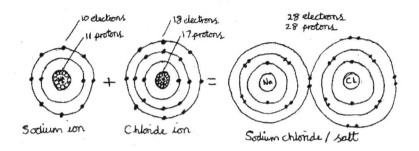

FIGURE 18 – Sodium Chloride Ion

In short, atoms always seek out a state of balance. An ion is an atom whereby the total number of electrons are not equal to the total number of protons, such atoms and molecules are attracted to, and stabilise, each other.

The Acid- Alkaline Base

Substances, such as sodium chloride, which dissolve in a liquid are known as solutes, and the liquid in which they dissolve within are called solvents. Basically, solutes dissolve in a solvent, and this is what is known as a solution. According to Eric Widmaier et al (2016), water is the most abundant solvent in the human body, making up about 60% of the body's total weight. As a result, most of the chemical reactions that occur in the body involve molecules that are dissolved in water.

A hydrogen atom consists of a single proton in its nucleus, orbited by a single electron. A hydrogen ion (H+), then, born at the loss of its only electron, is just a single proton. Molecules that release these hydrogen ions (single protons) are called acids. Obviously, due to being a single proton, these are positively charged. The acidity of a substance, thus, is referring to the number of free positively-charged hydrogen ions. This is termed 'pH' (potential Hydrogen). On the other hand, solutions which have a lower hydrogen ion concentration are referred to as alkalis. Any (negatively charged) substance which can accept a hydrogen ion is termed a 'base'. Bicarbonate is a common base in the body. In an oxygenated environment, hydrogen atoms are able to combine with oxygen atoms to form hydroxyl ions. These function as a base and are the alkaline molecules used to balance the body's overall pH. It is for this reason that deep breathing is one of the quickest and easiest ways to balance the body's pH. Grounding to the earth can also make the body more alkaline by absorbing electrons from the ground.

Measurements of pH are based on comparing the level of hydrogen ions to hydroxyl ions. This system ranks from pH 1 (extremely acidic) to pH 14 (extremely alkaline), with a pH of 7 being neutral. [NOTE: As acidity increases, pH decreases.] In blood, the physiologically normal pH range is 7.35 to 7.45 (marginally alkaline). Cerebrospinal fluid (CSF) is usually very slightly more acidic due to its minutely higher concentration of carbon dioxide, with a general pH of about 7.33, so still tilting more towards to alkaline side of the scale, overall.

Ergo, an acid substance is positively charged, whereas an alkaline substance is negatively charged. If the electrical charge on a molecule is altered, its interaction with other molecules is also affected, hence its function changes. As humans, our liquid pH is pretty balanced, just slightly tilting towards the alkaline- end of the scale, thus making us perfect antennas for dirty electricity and damaging radio waves from the modern environment, such as 5G.

To conclude so far, an acid is any substance that donates hydrogen ions into a solution whereas an alkali is a substance that donates hydroxyl ions into a solution. Homeostasis is the body's attempt to maintain a stable internal environment. Therefore, solutes are exchanged throughout the body in order to maintain this, often going to the area of highest need first. It is for this reason that cancer rates are so high in this day and age of toxicity, as the body is having to put the majority of its focus on surviving the immediate contamination of the body, such as pathogens and free radicals (unstable atoms abundant in processed foods, for example), that it hasn't time to deal with the growing tumour.

The Nervous and Endocrine System

Fluid balance is linked to electrolyte balance. Electrolytes are salts and minerals, such as sodium and potassium, found in blood, that turn into ions and become electrical conductors. It is the antidiuretic hormone (more commonly known as Vasopressin), that regulates the fluid balance within the body. This is produced by the hypothalamus and is stored within the pituitary, ready for use later. The pituitary is the master gland of the endocrine (hormone) system within the body, which produces and stores hormones to be released into the blood when signalled to do so. This signal typically comes from hypothalamic neurons. Therefore, a hormone is a chemical messenger that enables communication between the cells of the blood. With hormones being the chemical messengers of the blood, neurotransmitters are the messengers of the nerves. Neurotransmitters diffuse through the conductive (ion- rich) fluid between neurons. Thus, the nervous system works with the endocrine systems to control many body functions and maintain balance.

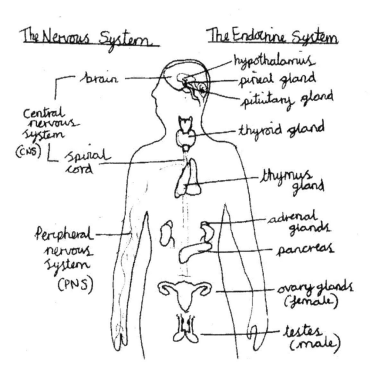

FIGURE 19 – The Nervous and Endocrine Systems

The nervous system can be split into two distinct systems: the Central Nervous System (consisting of the brain and spinal cord) and the Peripheral Nervous System (including the nerves that spread out throughout the body). Myelination (increased white, fatty coating) around these neurons improves their conductivity. This myelination occurs when actions- or thoughts- are repeated, making access to these easier and faster in the future. So 'muscle memory' isn't actually a real thing- it's just that the neurons responsible for that action are more myelinated.

Action Potentials

Voltage-gated **sodium** channels are employed by nerve and muscle cells to generate action potentials. As the body is an electrical furnace, each of these cells has a *comfortable* voltage. This is referred to as its 'resting potential'. These are maintained by ion pumps in the membrane of the cell. Some cells have extra ion channels, which give the cell the ability to produce signals that can be transmitted potentially long-distances when excited electrically. These long-distance signals are referred to as 'action potentials'. Action potentials are particularly important in neuronal cell membranes in order to communicate throughout the nervous system. Thus, the action potential occurs due to the movement of ions in and out of the neuron. It is the voltage-gated ion channels which give a membrane the ability to produce action potentials.

In short, these are pathways which open and close in response to the electrical potentials detected along the membrane, allowing ions to flow in. This communication system is super quick and can travel vast distances at lightning speed (especially along myelinated paths).

Voltage-gated **calcium** channels are utilised by cells to control a variety of cell functions, including secretion. Many cells release molecules they have synthesised into the extracellular environment. This is what is known as *secretion*. Hormonal secretions are regulated by the concentration of a substance that is continuously circulating in the plasma, like other chemicals. An example of this is insulin secretion, which is regulated by the level of glucose in the blood.

For any of these signals to be read, however, receptor sites are required.

Receptors

In order to receive messages (be they hormonal or neural), cells require the binding to a receptor site. Receptors are specific target-cell proteins that respond to these messengers. The abundance of receptor sites tend to adapt depending on environmental input. As such, the body can home all of the receptor sites it likes, but if the environment is not supplying the chemical signalling required for the DNA to go ahead and code for the molecule in the first place, then these will remain inactive.

Interestingly, neuroscientist Joe Dispenza claims that cells are 100-200x more sensitive to electromagnetic fields than chemistry (such as diet). This could lay the path for further research into the electromagnetic effect on genetic expression in the future, such as that by light codes. These electromagnetic signals are particularly conductive in fluid, such as that within the cell membrane and spinal column.

Cerebrospinal Fluid

Like the brain, the spinal cord is protected by bone and fluid. Cerebrospinal Fluid (CSF) is a liquid found in and around the central nervous system. The CSF is like blood plasma, but with different ion concentrations and less protein due to it being filtered in from the blood via the choroid plexus (from *choroid* meaning 'coloured' and *plexus* meaning 'network'). Within the choroid plexus, the choroid epithelial cells selectively transport ion and glucose from the blood and into the ventricles.

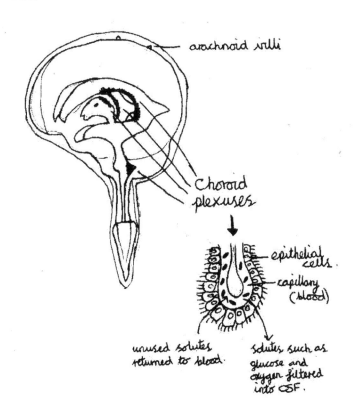

FIGURE 20 – Choroid Plexuses

Once produced, CSF moves freely through the ventricles of the brain before returning to the blood via the arachnoid villi. Most of this fluid flows around the brain, cushioning it. Some, though, travels down the central canal of the spinal cord towards the base of the spine, taking about 12 hours to reach the end of the spinal meninges. Here, there is a large lumbar cistern like a pool, which is filled with CSF. The fluid is forced back up the spine from here via a pump mechanism (see FIGURE 24).

Scientists have also found that during sleep there is as much as a 60% increase of CSF in the interstitial compartments (space around the cells), once again supporting melatonin reactions, cell health and cell reproduction. CSF also contains messenger molecules in the form of neuroactive substances. Therefore, not only do brain waves slow during sleep, but there is increased chemical flow and electromagnetic resonance. This could explain why prophets in the Bible often received messengers in their sleep.

There are two main pumps that support the flow of CSF in the body. The pump residing within the skull is called the craniosacral pump and the pump at the base of the spine is called the sacral pump. Each time these pumps activate, a surge of electrons is sent through the body, generating an internal response to environmental input. These signals often trigger hormonal responses from the endocrine system, too.

The King and Queen of Holy Land

As mentioned previously, the endocrine system is the hormone-regulating system of the body. In short, it enables the organs, etc, to send signals to each other via the blood. This system is an amalgamation of a range of glands that produce different hormones. The 'queen' of these glands is the pituitary, which is often referred to as the master gland. The pituitary is the size of a pea and secretes at least 9 major hormones, including growth hormone, gonadotrophins (for sperm and egg production), prolactin (for milk production) and oxytocin (the love hormone). The pituitary gland is a small, reddish organ associated with female energy- the Mother- and has magnetic properties. There are two parts to the pituitary: the anterior and the posterior. The anterior is responsible for metabolism, milk production in women, cortisol, growth and so on. The posterior of the pituitary stores the chemicals oxytocin and vasopressin, brought into existence by the hypothalamus. By releasing hormones into the body, the pituitary is able to influence the nervous system and alter emotions and cognition. The two distinct lobes of the pituitary in more detail are:

- The Posterior Pituitary stores the hormones oxytocin and antidiuretic (AKA vasopressin) ready made by the hypothalamus until required by the body, much like the womb of a woman 'storing' (protecting) a foetus until birth

[NOTE: Oxytocin can also act as a neurotransmitter in the brain, promoting nurturing, bonding, love and trust.]

- The Anterior Pituitary manufactures many essential hormones, such as growth hormone (essential for metabolism and tissue building), prolactin (for breast milk production) and thyroid-stimulating hormone (which stimulates further hormonal secretions from other glands in the endocrine system)

Another essential gland in the brain is the pineal. This tiny, pine-cone shaped gland hangs from the roof of the third ventricle (Brahma's Cave) and secretes pinealocytes (cells from the pineal). The name 'pineal' itself derives from *pine* based on its shape and *al* meaning 'god'. So *pineal* can literally be translated into **pine-god**. This gland is intimately linked to our body's perception of light. It is the size of the pinky-finger-nail and has the same wiring to the visual cortex part of the brain as the two eyes. For this reason, the pineal is believed to be the origin of non-physical connection. Energetically speaking, the pineal gland is associated with the masculine: the Father. It has electric properties and is synchronised with the pituitary, its sister gland.

The fact that the pineal gland lies within the fractal centre of the brain, is bathed in CSF (even owning its own noble path to secrete straight into the vibrant liquid) and receives more blood flow per cubic volume than any other organ of the body (including the heart), tells us that its role is of paramount importance as so much energy and attention is put onto it. Interestingly, the pineal gland develops in the human foetus at 49 days (7 weeks) after conception. This is also the same time that the first indication of gender develops and when, according to Buddhists, the reincarnated soul enters the physical body. Consequently, the pineal is often referred to as the 'antenna' to universal energy.

According to Marieb and Hoehn (2013), the endocrine function of the pineal gland is still a mystery. One thing that is confirmed, though, is the pineal's role in secreting melatonin (discussed in Chapter 2). It is due to the vast network of chemicals that can be made from the production of melatonin that earns pineal the title as the body's alchemy centre. The pineal floats in CSF, constantly moving in the waves of the salty liquid (sea). Consequently, it picks up on even the minutest vibrations and alteration in the electromagnetic field. What's more, the pineal exhibits the piezoelectric effect, meaning that when pressure is applied (such as by flowing CSF), it stimulates an electrical charge. This is one of the ways that the pineal is a transducer, as it receives a signal in one form and converts it into another (such as signalling between frequencies of 3D, 4D and 5D Earth).

Interestingly, research by Lohmann and Johnsen (2000) found that the human brain also contains bio-magnetite (a metallic mineral found in highest concentration within the pineal) that provides an electromagnetic link between the body, mind, Schumann resonance and geomagnetic frequencies. Similarly, Bryant Myers (2013) states that these bio-magnetite compounds are over one million times more responsive to external magnetic fields than surrounding cellular non-magnetic structures, claiming that magnetite is the biological antenna that connects the Earth and cosmos to the human mind and body. Kirschvink (1992) also discovered that bio-magnetite acts as a transducer, able to convert one form of energy into another.

When considering the anatomy behind the sacred secretion, one could conclude that the bio-magnetite within the pineal responds to the change in magnetic energy as the Moon moves into our sun sign, then able to convert this energy into signalling for the precursor of the spiritual seed and alters the entire electromagnetic output of the body.

Other Important Brain Structures

The Claustrum

Inside the brain is a thin, irregular sheet-like neuronal structure (cluster of brain cells) of grey matter that is attached to the underside of the neocortex in the centre of the brain, which is called the claustrum. Claustrum literally means 'hidden' or 'closed', like the hidden gates to God which one must find for themselves. Scientists describe the claustrum's function as *enigmatic* (meaning difficult to interpret and mysterious). Yet, as the most densely connected part of the brain, with the highest number of connections per millimetre cubed than any other, its function is unquestionably of upmost importance. According to Francis Crick and Christof Koch (2005), research shows that the claustrum receives input from almost all regions of the cortex and projects back to almost all regions. The same investigation results also speculate the claustrum's relationship with consciousness, which is also supported by Steifel et al (2014), Yin et al (2016) and Dillingham et al (2017), whose studies have all linked the claustrum to human consciousness as it branches out the entire circumference of the brain. In this way, all sensory information is sent to the claustrum in order for one, overall perception to be formed, which is then transmuted for reaction.

The Hypothalamus

From *hypo* meaning 'above' and *thalamus* meaning 'chamber', the hypothalamus is a small, cone-shaped structure in the brain that is directly connected to the pituitary gland via the pituitary stalk. Its most important function is to link the nervous and endocrine systems via the pituitary. The hypothalamus synthesises vasopressin and oxytocin before transporting them along nerve axons to the posterior pituitary, which stores them in axon terminals until stimulated to release them. This, in turn, aids the hypothalamus in controlling temperature, hunger, thirst, fatigue, emotions, growth, salt-water-electrolyte balance, stress and sexual-activity. Thus, the hypothalamus links the nervous system to the endocrine system by controlling the pituitary, supported by healthy fats, B vitamins and Vitamin E.

Scientific observations as well as brain imaging techniques show that brain activity depends on the physiological and behavioural states of a person. For example, if a person feels stressed then their brain perceives this as an immediate threat, without recognising whether that threat is a tiger or a debt. This activates the 'fight-flight-freeze' response. When a person is stuck in this state, the brain has to focus its energy on dealing with that immediate threat (manifesting as constant worry, stomach-butterflies, mood swings, etc). Consequently, it has no energy left for growth and repair. Instead, the brain must increase the production of hormones that will provide the body with a higher chance of immediate survival- such as adrenaline and cortisol [NOTE: Studies show that the higher the levels of cortisol in the body, the lower the levels of melatonin]. For many people, this threat can loom over for months on end, leaving the body in a state of panic and sickness.

Suprachiasmatic Nucleus

Supra means 'above' and *Chiasm* means 'crossing point'. The crossing point is that of the optic nerves coming from the eyes (known as the optic chiasm or optic chiasma). They meet in the middle of the brain and switch sides. The suprachiasmatic nucleus is located just above the intersection and 'samples' the light signal being sent from each eye, which it then uses to reset the circadian rhythm. Hence why the suprachiasmatic nucleus is referred to as the brain's clock.

Arising from the pons (brainstem), CSF surrounds this cross[ing point], which rests directly besides the pituitary gland and immediate inferior to the hypothalamus. It's 12mm horizontally and forms the anterior wall of the third ventricle. The CSF passes here before reaching the arachnoid granulations and being reabsorbed back into the blood via the superior sagittal sinus (a big brain vein). What is viewed by the two individual eyes and transferred through the optic chiasm is then sent to the corpus callosum, which brings the left and right together in order to form an overall picture of the world.

The Corpus Callosum

The corpus callosum is a large bundle of myelinated (hence, white) neuron axons that hold both hemispheres together. As the master communicator between the left and right (logic and creative, physical and spiritual) sides of the brain, the corpus callosum is the mediator of the human body. The corpus callosum is like a highway of about 200 million densely-packed nerve cells that integrate information from both sides of the body. If one considers the fact that the left side of the brain is the physical, logical side of the brain and the right side is the spiritual, creative half, the corpus callosum can be seen as the messenger between both worlds.

Clearly, the brain is full of overlapping areas with a variety of roles. As the focus of this book is on the sacred secretion, other than those already listed, some brain structures and terms that it would be useful to be aware of (and to refer back to) are:

- **White** Matter- myelinated cells
- **Grey** Matter- nerve cell bodies, also known as Soma
- **Neurotransmitters**- chemical messengers between neurons in the brain.
- **Neuropeptides**- chemical messengers that are like molecules of emotion that signal to hormonal centres.
- The **brainstem** is the posterior part of the brain, containing the pons and medulla. This is also referred to as the reptilian part of the brain as it is concerned with instinctual behaviours such as survival and reproduction.
- The **Pons**- containing nerve fibres which connect the 2 parts of the cerebellum (lower brain).
- Beneath the pons and flowing into the spinal cord is the **Medulla Oblongata**, which transmits the ascending and descending nerve fibres of the spinal cord. Surprisingly, there is another structure known as the renal medulla (medulla means 'middle'), which resides within the kidneys. Vasopressin from

the pituitary signals to the kidneys to retain water. As the kidneys are the body's filtering system that take waste products from the blood (producing urine), they can be seen to literally 'wash away sin'.

- The **fornix**- a C-shaped bundle of nerve fibres that look like an arch, or of Aries.

- The **Nigrostriatal Nerve Tract**- which is exceedingly sensitive to movement detection, even minute magnetic ones.

- The **Neocortex**- the seat of your conscious mind. This is known as the human part of the brain, concerned with logical thinking and abstract thought.

- The **Autonomic Nervous System**- responsible for creating balance through its control of hormonal secretions.

- **Ventricles** are spaces filled with CSF. Interestingly, the two lateral ventricles on both sides of the brain form the shape or wings. The 4th ventricle (shaped like a tent or pyramid) is continuous with the spinal line and the 3rd ventricle is a mysterious opening in the upper middle area of the brain, commonly referred to as the Cave of Brahma. This area in the 3rd ventricle has the thalamus as its walls, the hypothalamus as its floor and the plexus of the 3rd choroid ventricles as its roof. [See FIGURE 24]

- **Limbic** System- from the word *limbus*, Latin for 'border', this is the emotional centre for the brain. This section of the brain is also referred to as the mammalian part as it is responsible for emotions, such as empathy and parental bonding.

According to Saint Germain (2015), as we become resonant, further brain parts harmonise. Saint Germain advocated the necessity of a purity of heart in order to raise our 'sacred fire' (or *fire energy*, as advocated by Christ).

Alchemy

The Arabic word 'alchemy' has its roots in Egypt, literally meaning "the Egyptian way". Nowadays it tends to be used to describe the changing of one substance into another. For alchemy to be successful, balance between the mind and physical body is essential. (Balancing meditation with exercise is effective at anchoring your spiritual and physical body to this plane of existence.)

The physical senses allow for both physical and spiritual alchemy. The senses gather from the environment; neurons organise into networks and form a pattern; the brain releases a chemical reaction in response, which is sent throughout the body; then an emotional response is created. Thus, the stronger the emotional quotient, the stronger the change in internal chemistry. According to Dr Joe Dispenza (2017), this thinking-feeling loop also produces a measurable electromagnetic field: the aura. Therefore, we are always sending and receiving information frequencies and emit a frequency that resonates with your state of being. As such, most practitioners advocate the emotion of LOVE; the most powerful emotion in the world, both vibrationally and euphorically.

This seems to me the obvious message from the Bible: to return (synchronise) with the father (universal energy), one must emit (and share) the frequency of love and compassion. Alas, as the flow of electricity generates a magnetic field, humans also have an electromagnetic field, which is influenced by the chemicals within the liquid composition of the body. Therefore, thoughts become biochemical reactions which release chemical signals and energy waves, which attract likewise energy waves.

Major Hormones and Neurotransmitters

Melatonin is a natural hormone secreted by the body to regulate biorhythms and cycles, notably the circadian rhythm (sleep-wake cycle). Melatonin is produced by the pineal gland, increasing in concentration when it's dark. Exposure to light at night can block the production of this hormone, leading to a cascade of physical and mental health problems as the body's natural rhythm is affected. The precursor to melatonin is serotonin. Serotonin contributes to feelings of well-being and happiness, as well as playing a major role in the regulation of appetite, digestion, motor skills, cognitive function and several organ systems. Structurally, the serotonin molecule is twinned with that of DMT and can even share the same receptor sites. DMT is a chemical substance found naturally in all living things, both animal and plant. (Further details can be found in Chapter 12.)

Not far from the pineal, which can be seen as the father gland of the compounds described above, is the pituitary. The pituitary is the mother gland of the body, responsible for the production and storage of a vast number of hormones. A key one of these includes vasopressin. Vasopressin, also called *antidiuretic hormone*, is accountable for the regulation of fluids, salt and blood pressure.

In addition to vasopressin, the pituitary also stores oxytocin: the mother hormone. Oxytocin is calming and reduces fear and anxiety whilst improving love, peace, trust, calm and the sensitivity of the senses. Vast oxytocin receptors in the stomach increase nutritional uptake (just like Christ being able to feed the 5000 with such minimal bread and fish). Furthermore, skin-to-skin contact stimulates mass oxytocin release, hence Christ's touch having the ability to heal. Oxytocin also increases intuition by means of improved social interaction and ability to 'read' others. Thus, if the father hormones are lovingly nurtured by the mother hormones, the perfect environment is created for the spiritual seed.

Summary

From the information presented within this chapter, it is clear that the human body is a magnificent laboratory capable of the most profound and mysterious alchemy, influenced by as little as a single thought. An exploration of this magical capability is likely the root of the discovery of the sacred secret-ion preservation. Frequent preservation of the sacred secret-ion will stimulate the growth of more receptor sites on cells that welcome and use the all-healing spirit molecule, as well as myelinate (thicken and consolidate) the nervous system path for faster accessibility and conscious creation in the future.

Top Recommendations

Website: www.khanacademy.org

Book: Widmaier, E., Raff, H. and Strang, K. 2016. *Vander's Human Physiology*. MvGraw-Hill Education.

Article: Kirschvink, J. 1992. Magnetite Biomineralization in the Human Brain. *Proc Natl Acad Sci.* 89:pp.7683-7687.

Podcast: Instant Anatomy with Dr Robert Whitaker

Video: 'Anatomy & Physiology' Learning Playlist by CrashCourse [YouTube] 22 June 2015

Bibliography and References

Alberts, B., Hopkins, K., Johnson, A., Morgan, D., Raf, M., Roberts, K. and Walter, P. 2019. *Essential Cell Biology. 5th Ed.* Norton & Company.

Dispenza, J. 2017. *Becoming Supernatural.* Hay House.

Eiden, L., Mezey, E., Eskay, L., Beinfeld, M. and Palkorits, M. 1990. Neuropeptide Content and Connectivity of the Rat Claustrum. *Brain Research.* 523(2):pp. 245-250.

Harrell, K. and Dudek, R. 2019. *Anatomy.* Wolters Kluwer.

Kirschvink, J. 1992. Magnetite Biomineralization in the Human Brain. *Proc Natl Acad Sci.* 89:pp.7683-7687.

Lewis, D. 2015. *Saint Germain on Advanced Alchemy.* Meru Press.

Lin, L. and Sibille, E. 2013. Reduced Brain Somatostatin in Mood Disorders. *Frontiers in Pharmacology.* 4:p110.

Lohmann, K. and Johnsen, S. 2000. The Neurobiology of Magnetoreception in Vertebrate Animals. *Trends in Neuroscience.* 23(4):p.153.

Marieb, E. and Hoehn, K. 2013. *Human Anatomy and Physiology.* 9th Ed. Pearsons Education.

Martini, F., Nath, J. and Bartholomew, E.2015. *Fundamentals of Anatomy and Physiology.* 10th Ed. Pearson Education Ltd.

Myers, B. 2013. *PEMF: The 5th Element of Health.* Balboa Press.

Peate, I.and Nair, M. 2017. *Fundamentals of Anatomy and Physiology.* 2nd Ed. John Wiley.

Pocock, G. and Richards, C. 2008. *The Human Body.* Oxford.

Pocock, G., Richards, C. and Richards, D. 2018. *Human Physiology.* 5th Ed. Oxford.

Roca, C., Tung-Ping, S., Elpern, S., McFarland, H. and Rubinow, D. 1998. Cerebrospinal Fluid, Somatostatin, Mood and Cognition in Multiple Sclerosis. *Biological Psychiatry.* 48(4):pp. 551-556.

Ryan, S., McNicholas, M. and Eustace, S. 2011. *Anatomy for Diagnostic Imaging.* 3rd Ed. Saunders Elsevier.

Saladin, K. 2017. *Human Anatomy.* 5th Ed. McGraw-Hill Education.

Widmaier, E., Raff, H. and Strang, K. 2016. *Vander's Human Physiology.* MvGraw-Hill

Chapter 12

DMT:

Diet, Music and Tryptamine

The human body is an amalgamation of trillions of cells. These cells are based on a combination of molecules and can be altered according to the levels of various biochemicals they are exposed to. For example, when a person is under extreme stress, the body releases more cortisol and adrenaline. The aftermath of these chemical bomb-shells is exhaustion, which leads to a weakened immune system and corresponding sickness. Other hormones and chemicals produced within the body include melatonin, serotonin and tryptamine, the chemical family of DMT.

N, N- Dimethyltryptamine, or DMT, is a monoamine alkaloid (a molecule) found in all plants and animals. It is a structural analog of serotonin and melatonin (the body-chemicals responsible for mood, sleep and rhythms), all of which are regulated by the pineal gland. In large doses, DMT is a psychedelic compound that produces influences similar to those of intensive meditation. In small doses, it stimulates a relaxed and comfortable mental state. Endogenously, Strassman (2001) states that DMT is largely produced in the lungs, which is speculated to be a key component when reaching higher realms during deep meditation that focuses on the breath. This is due to the fact that a key atom within the DMT molecule is hydrogen, and the deep breathing during meditation as well as consuming hydrogen water and having an alkaline-balanced body supports this process of producing DMT molecules. It is the most effective psychedelic known to man and gives humans a supremely intense sensation... and it can be made internally, free of stigma and legalities. Endogenous DMT is termed *endouaska* by such researchers as John Chavez.

Psychedelics work by shutting down the materialistic, dominating five physical senses, allowing our spatial senses to take over and showcase what is hidden beyond the third dimensional veil. Intriguingly, although the brain puts up a fight against most drugs and chemicals, it takes a particularly interesting fancy to DMT, making the psychedelic molecule one of few that is actively transported to the brain tissue. Yet, by law it is illegal due to the fact that we live within a culture of prohibition, even though there has never been a case of overdose, abuse or recorded death from DMT. Furthermore, it is non-addictive and has been used within religious ceremonies for thousands upon thousands of years. Still, in the late 1960s- early 1970s it became classified as a Class A (Schedule 1) drug in most countries. It would be interesting to ask those who deemed DMT bad enough to be a Class A drug why, if it is so dangerous, are our cells abundant with receptor sites for it? According to Dr Ede Freska et al (2013), DMT binds to the sigma-1 receptor, found

277

throughout the body, which plays a key role in protecting cells when oxygen is low. Hence, the receptor that seeks DMT is the same receptor that keeps the cells of the body alive during times of near death. One could speculate that this is also a connection to 'near death experiences', whereby people claim to leave the body and see visions from higher dimensions, and possibly even the inspiration behind the stories of Jesus bringing people back from the dead.

Interestingly, the gene that synthesises DMT is highly active in the retina and visual organs, as recorded from a study by Cozzi et al. (1999). Seeing as the pineal regulates DMT and also expresses cones and rods similar to those of the eyes, it seems only fair that the pineal is given the title as the Third Eye.

Like most psychedelic compounds, DMT stimulates neurogenesis (brain cell growth and development). It is for this reason that psychedelics such as truffles, mushrooms and ayahuasca, have been said to be the missing link in our evolution by such influential figures as Terence and Dennis McKenna (as discussed in Chapter 1). This is particularly interesting as there is some current emerging evidence, although not completed or common knowledge yet, that there was a thriving civilisation in Brazil that could in fact be the oldest known human remains. The reason this civilisation has remained hidden for so long is that it is hidden below the now Amazon Rainforest. It can be seen from this, then, that humans may have evolved where the Amazon now is (and where ayahuasca is found abundantly).

As it is a rainforest, it's possible that there is more to the 'snake' analogy than currently in our awareness. Maybe serpents lived in the trees which homed the psychedelic DMT, which is how the shaman in the past knew where to look, which gave way to increased knowledge through neurogenesis? But I'm just speculating here. And with such a mass rainforest growing over these ancient remains, it's unlikely we'll know much more during this lifetime. Still, the power of the compound is undeniable.

Because of its profound healing effects- both physically and mentally- DMT has been consumed orally within Amazon shamanic brews for over 5000 years. Although fungus has its own DMT-like compounds (4-HO- DMT), the most potent form of DMT known today is through the use of Ayahuasca (pronounced aya-waska), which is used by shaman for both spiritual and medicinal use. However, as the body takes in these DMT molecules so quickly, the felt effects often go unnoticed. That is, unless inhibitors are consumed at the same time to slow this absorption rate down.

MAO Inhibitors

According to a recent study by Dean et al (2019), DMT itself is biosynthesised from aromatic-L-amino acid decarboxylase (AADC, a tryptophan enzyme which also has the ability to make neurotransmitters such as serotonin and dopamine) and indolethylamine-N-methyltransferase (INMT). The transcription of both of these can be found in the mammalian brain. [NOTE: Tryptophan must be obtained from diet as it cannot be synthesised in the body. As it is the precursor to serotonin, it is essential for mood-regulation and feeling calm.

Moreover, it is also required for the synthesis of Niacin, which increases energy levels. According to Jullian Levy (2018), tryptophan-rich foods include bananas, legumes, seeds, nuts, spirulina, raw dairy and pasture-raised eggs.]

However, the effects of DMT are counteracted by MAO (mono-amino-oxidase) acids in the digestive system. These MAOs are bound to the outer membrane of mitochondria in most cell types in the body and are involved in removing neurotransmitters such as norepinephrine, serotonin, dopamine and DMT from the brain. It is necessary for these chemicals to be inhibited in a dangerous world so that the more survival-enhancing molecules, such as cortisol and adrenaline, can take over. At the end of the day, serotonin isn't going to help you to escape from that tiger! In the modern world, though, we are returning to a state of homeostasis, whereby the levels of DMT produced within the body are balanced with MAO- inhibitors in order for its effects to bloom.

The rainforest tribes discovered that adding the Ayahuasca vine (Banisteriopsis Caapi, containing MAO- inhibitors) to their brew of Chachruna Leaves (which contain high levels of the DMT molecule) provided a harmonising effect that allows the body to absorb the DMT more slowly so that the effects can be felt. There are two types of MAOs found in the human body: MAO-A (found in the gut) and MAO-B (found in the blood). Both types are also found in brain cells. MAO-A is a major enzyme which breaks down and deactivates serotonin and DMT. So inhibitors of MAO-A cause a build-up of these neurotransmitters.

Interestingly, not only does the human body naturally produce DMT, but it also produces MAO inhibitors (MAOIs) in the process, notably pinoline, harmaline and tryptoline, to name a few (Chavez, 2017 and 2018). Therefore, the body is able to produce its own all-healing, all-enlightening, all-cosmically-connected internal ayahuasca brew. DMT specialist Rick Strassman (2014) claims that the effects of consuming external DMT provides similar effects to those experienced from DMT brewed internally. He also supports the hypothesis that the production of endogenous DMT is influenced by magnetic field shifts. This could explain why DMT levels sky-rocket at the point of death (or near death) as the spiritual soul leaving the physical body would naturally have an effect on the body's magnetic field (which then bind to the Sigma-1 receptor site mentioned previously).

Visions

People who have experienced the psychedelic effects of DMT claim to visit other dimensions with different shapes and laws. They also state that they meet foreign entities and communicate with them telepathically. Furthermore, those who have had a DMT trip strongly exert that it feels as if the mind has separated from the body and that the experience triggers an overpowering array of emotions, particularly those of excitement, euphoria and pleasure. Research also shows that lower dosages produce calm, psychological effects, whereas higher dosages induce psychedelic experiences with four- dimensional awareness. Humans who are familiar with DMT use also describe extremely bright colours, geometric patterns (like those commonly associated with the Mayan and Aztec cultures) and a sense of timelessness.

The 'trip' experienced whilst on DMT often appears universal, meaning that the sights and feelings are often very similar. It is this similarity, alongside strong belief in the validity of the experiences being real, that has led to DMT's popularity and use by shamans all over the world as an access portal to other dimensions. The same shamans even claim that it is our severed connection with spirit that is causing western sickness. Dr Rick Strassman, who famously dedicated his career to studying the effects of DMT, nicknamed the psychedelic *The Spirit Molecule* and beautifully described it as a 'Reality Thermostat'. His research led him to the conclusion that the body produces just the right amount of the psychedelic DMT molecule to keep us in this level of existence. Fortunately, thermostats can be adjusted.

DMT researcher Andrew Gallimore sees this molecule as more of a technology, like a TV remote control, able to enable conscious intelligences, such as ourselves, to emerge within a cosmic game of life and switch channels in between. Gallimore claims that the brain's model of reality begins to build at conception, learning which aspects of the world to exclude, ignore and distort in order to build an informational representation of reality. Interestingly, he explains how the cortex of the brain is actually a flat sheet made of columns, with connections that strengthen or weaken depending on conscious perception. It is because of this that Gallimore states that the brain cannot just make up a reality, such as those experienced on DMT. His belief is that there must be some memory associated within these columns to such states of awareness. According to Gallimore, DMT has likely been present throughout our evolution, probably acting as the dominating neurotransmitter at night whilst we sleep, which then hands the baton to serotonin during the light of day. This ideology supports the *matrix* theory, whereby the universe is comprised of vast arrays of frequencies and levels of reality which overlap. The beings within each strand of reality are aware of each other due to sharing the same chemical soup and DNA/ light code potentials, contributing to the collective consciousness. These various dimensions are just a slice of the *real* world, with beings able to tap into other frequencies when they adapt their own awareness in order to resonate with different dimensions of collective consciousnesses.

So, we have the biochemistry of *heaven* waiting to be unlocked and fully lived here on Earth.

The sacred secretion is a way of preserving the molecule and working with the natural biological cycles of the body and astrological rhythms of the stars to enhance the levels of DMT, thus turning up our thermostat and raising our unique awareness. As humans are the only known species of animal who can consciously alter their vibrational output, removing themselves from survival mode and into spiritual enhancement, we are in a perfect line of consciousness to be able to raise our vibration naturally. It is worth remembering that the human brain only perceives that which it believes to be important. This is an evolutionary survival mechanism. As children, we are often conditioned to see the physical world for 'what it really is'. This conditioning strips us of our non-physical senses as our brain learns that it only needs to observe through the five basic senses to survive. Some people do maintain this higher awareness, evidenced by powerful psychics and mediums, but this is rare in modern society. Fortunately, by regularly returning to support the preservation of the secretion, the neuronal structures within the brain re-wire to support this process, as your conscious actions force the subconscious reactions to deem this important for your survival. Consequently, the reality thermostat kicks up a permanent notch! Through correct procedure (AKA. the natural life-style that human rhythms evolved to follow), the flow of DMT within the body can be raised, re-tuning the Reality Thermostat. As the Moon enters the sun sign that harmonises our biorhythms, the vibratory energy of these naturally occurring molecules increases.

When released, the individual experiences a more advanced perception of reality. This theory is not only supported by scientific research, but has been documented throughout the text-books of religious history. Those who study Ancient-Astrophysics admit that our modern understanding of human brain and body function has come full-circle back to the ways of the Ancients. This includes the realisation that the Bible is in fact full of metaphors, intended for story telling that enhances visual comprehension of these functions rather than to be taken literally.

Most chemicals within the body are amino acid-based, typically opening and closing ion channels to change a cell's electrical state, to synthesise proteins and the activate enzyme production. These circulate in the blood but can only exert their effect on cells that have receptor sites for that transmitter or hormone.

Above Genetics

As explained in Chapter 1, epigenetics literally means "above genetics" as it is based on tiny flags and tags that are above the DNA strand, waiting for certain chemicals to attach to these receptors and regulate the expression of genes. This is the biological action that allows us to pass cultural beliefs, individual ideas, phobias and fears, emotional control and even food preferences down to our offspring. Psychedelic plants, then, likely sped up evolution, which would have otherwise taken much, much longer, by providing humans with enhanced neurogenesis, creativity, problem solving ability, sex drive and access to universal information such as tool manipulation, the invention of fire to advance food nutrition, natural laws, etc. As these evolving people repeatedly operated these experiences, their own ideologies and philosophies would have altered. Naturally, these would have been passed down through the generations due to epigenetics.

Fascinatingly, the aromatic L-amino acid decarboxylase (AADC) enzyme which synthesises endogenous DMT is regulated by l-dopa decarboxylase (DDC), a protein-coding gene, which is involved in the development of the nervous system and is even found throughout the peripheral system. What is interesting about this particular gene is that it can undergo splicing (editing), able to fashion one of two different isoforms (proteins that originate from the same gene), referred to as AADC480 (which can decarboxylate) and AADC422 (which cannot). Now, a study by Jacob and Presti (2005) shows that it is the expression of this gene that can either encourage or discourage endogenous DMT production by means of the decarboxylation (a chemical reaction which releases carbon dioxide from a molecular chain) process.

Therefore, by upregulating this gene and encouraging the production of the AADC480 isoform, the preservation of the sacred secretion can promote endogenous DMT production that can be called upon continuously, not just once a month when the Moon is in your sun sign. Similarly, research by Sangah, Gomex and Domino (1979) had previously demonstrated that the brain has a re-uptake mechanism for DMT based on active transportation of the molecule in nerve cells. Ergo, any un-used DMT can be reabsorbed for later. In addition, a study by Chu et al (2014) found that another protein-coding gene called Indolethylamine N-Methyltransferase (INMT) also regulates the receptors for DMT. Importantly, both the DDC and INMT genes are found throughout the cerebral cortex, as well as within the pineal gland and the choroid plexus.

Consequently, it is this particular gene expression and increased receptor sites which I believe is able to tune the DMT thermostat advocated by Rick Strassman. The more this transmitter is activated, the more receptor sites can be upregulated to increase cellular response and the more connected we can feel to source energy as our internal DMT brew becomes more consciously metabolised. As the genes which dominate the coding of DMT are also found abundantly throughout the brain, particularly within the pineal and choroid plexus which directly feed into the CSF, it seems reasonable to conclude that the change in cosmic influence on our bodies when the lunar energy shifts into our dominating star sign does, indeed, have an impact on endogenous DMT production.

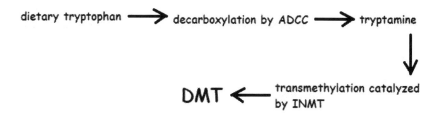

FIGURE 21 – DMT Synthesis

The Power of Vibration

DMT, like all matter of energy, is affected by sound vibration. It is because of this that traditional tribes include musical instruments and chanting within their ceremonies and rituals. The Shaman will often chant, hymn and throat sing to allow for successful achievement of the transcendental state. This is because of the way these very specific vibrations harmonise with the rhythms of the body and the frequency of the DMT molecules. It also stimulates the Vagus nerve (the "wandering" nerve, connecting the brain to all organs of the body) to a state of calm or excitability. Hence why there's a difference in sympathetic response between singing and shouting and explains why different songs produce varying emotions. How we respond to this stimulus depends on our own level of resonance and receptivity.

Colours even vibrate to resonate with specific cords, a phenomenon commonly applied within Colour Therapy. According to specialist Mary Bassano (1993), these include: Red – Middle C ; Orange – D ;

Yellow – E ; Green – F ; Blue – G ; Indigo – A ; Violet – B. All of which clearly correlate with a chakra, thus emphasising the role of the energy centres.

Therefore, it can be inferred that varying frequencies and vibrations, such as those processed within the brain as sound and colour, impact the rate at which DMT is produced and modulated. These also resonate with the different chakras, which would naturally lead to resonance and a clearer path laid out in between, enhancing the level of received cosmic signalling.

Summary

The main down-side to reincarnating into a human body is that it has genetic inclinations towards the development of an ego in order to survive physically on this plane. Fortunately, the body also homes the pineal gland, which can produce the spirit molecule DMT after puberty so that, once we have survived into adulthood, we can begin to reconnect with the universal source. As DMT can be produced endogenously, the potency of which can be effected by diet, light and magnetic fields, the sacred secretion can be used to enhance our body's capability of upregulating the genetic expression of the enzyme required for the synthesis of this psychedelic molecule. Engagement with sensory stimulus, such as watching colour and/ or listening to shamanic chanting is commonly used to heighten to effects of DMT as these influence the molecular structure of the compound.

Top Recommendations

Website: www.metatoninresearch.org and www.dmtquest.org

Book: Strassman, R. 2014. *DMT and the Soul of Prophecy.* Park Street Press.

Article: Dean, J. et al. 2019. Biosynthesis and Extracellular Concentrations of N,N- dimethyltryptamine (DMT) In Mammalian Brain. *Scientific Reports.* 9:9333.

Barker, S., McIlhenny, E. and Strassman, R. 2012. A critical review of reports of endogenous psychedelic N,N,-dimethyltryptamines in humans:1955-2010. *Drug Testing and Analysis.* 4:pp.617-635.

Podcast: 'Mind Meld 162- Dr Bruce Lipton' by Third Eye Drops. 13 June 2019.

Video: 'The Spirit Molecule' documentary, available on YouTube

Bibliography

Barker, S., McIlhenny, E. and Strassman, R. 2012. A critical review of reports of endogenous psychedelic N,N,-dimethyltryptamines in humans:1955-2010. *Drug Testing and Analysis.* 4:pp.617-635.

Bassano, M. 1993. *Healing With Music and Colour.* Red Wheel.

Borowsky, B., Adham, N. and Jones, K. et al. 2001. Trace Amines: Identification of a Family of Mammalian G-Protein- Coupled Receptors. *Proc Natl Acad Sci USA.* 98:pp. 8966-8971.

Chavez, J. 2017. *Questions for the Lion Tamer 1.* Independently Published.

Chavez, J. 2018. *Questions for the Lion Tamer 2.* Independently Published.

Cozzi, , N., Mavlytov, T., Thompson, M. and Ruoho, A. 1999. Indolethylamine N-methyltransferase expression in primate nervous tissue. *University of Wisconsin: School of Medicine and Public Health.*

Dean, J. 2018. Indolethylamine-*N*-methyltransferase polymorphisms: Genetic and biochemical approaches for study in endogenous N,N,-dimethyltryptamine. *Frontiers of Neuroscience.* 23 April 2018.

Dean, J. et al. 2019. Biosynthesis and Extracellular Concentrations of N,N-dimethyltryptamine (DMT) In Mammalian Brain. *Scientific Reports.* 9:9333.

Devlin, T. 2011. *Textbook of Biochemistry.* 7th Ed. Kaye Pace Publications.

Frecska, E. et al. 2013. A Possible Sigma-1 Receptor Mediated Role of Dimethyltryptamine in Tissue Protection, Regeneration and Immunity. *Journal of Neural Transmission.* 120(9): pp.1296-1303.

Hancock, G. *The Divine Spark.* Hay House.

Jacob, M. and Presti, D. 2005. Endogenous Psychoactive Tryptamines Considered: An Anxiolytic Role For Dimethyltryptamine. *Medical Hypothesis.* 64(5):pp. 930-937.

Levy, J. 2018. *Get More Tryptophan for Better Sleep, Moods and Fewer Headaches.* Available online at: <www.draxe.com>

Luke, D. 2018. *DMT Dialogues.* Park Street Press.

McKenna, T. 1992. *Food of the Gods.* Rider.

McKenna, . 1994. Ayahuasca Increases Serotonin Receptor Sensitivity in the Brain.

Pless, G. et al. 1999. Pharmacological aspects of N-acetyl-5-methoxytryptamine (melatonin) and 6-methoxy-1,2,3,4- tetrahydro-B-carboline (Pinoline) as antioxidants: Reduction of oxidative damage in brain region homogenates. *Journal of Pineal Research.* 26:pp. 236-246.

Rommelspacher, H. et al. 1977. Pharmacological properties of tetrahydronorharmane (Tryptoline). *Archives of Pharmacology.* 298:pp. 83-91.

Sangiah, S., Gomez, M. and Domino, E. 1979. Accumulation of N,N-Dimethyltryptamine in Rat Brain Cortical Slices. *Biol Psychiat.* 14:pp.925-936.

Strassman, R. and Qualls, C. 1994. Dose Response Study of N,N-Dimethyltryptamine in Humans. Part 1. Neuroendocrine, Automatic and Cardiovascular Effects. *Arch Gen Psychiat.* 51:pp. 85-97.

Strassman, R., Qualls, C., Uhlenhuth, E. and Kellner, R. 1994. Dose Response Study of N,N-Dimethyltryptamine in Humans. Part 2. Subjective Effects and Preliminary Results of a New Rating Scale.. *Arch Gen Psychiat.* 51:pp. 98-108.

Strassman, R. 2001. *DMT: The Spirit Molecule.* Park Street Press.

Strassman, R. 2014. *DMT and the Soul of Prophecy.* Park Street Press.

Wyatt, R., Saavedra, J. and Axelrod, J. 1973a. A dimethyltryptamine- forming enzyme in human blood. *American Journal of Psychiatry.* 130:pp.1359-1361.

Zeng, H. and Xu, W. 2015. *Enzymic Assays of Histone Methyltransferase Enzymes.* Epigenetic Technological Applications.

Summary of Part 1

The human body is an alchemical factory of divine creation. Part 1 of this book aimed to emphasise the clear intelligence behind the human-design and provide the background understanding necessary for a full comprehension of the science and philosophies behind the ancient practice of preserving the sacred spiritual seed. So far, we know that the body has the ability to communicate with source energy through the electromagnetic properties of its structures, change its own frequency through conscious thought and can even pass ideas, beliefs and epigenetic adaptations down to offspring.

As humans form part of the ecosystem of Earth, much alike our own internal ecosystem consisting of such organisms as cell mitochondria and gut flora, we are as much responsible for the health of the overall planet as it is for us. The fact that each human being is unique both physically and energetically, evident by our vast differences in characteristics and preferences, means that even our path to enlightenment is tailor made. You will naturally gravitate towards teachings which resonate with you and your path in life, so make a note of any information which particularly excites you as areas for further research.

Alan Watts once proclaimed that you cannot have an environment without an organism, and you cannot have an organism without an environment. In the same way, the great Garden of Eden cannot exist without humans, as humans cannot exist without the Garden of Eden. A world needs creatures and creatures need a world. It is a relationship based on balance. Consequently, people and Gaia share a reciprocal give-and-take relationship, which is powered by the universal frequency of love and connection. By saving the sacred secret-ion, we can strengthen our own vibration and return this to Gaia in order to support her cleansing and ascension from the damage done in the past. This, in turn, will allow us to reconnect to the Father and giver of all life (the universe) with a pure heart (much akin to the ancient Egyptian stories of life after death).

The aim of Part 1 was to show how intrinsically connected all things are; how the microcosmic human is a reflection of the macrocosmic universe and how both follow the same cycles just at varying time lapses. Humans are clearly of intelligent design and are the perfect powerhouses for the planet. When we heal ourselves, we heal the world. As God-seeds on Gaia, we hold the ability to feel the Matrix of things and navigate through the various realms of existence.

Part 2 of this text will explore the evidence of, process and purpose of sacred secretion more specifically. It is recommended that you go back and read all of the short summaries from each chapter in Part 1 to consolidate your understanding before moving onto Part 2.

Victoria Loalou
THE ART OF PRESERVATION

Part 2

Evidence of the Sacred Secretion

Chapter 13

In DNA

At conception, the nuclei of a woman's egg and a man's seed combine to form a zygote and begin the process of cell division. Eventually, these cells differentiate into various roles (such as a heart cell or a nail cell) but the entire genetic imprint and potentials are still laid inside, it is just that the cell is signalled by the body to express itself specifically in this way. (Stem cells are those which have not yet been differentiated into specific roles, which is why menstrual blood is full of them.)

Contained within the nucleus of cells are chromosomes, of which 23 are passed down from each parent, equalling a total of 46 chromosomes organised into 23 pairs. These contain genes and are the basic units of inheritance. Chromosomes are also composed of an array of structural proteins called histones, which help to pack the extremely long, coiled lengths of DNA into the small space of the cell nucleus. So all of our inherited potential is stored like a spiralled, sleeping serpent within cell nuclei and is synthesised in response to signals from the cell membrane (such as ion influx). Thus, DNA is able to replicate, recombine and repair in response to the environment.

Deoxyribonucleic acid (DNA) is one of the most controversial mysteries to science even to this day as, not only does DNA govern all cell function, but it stores genetic information, both ancestrally and epigenetically. In essence, the double-helix DNA is a coiled chain whose bases are bonded together by hydrogen (and looks incredibly similar to a ladder).

Ancestral DNA

Our genetic DNA is a library of our history, which only our internal, secret world currently knows how to read. Interestingly, the coiled DNA has to uncoil (like a serpent) in order to be transcribed and replicated. Note, however, it is not the entire DNA which uncoils, just the codon (sequence of nucleotides that are part of the genetic code, specifying the synthesis of a particular protein) being transcribed and replicated; it's like going to a library but only gaining knowledge from a specifically desired book or opening a cook book in order to follow one recipe.

Research by Vladimir Poporin (1995) and Luc Montagnier (2010) proved the ideology that the coils of DNA store data like a library and can emit electromagnetic signal which imprint onto other molecules. So all of the ancestral genetic potential stored in our cells are able to release signals which projects themselves from one cell to the next, like quantum teleportation. On an external level, this could explain how one person is able to signal light codes to activate another.

Located in the cytoplasm (cell material excluding the nucleus) of the cell are organelles called ribosomes, which synthesise protein. Proteins are assembled from a set of 20 amino acids. These can be linked together within an infinite number of possible structures. As a person's biological characteristics are determined by which proteins are synthesised, the number of possible human characteristics are also infinite. So the genetic data is held within the DNA of the cell nucleus, but the ribosomes required to code this into proteins that the body can use are constricted to the cytoplasm. As DNA is too large of a molecule to leave the nucleus, information from this has to be copied (transcribed) into a single-stranded nucleic acid similar to DNA called messenger RNA (mRNA).

This transcription, which originally takes place in the nucleus, can then migrate to the cytoplasm within the more transportable mRNA strand. Next, this attaches to a ribosome (protein synthesiser) within the cell. It is the base sequence of mRNA that specifies the sequence of amino acids in proteins which constitutes the genetic code. The amino acids must then be assembled in the correct order dictated by the code. This process is called translation and involves another kind of RNA: transfer RNA (tRNA). Finally, the original message relayed by the DNA becomes proteins which can be read and used by the rest of the body.

In simple terms, DNA (which holds all potentials and does not change) makes RNA (strands of itself replicated in response to stimuli), which signals the production of proteins that can be used for maintenance in the body. But how does the DNA know which information to code into protein? This question is answered in a field of science referred to as epigenetics.

Epigenetic DNA

According to Ko and Susztak (2014), epigenetics refers to the modification of the genome (without changing the nucleotide sequence) in response to environmental input. Basically, there are tiny chemical flags and tags that are layered on top of your DNA. These tell the DNA which genes to code for and which to methylate.

Methylation is the process by which methyl groups (hydrocarbon molecules) are attached to certain genes in order to inactivate them, making these dormant to expression. In this way, genes are modified without changing the DNA itself. This means that our genetic library is capable of storing extremely vast quantities of information and only expressing proteins which increase our chances of survival within whatever environmental circumstances we find ourselves in, whether in physical reality or imagined mentally. This means that both the outer (cosmos) and inner (physiology) selves must be synchronised in order for the sacred secretion to rise to its full potential.

A more recent area of research is 'nutrigenomics', whereby scientists are discovering the undoubtable connection between nutrient-gene interaction. That is, how nutrition effects which DNA strands are expressed. Nutritional epigenetics describes how what we eat induces changes in DNA methylation. Therefore, there is no 'one-size-fits-all' plan for humans. We all carry genetic coding from diverse ancestral backgrounds, some containing more DNA strands from extinct species of humans (and possibly extra-terrestrial origin) than others. Thus, DNA transcription is regulated by the epigenome to allow the organism to adapt to fluctuating environments. Which of these genetics is expressed depends on what information is received by the receptors.

Receptors

Receptors are bound to the cell membrane, which can then respond by activating enzymes, releasing molecules or opening ion channels. The number of receptors can be upregulated to increase the cellular response. In order to adapt to the current inner environmental situation so that the organism can reproduce and survive, inherited DNA strands can either be awakened or made dormant (methylated) in response to stimuli. According to Strachan and Read (2019), these methyl groups can attract methyl-binding proteins that affect gene expression. Hence, although dormant, DNA is ready and waiting to be re-awakened within the right environment. These genes also carry an 'imprint' (memory) of their (parental) origin, thus supporting the idea that not only is our DNA a library of information passed down over millennia, but it is also fully referenced, enabling entanglement of energies along the ancestral line and access to ancient knowledge via the subconscious and raised awareness.

Yet, only about 2% of DNA can actually code for protein. The other 98% was previously referred to as 'Junk DNA'. Nowadays, we know that this non-coding DNA acts more like law-enforcers, telling the coding part of the DNA the pace and repetitions required. Interestingly, a study done on yeast found that junk DNA was essential for the organism's survival when food was scarce. Although the human is a long way off of being yeast, this study could suggest that more DNA becomes available through fasting- a practice actively encouraged throughout most religions.

One study (Rose et al, 2018) even likened junk DNA to that of a door-knob (or thermostat) for gene expression, turning this up and down. From this it can be seen that 'junk' DNA is the regulator of coding DNA and can be made more responsive during fasted states. These strands of DNA are packaged into thread-like structures called chromosomes. Each chromosome is made of DNA which is tightly coiled many times around proteins called *histones*, with protective caps at the end called *telomeres*. Chromosomes are shaped like crosses and each strand of DNA within a chromosome holds 33 complete turns; the same age as Christ at crucifixion. Hence, one could deduce that Christ is literally birthed, grown, killed and returned all within our genetics.

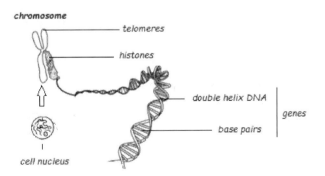

FIGURE 22 – Chromosome

Christ DNA

DNA is commonly described as comprising of four 'letters' (A,T,G, C) which combine together to form different 'words' or 'codes' (strings of letters). In the Bible, Jesus is described as *the word made flesh* (John 1:14). The physical body, then, is the alchemist able to turn *words* into *flesh*. Preserving the sacred secretion is a way of accessing the words/ codes for Christ Consciousness (the ability to tap into the higher realms and powers, deeming a person what mythologies refer to as *demi-god*). Here, I will repeat some of the details from Chapter 12 for emphasis.

The production of the L-amino acid decarboxylase (AADC enzyme) is regulated by the DDC gene, which is able to express one of two different isoforms: AADC480 (which can decarboxylate) and AADC422 (which cannot). As Jacob and Presti (2005) showed that it is the expression of this gene that can either encourage or discourage endogenous DMT production by means of the decarboxylation, it is reasonable to assume that this is the specific gene encoded within our ancestral DNA that dictates the 'temperature' upon our 'reality thermostat' (DMT production). Therefore, by awakening this gene and encouraging the production of the AADC480 isoform, the preservation of the sacred secretion can promote endogenous DMT production that can be called upon continuously, not just once a month when the Moon is in your sun sign. As it proclaims within the Book of Revelations:

"There will be no more night in the city, and they will have no need for the light of a lamp or of the sun. For the Lord God will shine on them, and they will reign forever and ever." [Revelations 22:5]

Similarly, research by Sangah, Gomex and Domino (1979) had previously demonstrated that the brain has a re-uptake mechanism for DMT based on active transportation of the molecule in nerve cells. Ergo, any un-used DMT can be reabsorbed for later. In addition, a study by Chu et al (2014) found that INMT (a protein-coding gene) regulates the receptors for DMT. So the more DMT synthesis is activated, the more receptor sites can be upregulated to increase cellular response and the more connected we can feel to source energy as our internal DMT brew becomes more consciously metabolised.

To sum: within our genetic blueprint are dormant genes that specifically code for the production of DMT and increase cell receptor sites for its practical use. Thus, preserving the sacred secret-ion each month will not only increase connection with the Father and Mother energies at this time, but will eventually lead to overall awakening which can be tapped into at will. From the Bible, this is evidenced by the aging of Jesus, whereby he began his life with initial blessings to those who residing within his presence, until he was eventually able to spread word of his miracles to all, even psychokinetically.

It would be intriguing here to look at research by Montagnier, showing that DNA is able to teleport. According to a team lead by Luc Montagnier, DNA sequences have been found to induce low frequency electromagnetic waves, even in solutions of water, triggered by the ambient electromagnetic background. The idea of DNA teleporting through fluid is one that holds some relevance to Christ being able to travel on water. If the background electromagnetic frequency of Christ DNA can teleport through and into water, and our bodies are filled with water, we all hold the potential for storing Christ DNA and being 'brothers and sisters', even able to electromagnetically resonate with and be imprinted by such structures. This could also explain why, when one's internal waters begin to vibrate at a higher level during the time of the sacred secretion, we feel more connecting as we are literally able to feel (via the transferable electromagnetic frequency of DNA) the inner perceptions of others.

When speaking of Akashic records, or the Library of Akasha, reference is being made to the great web of memories and creative potentials; a hidden aetheric library. These records include what has happened, is happening and what will happen. It is weaved through the grid of Gaia and includes consciousness codes that can be tapped into and accessed. Within this great library, you may access not only your own records but those of others who grant you the necessary permissions. Akashic records and the consciousness of the historic figures of Yeshua and Magdalene are stored here, often accessed as a Christ Couple Coding due to their sacred union bonding. Both of these energies, as well as those of many ascended masters and gods/goddesses, are coming through incredibly strongly at the moment to support the ascension of Gaia. Preserving the sacred secretion with the intent of granting permission to access their Christ Consciousness light codes from the Akasha is one way of awakening such DNA potentials.

If we remember the magic of biophotons discussed in Chapter 6, it can be seen that DNA also holds the potential for creating worm holes within reality, allowing for alternate states of consciousness to be felt, extra-terrestrial information to be received and enhanced connectedness to the collective as the portals exchange and share energy between each other, like the black holes of the universe. According to Bertrand and Bertrand, these black holes/ worm holes are more akin to *womb holes*, whereby they connect the cosmic womb of the universe with the earthly womb of Gaia and the microcosmic womb of humans. In this way, all creative matter is connected and built *in the image of the creator/ creatrix*. It is for this reason that so many ancient cultures believed in a great grandmother *spider* energy, that weaves all of the universe in and out of creation within her magical tapestry.

Thus, the copying of genes is not only physical but also spiritual, evolving metaphysically within the gene pool of the collective consciousness, as is the law of creation. This correlates with the theory of light codes, whereby Christ as *the light of the world* is able to actively awaken our Christ DNA via our solar-lunar influences, vibrant, internal waters (CSF).

Michael Hayes links the hermetic code (discussed in Chapter 5) of the ancients to our modern human DNA, showing how we are genetically predisposed to use and abide by the natural laws of the universe. According to Hayes, this means that all of creation happens in threes: the father, son and holy spirit; mother, father and child; electrons, protons and neutrons; acid, alkaline and neutral; Isis, Osiris and Horus; the Moon, the Sun and the Earth. With regards to the sacred secretion, the creation of the spiritual seed can be seen as physical (endogenous DMT synthesis), spiritual (engagement with the frequency of and vibratory connection to the cosmos and Akasha) and mental (through the process of visualisation and conscious awareness of emotions). The understanding of which can be comprehended, depending on one's genetic preferences, kinetically (through the felt experience), auditorily (via storytelling and music) and visually (through imagery and art).

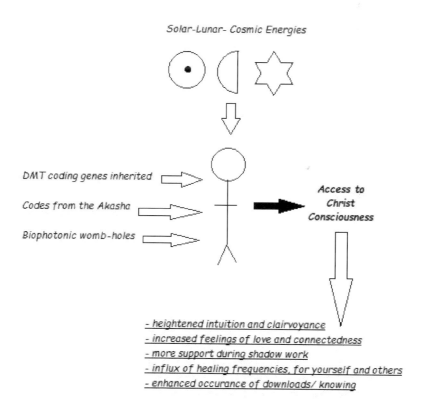

FIGURE 23 – Christ Consciousness

Summary

DNA can create wormholes in the matrix of reality via light and energy potentials. As altered states, such as those induced through the consumption of psychedelics, can allow us to see other aspects of this matrix, the fact that our DNA is able to code for such compounds shows clear evidence for their role within our evolution. The ancients, then, did the hard work. They made the connections within our DNA structure and established the spiritual potentials. They knew that the world followed cycles/ biorhythms and they needed to secure these spiritual potentials within our DNA so that the foundations would always be laid for those ready to wake up and activate them during a time when it was safe to re-awaken. They did the work- we just have to gratefully return home to ourselves.

Bibliography and References

Blanco, D. 2019. *Our cells are filled with 'junk DNA'- Here's why we need it.* [online] Available at: <www.discovermagazine.com>

Currivan, J. 2017. *The Cosmic Hologram.* Inner Traditions.

Gariaev, P., Tertishny, G, and Leonova, K. Journal of Non-Locality and Remote Mental Interactions. Available online at: < https://www.slideshare.net/INVERTONE/the-phantomdna-wave-p-garjajev-v-poponin>

Hayes, M. 2008. *The Hermetic Code in DNA.* Inner Traditions.

Ko, Y. and Suszak, K. 2014. Epigenomics: The science of no-longer-"junk" DNA. 33(4). *Seminars in Nephrology.*

Montagnier, L. 2010. DNA Between Physics and Biology [video]. Available online at: < https://www.mediatheque.lindau-nobel.org/videos/31544/dna-between-physics-and-biology-2010/laureate-montagnier>

Montagnier, L. 2011. DNA "Teleportation". Summary available online at: < http://www.rexresearch.com/montagnier/montagnier.htm> Full article: Montagner,L. et al. 2011. DNA waves and water.

Poporin, V. 1995. The DNA Phantom Effect. Available online at: < https://www.bibliotecapleyades.net/ciencia/ciencia_genetica04.htm>

Rodwell, M. 2016. *The New Human*. New Mind Publishers.

Rodwell, V., Bender, D., Botham, K., Kennelly, P. and Weil, P. 2018. *Harper's Illustrated Biochemistry*. 31st Ed. McGraw-Hill Education.

Rose, A. et al. 2018. MSR1 repeats modulate gene expression and affect risk of breast and prostate cancer. *Annals of Oncology*. 29(5):pp.1292-1303

Suleyman, S. 2015. *Cell Biology and Genetics*. Elsevier Ltd.

Chapter 14
In Physiology

According to Manly Hall: "There is no doubt that the Old Testament is a physiological and anatomical textbook to those capable of reading it from a scientific viewpoint." He claims that, in order to simplify the great laws of nature (e.g. alchemy, anatomy, physics), the ancients personified them and expressed gratitude and intent via offerings, etc. However, such practices became redundant when such *magic* as pharmacy took the place of the divine.

Many of the resources on the internet claim that the Christos originates from the *claustrum*. After delving into the research available on this part of the brain, it was discovered that, in recent years, Reardon (2017) reported that Koch discovered a giant neuron emanating from the claustrum which wraps around the entire brain, resembling a 'crown of thorns', like that which was worn by Jesus Christ prior to crucifixion. What's more, it's even reported that the claustrum, unlike all other areas of the cortex, holds no specific organisation of cells. If the claustrum really is linked with human consciousness, the vast variations in cell type division and differentiation here could be the physical counter-part to our spiritual path, thus highlighting that we each have our own unique way of getting close to God again; our own divine blueprint. Note that the word 'claustrum' literally means *door*, so could indeed be the literal door/ gate to heaven (and god-consciousness).

Eiden et al (1990) have discovered that the claustrum also concentrates the neuropeptide levels of somatostatin (SOM), cholecystokinin (CCK) and vasoactive intestinal polypeptide (VIP). Intriguingly, SOM is a chemical messenger which regulates the endocrine system and neurotransmission, CCK supports digestion and suppresses hunger and VIP controls the secretion and can inhibit the absorption of essential electrolytes (including cell salts). In particular, SOM[A] is released to the pineal to modulate variations in light levels during seasonal (environmental) adaptation and the pituitary to regulate hormone secretions, with an ability to demonstrate inhibiting factors. [INTERESTING NOTE: Optimal somatostatin levels in CSF has been linked to higher cognitive functioning and mental well-being.]

To summarise, based on the information here and from Chapter 11, the claustrum's essential roles appear to be:

- To create a coherent picture of what is happening by bringing all information from the senses together (perception)
- To signal to the pituitary and pineal glands to release their secretions (milk and honey)
- To release neuropeptides which support optimal digestion and fluid balance, particularly of the cell salts (creating clear paths)
- To release neuropeptides which inhibit the release of the 'seed' during the 2.5 days of preservation (preparing the 'body')

Following the neuropeptide release form the claustrum, physiologically, this sacred, spiritual oil is evident within the Cerebrospinal Fluid (CSF). The composition of CSF is dependent on the activity of surrounding brain tissue due to the fact that the structures of the brain are so closely interconnected. Therefore, even our current thoughts and mood can alter the quality and quantity of hormones and neurotransmitters that enter the flow of internal liquids.

Cerebrospinal Fluid is produced by the choroid plexus, a network of cells connected to the claustrum, and has a salty-chalky taste (due to its high sodium content). The choroid plexuses also hold cells with both known DMT-producing genes: DDC and INMT. Scientists state that the three main functions of CSF are to protect the brain and spinal cord from trauma, supply nutrients to the nervous system and remove waste products from the cerebral metabolism (brain- blood flow). About 80% of CSF is from blood-derived proteins, with the other 20% being from proteins originating from within the central nervous system itself.

Changes in behavioural states, which have a direct impact on physiology, require a complex rearrangement of neural activity. Therefore, during the rest days of the sacred secretion, the brain requires more energy to focus on re-wiring the neurons that control your behaviour and physiology for the better. The hypothalamus part of the brain, which is responsible for signalling the release of hormones and regulating body temperature as well as preserving the oil, is strongly involved with these motivational state changes. What's more, once the pituitary hormones intertwine with and protect the body in birthing the sacred seed, the spirit returns to the thalamus and lateral ventricles, which home the Christ seed during the preservation days. It could therefore be speculated that the hypothalamus is the Holy Spirit, delivering the spiritual child to the mother (gland) and bringing the father and son back into unity again within the holy trinity, with the 'above chamber' (hypothalamus) being the literal 'heaven'.

Within the pineal gland are cells known as pinealocytes. These use enzymes (proteins that increase the rate of chemical reactions) to convert tryptophan (an amino acid) into melatonin (the biorhythm maintaining neurotransmitter). But, in a well oxygenated, alkaline, harmonised body, a cascade of other biochemical reactions can take place in an effort to create equilibrium. The pineal also holds cells which contains both the DMT-producing DDC and INMT genes, as well as having the ability to emit varying levels of MAOIs.

Mainly, there are two ways that the body can produce endogenous DMT. These are from either melatonin (via dialkylation) or from tryptamine. Tryptophan (an amino acid from food) can be converted into tryptamine when carbon dioxide is removed (referred to as decarboxylation). This tryptamine can then be turned into DMT following a process called *transmethylation* or *dimethylation*-'di' meaning 'two' and 'methylation' referring to a form of alkylation.

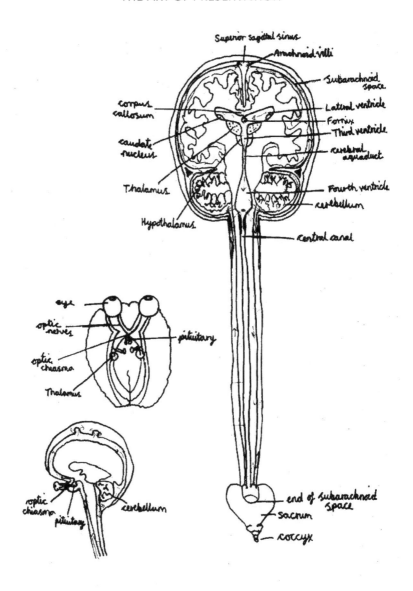

FIGURE 24 – CSF Flow

Thus, via both routed, DMT synthesis follows a similar fashion through the introduction of alkylation (see FIGURE 21). Fascinatingly, alkylation refers to the action of an alkyl group replacing a hydrogen atom. Now, this is the really interesting part: alkyl groups are constructed from alkane molecules, which are a paraffin (oil), and the synthesis of DMT is the same process used to refine oil. Therefore, I believe this to be why the ancients referred to the physical sacred secretion as an *oil*; a sacred, spiritual oil, capable of inducing awakening and rebirth of the psyche.

Furthermore, oil is defined in the Collins Dictionary as *a smooth, viscous liquid that in insoluble in water, often obtained from mineral deposits and synthesis*. Endogenously, these can be used as the raw materials in biochemistry. The preservation process, then, can be seen as one where, in a well-oxygenated, alkaline-balanced, harmonised body, electromagnetic signals trigger the tryptamine conversion into an oil-like DMT compound (the spirit molecule). The entire process, of which, begins with father energy in the pineal.

The Alchemical Centre

The pineal shows us that the timing of physiological events is critical to health as it adjusts the entire organism in response to the environment. The main hormone of the pineal is melatonin, the rest are typically assumed to be by-products in response to this chemical reaction. Interestingly, it can also be seen that the pineal is not only able to stimulate the production of DMT, but also internal MAO inhibitors;

both required for the generation of the psychedelic properties associated with DMT.

The essential chemicals concentrated within or produced by reactions from the pineal include:

- Melatonin (responsible for the maintenance of body rhythms)
- DMT (able to enhance clarity and creativity)
- Mexameme (an anti-oxidant with healing properties)
- Pinoline (also known as pineal beta-carboline, an anti-inflammatory, also with healing properties. It is also an MAOI)
- Harmaline (a fluorescent beta-carboline which stimulates dopamine release and also acts as an MAOI)
- Tryptolines (supports the reuptake of serotonin and DMT, tryptolines are also MAOIs)
- Lucifrin (from the Latin word 'Lucifer', meaning "Light Bringer", a bioluminescent light- emitting compound able to create inner light. The purpose of which is to enhance our relationship to the light spectrum, as well as to improve cell-to-cell communication, telepathic communication and navigation.)
- Bio-Magnetite (a ferrous, magnetic mineral particularly concentrated in the pineal that is affected by astronomical phenomena. This mineral can be seen as paramount to the Sacred Secretion as its magnetic properties are affected by the magnetism of the Moon, thus stimulating a chemical response from the pineal.)

The pineal is also lined with cilia (tiny, eye-lash-like hairs), which further simulate the pineal when CSF flow tickles these hairs. The pineal requires both the full spectrum of light in the day and darkness at night to work at its most optimal. Furthermore, the gland is strongly affected by electromagnetic fields (EMFs) which can interrupt its natural vibration, as well as being susceptible to calcification.

Calcification of the Pineal

Unfortunately, many modern dietary habits prevent the pineal from reaching its full potential. One of the biggest inhibitors is pineal calcification. According to Song (2019), pineal calcification is the result of calcium deposition in the pineal gland, a result from environmental factors, the most well-known being from fluoride intake. Fluoride concentrations are highest in the pineal gland than anywhere else in the body, including the rest of the brain and even bone, which cause the gland to solidify with calcium crystals. The pineal has the highest calcification rate amongst all organs in the body due to the high volume of blood flow here. These calcification deposits which engulf the pineal are similar to those found in the enamel of teeth. Although calcification of the organ can be prevented by reduced toxin intake and increased sun exposure, it is becoming an increasing problem globally.

Pineal calcification not only jeopardises melatonin synthesis, which correlates with sleep disorders (as melatonin regulates biorhythms), mental illness (due to reduced serotonin) and neurogenerative diseases such as Altzeimer's (caused by less neurogenesis), but also suppresses the immune system and weakens the body as a whole (as melatonin also works as an anti-oxidant which reduces free radicals), leading to increased inflammation and frailty, such as arthritis. Increase fluoride concentrations within the pineal are also connected with shortened time to puberty.

In addition, the crystals within the pineal's flowing water get bound up by these harmful substances, such as the fluoride and chlorine, which cause blockages. Obviously, the less water getting to the pineal, the less access you have to your astral body due to the pineal being the transmuter between spirit and physical. For this reason, calcification of the pineal is also linked with mental health issues. In fact, pineal calcification occurs in an estimated 40% of Americans by the age of 17. (Personally, I believe the figure to be closer to double that.)

This clearly demonstrates a direct connection between pharmaceuticals which are known to be high in toxins, as well as the daily consumption of modified food and impure water, with increased mental health issues in children and adults alike. The pineal is also largely associated with our gender identity and the onset of puberty, which could also be a possible route to gender dysphoria. On a more positive note, the human body is constantly re-generating, self-healing and adapting. Through a developed awareness and conscious action, de-calcifying and activating the pineal gland is actually very simple. Calcification significantly damages the pineal's ability to function effectively, which clearly leads to a range of malfunctions throughout other areas of the body through the domino effect. Hence, preventing calcification of this essential gland is of paramount importance (how to do this is explained in Chapter 20).

Lifestyle changes always seem difficult at first, but after a while they become normal; a part of everyday life. To reach higher realms of consciousness, it is important to keep the heart and third eye open and stay connected to universal energy. To feel the health of the pineal, a buzzing can be felt in the head when the pineal vibrates, which Joe Dispenza (2017) describes as a 'head orgasm'. During this time of stimulation, Manly Hall (2010) claims that the pineal is said to stand up right like the head of a cobra and move as rapidly as a serpent's tongue. This erection of the pineal also increases the flow of energy through the ventricles, thus improving the quality and quantity of pre-cursors available for spiritual alchemy. Hence, the vast array of representations of male genitalia throughout the ancient world could, arguably, be symbolic depictions of the erect pineal gland.

So, after the male and female energies (pineal and pituitary secretions) have travelled by beast (donkey= cancer= water) and overcome the animal urges of the root chakra, they rest in the sacred place (sacral chakra) and combined their energies with oxygen (the Holy Breath), forming the sacred secret-ion (the spirit molecule), before seeking salvation within the land of light (Egypt- the solar plexus).

'The Land of Honey and Milk'

Together, the male and female energies raise the spiritual seed. George Carey refers to this as the bread, ready to be eaten in the Father's kingdom (the brain). This coming together of the pineal and pituitary energy has many names, including the Sacred Royal Marriage and the

319

Land of Honey and Milk. The ideology of the Land of Honey and Milk derives from the Biblical story of Moses, whereby the prophet is said to have led the Israelites out of slavery in Egypt and towards a sacred land, *flowing with milk and honey.* With regards to the sacred secretion, this is commonly believed to refer to the pineal's excretion (honey) and the pituitary's (milk). [The idea of milk and honey can also be easily linked to the Moon and Sun. The Moon is silver and symbolised as the sign Cancer, which resonates with the breast (milk) and the Sun releases its golden sweetness onto the Earth, enabling the growth and pollination of all life (honey).] Moreover, during their long travel towards this sacred land, the Israelites are known to have fed from Manna, which Bill Donahue likens to the sacred secretion. If so, it can be seen that the believers of God survived off of this mystical dew until full salvation (awakening) was given.

The Wandering Nerve

There are 12 cranial nerves (followers/ disciples) coming from the brain which are connected to various parts of the body. These include: Olfactory, Optic, Oculomotor, Trochlear, Trigeminal, Abducens, Facial, Vestibulo-Cochlear, Glossapharyn-Geal, Vagus, Accessory and Hypoglossal. With regards to the sacred secretion, the vagus nerve is the most necessary. The Vagus Nerve derives from the Latin 'Wandering Nerve' as it starts at your brain stem and *wanders* throughout the body, connecting your brain to vital organs. The vagus nerve's main job is to monitor what's going on in your body and report information back up to the brain. It is a key component of the parasympathetic nervous system, which is responsible for calming the body after an emotional response excites it.

The vagus nerve has also been allegorised with The Tree of Life due to its nerve-wandering nature. This receives messages from the brain stem, which is the pivot point between higher brain structures and bodily organs. It is in this way that the flow of CSF past the brainstem can be seen as an internal baptism by *water*. Once the sacred secretion has been successfully preserved, one becomes baptised by *oil*. Eventually, a crystalline light body is formed, hence the baptism by *fire* advocated in numerous spiritual traditions.

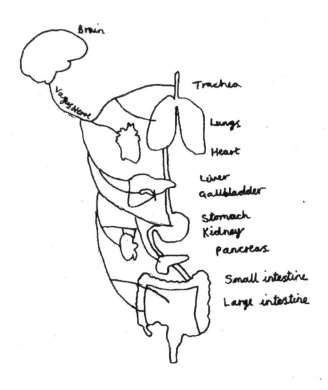

FIGURE 25 – The Vagus Nerve
321

The strength of your vagus nerve activity is known as your vagal tone. If you have a high vagal tone, your body will be able to relax more quickly after experiencing stress. Obviously, a low vagal tone will do the opposite. The sacred oil strengthens the vagus nerve, stimulating a high vagal tone, by using DMT's maintenance effects to signal healthy levels of oxygen to the body. A similar ideology is promoted by Wim Hof. The Wim Hof Method consists of breathing strategies which optimise oxygen levels in the body, thereby effecting the chemical and physiological output, notably for the autonomic nervous system and ATP production. It is even reported that success in this program feels identical to DMT kicking in. This isn't surprising, considering the decarboxylation process involved in producing the psychedelic compound.

Moreover, according to Dr Porges (2009), vagal tone can also be heightened through social interaction and gratitude, which release harmonising hormones throughout the body. Note that the roots of the vagus nerve are connected to the medulla oblongata. The medulla oblongata is located in the brain at the top of the spinal cord and is the entry and exit point for the vital fluids from the brain to the body, and vice versa. The medulla is cone-shaped and controls basic functions such as breathing, digestions, heart and blood vessel function. I personally find it no coincidence that medulla, with so many nerves emitting from it, sounds similar to 'Medusa' from Greek mythology, who had a head of snakes. [NOTE: The basilar artery, which ascends from the medulla, spreads throughout the brain and looks just like a woman with a head of snakes.]

Initially, Medusa was a mortal woman who, as a consequence of her egotistical nature and promiscuous sexuality, was transformed into a monster. If the Greek myth is to be taken factually, it can be seen that an immoral lifestyle can lead to one becoming cold-hearted and lose control of their own bodily functions (or hair of serpents!) which will devour the spiritual child. As storytelling is innate in the human genome, evidence of the sacred secretion is everywhere in mythology- which is where we will turn our attention to in the next chapter.

<u>Summary</u>

The human body is an alchemical factory built in the image of God/ Source, evident by its ability to constantly regenerate, convert one frequency into another and access vast levels of altered states of consciousness and realities/ dimensions. Specifically, this chapter has sought to present evidence for how Heaven on Earth can be reached via to preservation of the sacred secretion, and explained how the human body is perfectly build by clear intelligent design in order to produce these all-enlightening compounds once our physical vessel is in an environment safe to do so. Although there are many attacks on our divine ability to access such possibilities, the Book of Revelations clearly states that those who stay faithful to themselves and their belief in the good will be granted access to the new world (Gaia in 5D and beyond).

Bibliography and References

Bayliss, C., Bishop, N. and Fowler, R. 1985. Pineal Gland Calcification and Defective Sense of Direction. *British Medical Journal.* 291(6511):pp.1758-1759.

Carey, G. and Perry, I. 2013. *God Man: The Word Made Flesh.* Martino Publishing.

Chang, P. 2017. Biophotons: The Human Body Emits, Communicates with, and is Made From Light. *Omnithought.org.*

Crick, F. and Koch, C. 2005. What Is The Function Of The Claustrum? *Philosophical Transactions of the Royal Society of London Biological Sciences.* 360(1458):pp.1271-1279.

Crossman, A. and Neary, D. 2015. *Neuroanatomy.* Churchill Livingstone Print.

Devlin, T. 2011. *Textbook of Biochemistry.* 7th Ed. Kaye Pace Publications.

Diamond, M., Scheibel, A. and Elson, L. 2000. *The Human Brain Colouring Book.* Collins Reference.

Dillingham, C. et al. 2017. The Claustrum: Considerations Regarding Its Anatomy, Function and a Programme For Research. *Brain and Neuroscience Advances.* 1:pp.1-9.

Dispenza, J. 2017. *Becoming Supernatural.* Hay House.

Edsbagge, M., Tisell, M., Jacobsson, L. and Wikkelso, C. 2004. Spinal CSF Absorption in Healthy Individuals. *American Journal of Physiol Regul Integr Comp Physiol.* 287:pp.1450-1455.

Hall, M. 2010. *Man: The Grand Symbol of the Mysteries.* Kessinger Legacy Reprints.

Hall, M. 2018. *The Occult Anatomy of Man.* Muriwai Books.

Hardeland, R. et al. 1993. The Significance of the Metabolism of the Neurohormone Melatonin: Antioxidative Protection and Formation of Bioactive Substances. *Neuroscience and Biobehavioural Reviews.* 17(3):pp.347-357.

Hattingh, C. 2014. *Neuroanatomy of Affect*. Video on YouTube.

Hof, J. 2015. *The Wim Hof Method Explained*. [pdf] Available online at: www.wimhofmethod.com

John St. Julien Bab Wanyama. *Sacred Secretion/ Pineal Activation/ Chrism/ Christ Within, Pineal Lunar Cycles*. 18 March 2018. Available at: <https://www.youtube.com/watch?v=x82MGr1PZXQ>

Krebs, C., Weinberg, J., Akesson,E. and Dilli, E. 2018. *Neuroscience*. 2nd Ed. Wolters Kluwer.

Kobayashi, M., Kikuchi, D. and Okamura, H. 2009. Imaging of Ultraweak Spontaneous Photo Emission from Human Body Displaying Diurnal Rhythm. *PLoS ONE*. 4(7):e6256.

Laterra, J., Keep, R., Betz, L. and Goldstein, G. Blood-Cerebrospinal Fluid Barrier. *Basic Neurochemistry*.

Luke, J. 1997. The effect of fluoride on the physiology of the pineal gland. *PhD Thesis*. University of Surrey.

Michael-Titus, A., Revest, P. and Shortland, P. 2010. *The Nervous System*. 2nd Ed. Elsevier Ltd.

Moberg, K. 2013. *The Hormone of Closeness: The Role of Oxytocin in Relationships*. Pinter and Martin Ltd.

Peake, A. 2013. *The Infinite Mindfield*. Watkins Publishing LTD.

Peate, I.and Nair, M. 2017. *Fundamentals of Anatomy and Physiology*. 2nd Ed. John Wiley.

Perez-Figares, J., Jimenez, A. and Rodriguez, E. 2001. Subcommissural Organ, Cerebrospinal Fluid Circulation and Hydrocephalus. *Microsc Res Tech*. 52:pp.591-607.

Porges, S. 2009. The Polyvagal Theory: New Insights Into Adaptive Reactions of the Autonomic Nervous System. *Cleveland Clinic Journal of Medicine*. 76(2):s86-90.

Preston, J. 2001.Ageing Choroid Plexus- Cerebrospinal Fluid System. *Microsc Res Tech.* 52:pp.31-37.

Randal, W. 1990. The Solar Wind And Human Birth Rate: A Possible Relationship Due To Magnetic Disturbances. *Internal Journal of Biometeorology.* 34:p.42.

Reardon, S. 2017. A Giant Neuron Found Wrapped Around Entire Mouse Brain. *Nature.* 543:pp.14-15.

Reiber, H. 2003. Proteins in Cerebrospinal Fluid and Blood: Barriers, CSF Flow Rate and Source- Related Dynamics. *Restor Neurol Neurosci.* 21:pp.79-96.

Song, J. 2019. Pineal gland dysfunction in Alzheimer's disease: relationship with the immune-pineal axis, sleep disturbance and neurogenesis. *Molecular Neurodegeneration.* 14(28)

Stifel, L. et al. 2014. The Claustrum's Proposed Role in Consciousness is Supported by the Effect and Target Localized of Salvia Divinorum. *Frontiers in Cellular Science.* 8:p.20.

Strachan, T. and Read, A. 2019. *Human Molecular Genetics.* 5th Ed. Taylor and Francis Group.

Tan, D. et al. 2018. Pineal calcification, melatonin production, again, associated health consequences and rejuvenation of the pineal gland. *Molecules.*

Tricoire, H., Locatelli, A., Chemineau, P. and Malpaux, B. 2002. Melatonin Enters The Cerebrospinal Fluid Through The Pineal Recess. *Endocrinology.* 143(1):pp.84-90.

Walker, M. 2017. *Why We Sleep.* Penguin.

Yin, B. et al. 2016. Claustrum, Consciousness and Time Perception. *Current Opinion in Behavioural Sciences.* 8:pp.258-267.

Chapter 15

In Mythology

With a brain programmed to only remember that which is necessary for survival, humans have adapted their modes of communication in order to preserve essential knowledge. Story telling is repeatedly proven as a means of storing teachings into the long-term memory bank and was positively advocated by the ancient Druids (spiritual teachers) for storing as much knowledge as possible and passing it on in the simplest way. According to Giorgio De Santillana (1977), ancient masters used hidden metaphoric language to explain cosmology and preserve sacred, secret knowledge.

The work of Jonathan Levi has shown that the quickest and most efficient way of learning is to create visuals and stories surrounding a phenomenon. This process includes what he terms *tagging* (associating words to trigger memories) and *pinning* (linking ideas to something you already know) in order to develop schemas (neurons that fire together). Levi demonstrates that this process works especially well when learning anatomy. This isn't a new age method, though. Humans have always known this to be the most efficient way of learning and making knowledge stick. Furthermore, Levi explains that when we learn something, we're not actually learning to remember; we are learning not to forget. This is because each time we are reminded of something, the length of time it takes to forget it is lengthened. But that means that no knowledge is set-in-stone for a whole life. It is for this reason that important information is embedded in tales and fables, designed to be repeatedly retold across all generations.

Interestingly, due to mirror neurons, storytellers and listeners have the same regions of the brain active. When we listen to stories, we rehearse our human response. Jonathan Gottschall (2012) states that, "the constant firing of our neurons in response to fictional stimuli strengthens and redefines the neural pathways that lead to skilful navigation of life's problems." This is another reason why storytelling is so innate in human biology; it enhances survival. So when we repeatedly hear and read stories of prophets acting a particular way in order to reach the highest quality way of being, it becomes part of the brain's wiring response system. As our DNA holds ancestral memory and stories hold encrypted codes from the collective conscious, reading and hearing these can also act as light code activations.

What's more, humans are known to use symbols in the form of images and texts to represent vast information in order to make abstract concepts more accessible and comprehensible. For example, the shredding of serpent skin is associated with re-birth; an essential aspect of awakening/ enlightenment. The idea of rebirth is so foundational to human growth and development that the theme occurs in the vast majority of fairy tales, from the Lion King to Red Riding Hood. This is particularly effective as metaphors create visuals and increased synaptic connections, so bypass the processing stage. It is innate.

Historian and theologian Barbara Thiering claims that biblical texts were written for 2 audiences: common people who would read it as a story and the inner circles who could read between the lines. She believes that the texts were written as a way of holding secrets from the outer circle, such as the Romans or sceptics and elites who would otherwise murder them (seen through the killing of John the Baptist, Jesus Christ and the Witch hunts of the dark ages). These texts, retold over generations in evolving tongue, are often a translation of a translation of a translation. This makes it obvious that some misinterpretation would occur, especially if stories were exaggerated for increased profit, as evidenced by biblical researcher Ralph Ellis. Nowadays, this exaggerated text has no place in the modern world, hence an increasing rejection of it. Fortunately, this rejection of the tales has also brought more esoteric interpretations to light, whereby biblical stories are read as metaphors of greater knowledge. The tale of the sacred secretion is foretold in a variety of mythology throughout history. This chapter will include some examples of text that evidence the value of the Christos around the globe.

The Bible

Of all the texts, the Christian Bible is most commonly linked to human anatomy and physiology. Teachers of the sacred practice of preservation (represented as John the Baptist and Jesus Christ) were killed, highlighting the need to keep it a secret by means of fictional-appearing Bible stories. Some examples that link the Bible to the sacred secretion include:

- The Garden of Eden (cortex means 'bark') homes the Tree of Life (brain stem) which bears 12 manner of fruit (the cranial nerves) [Genesis 2:16-17]

- Cain and Abel were the first two sons of Adam and Eve, representing the two lobes of the cerebellum and the inner battle of the psyche [Genesis 4:1-16].

- God commanded Abraham to sacrifice his own son (Isaac) after a 3-day journey. A ram (Aries) appeared and was sacrificed instead [Genesis 22].

- Jacob's ladder as the stairway to heaven (AKA the spine and DNA) [Genesis 28:12]

- But before he had that dream, Jacob put a stone under his pillow. After this awakening, Jacob set up a pillar with the stone, poured oil over it and then renamed the place 'Bethal', meaning house of God, of which he set up tithes [Genesis 28:11]. The thalamus of the brain appears like a stone within [under] the head, to which the sacred secretion pours.

- Later, Jacob wrestles with God, which is evidently the pineal as, not only does Jacob state that the place will be called Peniel, but 'God' told Jacob: "Let me go for it is daybreak", for it is at night that the pineal does most of its work [Genesis 32:24-30].

- We know that Jacob's (Israel's) sons are the stars because the Bible literally says that Jacob's son Joseph had a dream: "The

Sun and Moon and 11 stars were bowing down to me". And his father's reply was: "Will your mother and I and your brothers actually come and bow down to the ground before you?" [Genesis 37:9].

- David defeated Goliath (the beast) by throwing 5 smooth stones at the creature's forehead; the stones representing the release of the 5 physical senses in order to conquer the ego.

- Moses (meaning 'to draw out') speaks with God in the form of a burning bush [Exodus 3] before his staff turns into a snake [Exodus 4]. Thus, preserving the oil frequently enough to create fire consciousness (enlightenment) allows one the ability to call upon their serpent energy at will.

- During dealings with the pharaoh, Moses and God covered all of Egypt in complete darkness for 3 days, only the Israelites had light [Exodus 10:2]. Hence, inner light will generate during the 3 days of preservation within all who listen.

- The Holy Land is described as flowing with 'milk and honey' (the pineal and pituitary secretions/ synchronised solar and lunar energies).

- There were 12 stones (mineral cell salts), 1 for each of the names of the sons of Israel and engraved like a seal with the name of 1 of the 12 tribes [Exodus 39:14].

- Elijah is taken up to heaven. Elish looks for him for 3 days before throwing salt into the Jordan (CSF) to clean and heal it [2 Kings:2]

- "… the almighty was still with me… when my path (CNS) was drenched with cream (milk) and the rock (thalamus) poured out for me streams of olive oil" [Job 29]

- "The Lord is my rock, fortress and deliverer to whom I take refuge, my shield and the horn (Aries- ventricle) of my salvation… who drew me out of deep waters." [Psalm 18]

- The ventricular system looks just like a giant fish, with the lateral ventricle as the belly of the fish. Interestingly, this is also where the 'spiritual seed' (also likened here to Jonah) rests for 3 days [Jonah].

- The fluffy choroid plexus (which produces CSF) can be seen as symbolic of John the Baptist, who was clothed in camel hair, preparing the way for Christ) [Matthew 3:4].

- The lateral ventricle looks like the ram or lamb, and Jesus is often referred to as the *lamb of God*.

- The three wise men (gifts) saw the star, signalling the birth of Jesus, in the East- where the Sun rises [Matthew 2:2]

- "You are the salt (gatherer) and light (preserver) of the earth… but if the salt loses its saltiness, it is no longer good for anything" [Matthew 5:13-14]. Just as each zodiac sign affects corresponding cell mineral salts within the body, the preservation of the sacred secretion is a physical way that we can control these vibrations in response to astronomical influences.

- Let thy kingdom come, let thy will be done, on earth as it is in heaven [Matthew 6:10]. All living matter is made of the same building blocks from within the cosmos. By following the way of the heavens, we are given internal peace.

- The eye (of Horus) is the lamp of the body [Matthew 6:22] – discussed later in this chapter

- The house (of God) won't fall when on a foundation of rock [Matthew 7:24]

- New wine (blood) must be poured into new wineskins (body) so that both are preserved [Matthew 9:17]

- Enemies (egotistic thoughts) are within your own household (you must conquer your own shadows) [Matthew 10:36]

- Whoever has (preserved the oil) will be given more, and they will have an abundance [Matthew 13:12] because of the increase in the DMT Thermostat

- Through seeing they do not see, through hearing they do not hear (you must try the practice for yourself in order to understand it) [Matthew 13:13]

- Christ transfigured up the highest mountain (brainstem) with his three closest disciples (deficient birth cell salts) and awoke ancestors (knowledge) [Matthew 17]

- The kingdom of God does not come with observation; nor will they say, 'See here!' or 'See there!', for indeed, the kingdom of God is within you [Matthew 17:21]. Thus, awakening cannot be seen, it is felt inside.

- Become like children- full of faith, joy and forgiveness [Matthew 18:3] in order to achieve 5D consciousness

- The first (preserver) will be the last and the last will be the first (all are equal, regardless of when they start their journey) [Matthew 20:16]
- Jesus Christ was able to heal the sick, mute and death, representing the power of the preservation process and this powerful DMT solute
- The Christ (oil) can save others, but he cannot save himself (you must!) [Matthew 27:42]
- At the point of death during crucifixion, curtains tore in two (clearer vision), the earth shook (a feeling in the brain), rocks split (blockages released), tombs broke open (ventricles where CSF is stored) and the bodies of many holy people who had died were raised to life (dormant brain cells and DNA awakened), whilst many women were watching, including the two Marys (both parts of the pituitary).
- Behind the sheet of cells covering the CSF-filled lateral ventricle (where the spiritual seed preserves for 2.5 days), a dissection would reveal what appears to be a hole (a tomb) with a 'body' inside. This 'body' is in fact the caudate nucleus.
- Peter (rock) lives in a tent (ventricles) of this body, awaiting the day (of preservation) that dawns the morning star (energy) to rise in our hearts [2 Peter 1:19]
- "When you make the two into one, and when you make the inner like the outer and the outer like the inner, and the upper like the lower, and when you make male and female into a single one, so that the male will not be male nor the female be

female, when you make eyes in place of an eye, a hand in place of a hand, a foot in place of a foot, an image in place of an image, then you will enter the Kingdom" – From The Gospel of Thomas, 22. Here, the combining of the masculine and feminine energies and the honouring of one's temple in order to merge the light body into the physical, seems to be evident for pathing the way to Heaven on Earth. We need to *be like little children*, innocent and receptive to the magic of spirit.

1 Corinthians onwards literally reads like a preservation manual. Here are some highlights:

- The (day) will bring (the seed) to light. It will be revealed with fire (energy) and the fire will test the quality of each person's work. If what has been built survives, the builder will receive a reward [1 Corinthians 3:13-14]

- Those who preserve and become baptised by the oil will be given spiritual gifts by the Lord [1 Corinthians 12:4-14]

- If sown in a natural body, there will also be a spiritual body [1 Corinthians 15:44]

- There are three versions of the Christ substance: blood, water and spirit [1 John 3:8]. Thus, the practice of preservation includes the raising of enlightening neurotransmitters (in the CSF waters- DMT), balance and healing of the body (endocrine system- clean blood) as well as raised vibration (aura- energetic field).

- He (God/ good) saves us, not because of righteous things we have done, but because of his mercy (forgiveness). He saved us through the washing of rebirth and renewal by the Holy Spirit, whom he poured out on us generously through Jesus Christ our saviour [Titus 3:5-6].

Similarly, Revelations reads as a prophecy of how it will feel to become awakened. Obviously, there will be some anxiety over the unpredictability of the effect of awakening on one's awareness, but the result is always of love and positivity:

- In heaven God was surrounded by 7 lamps, 7 churches and 7 stars (representing the balancing and purity of the main energy centres along the spine) and a rainbow encircled his throne (like the chakras release a rainbow of colourful energies within our surrounding aura). See FIGURE 26. Interestingly, in many ancient texts, a mansion with seven rooms is used as a metaphor for God.

- By God's throne were four creatures, each with 6 wings (4x6=24) who constantly praise the Lord, day and night (24 hours).

- There are also 24 elders around the throne; 12 cranial nerves which double on each side= 24.

- Eden is the body. The water of life (CSF) runs up the middle, with a Tree of Life (brainstem) on each side, which bear 12 crops (cranial nerves) and yields its fruit (seed) every (lunar) month [Revelations 22:1-2].

- Jesus said he is the Root (chakra), the offspring of David (star) and the bright morning star (Sun) [Revelations 22:16]. Thus,

Christ is within (the seed), without (star energy) and above (Sun).

From these few examples alone, we can infer that us, as human beings who evolved in connection and correlation with the cosmic energies of the universe (father), are created "in the image of God." I would recommend Bible Journaling to everybody as, once aware of the Chrism, one cannot read such detailed texts without constant revelations. Specifically, you will notice that there are clear links between the rising of the sacred oil and the story of Christ. The repetition of the need to honour God and love God throughout the Bible is therefore referring to the divine creator which is the universal energy field. As demonstrated by the Hermetic Principles, the universe is conscious and aware, and in this way we reap what we sow.

Feelings of love and gratitude are the ultimate connecting energies, as expressed by Christ himself when he claims that the Greatest Commandments are: *Love the Lord* and *Love your neighbour as yourself.* The questioning of the disciples actions in the Bible are a perfect way of demonstrating that it does not matter what you eat or how you work and rest, for if you are not expressing love, you cannot reach enlightenment and you cannot hear the father (universal energy). Hence, we are all children of God but we can only return to God by expressing unconditional love and compassion.

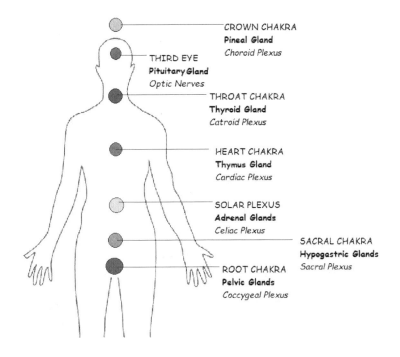

CROWN CHAKRA
Pineal Gland
Choroid Plexus

THIRD EYE
Pituitary Gland
Optic Nerves

THROAT CHAKRA
Thyroid Gland
Catroid Plexus

HEART CHAKRA
Thymus Gland
Cardiac Plexus

SOLAR PLEXUS
Adrenal Glands
Celiac Plexus

SACRAL CHAKRA
Hypogastric Glands
Sacral Plexus

ROOT CHAKRA
Pelvic Glands
Coccygeal Plexus

FIGURE 26 – The Seven Lamps, Churches and Stars

Jesus Christ

It would be a major omission not to compare the progression of Jesus' life to that of the spiritual seed. I will take this opportunity to say that, personally, I do believe that Jesus was a real person, or maybe even a number of people at different periods of time who have had their lives intertangled within mythology, who had a divine connection with the Father (source energy) and endeavoured to teach people the way of the stars and 5D consciousness. Specifically, one of these incarnations was as Yeshua, an Essene, who was in a sacred union relationship with the divine priestess, Mary Magdalene, whom travelled together on pilgrimages throughout Europe, spreading love and light and awakening as ascended masters for the planet. [Note, that the Biblical name 'Jesus' is a Latin translation from the original Hebrew name 'Yeshua', which is why both are therefore used interchangeably within this book.]

In Greek the name Christ means 'anointed one'. Similarly, the ancient Essenes (detailed in Chapter 17) also speak of Christ as an oil-like substance. As oil is commonly classified based on its inability to mix with water, it can be seen that the inner Christ is a substance that remains separate from the waters it resides in (such as the CSF). Oily substances can also be compared to gel or plasma-like texture, similar to that of aether. From this, one could use the term 'oil' in a range of situations to communicate phenomena metaphorically, much like the ancients are known to have done. Consequently, the Christ body can exist in a myriad of layers, depending on whether he is being compared to the outer solar god or the inner. According to Kelly-Marie Kerr (2019), there are four layers of God: God as divine energy in all things; God as space including our closest planets; God as the physical human; and God as the spiritual human whereby the seed is birthed. Jesus Christ is equated to all four layers, illuminated by unconditional love.

By a range of stories regarding similar sounding phenomenon (microcosmic and macrocosmic) coming together we get tangled tales with many interpretations. Take the story of Jesus. This can be read as a real man who completed miracles, of our own Sun moving through the sky or even of internal oil which raises connectedness with mother and father universal energy. Some examples for the latter can be seen within the following:

Jesus was born in Bethlehem which, in Hebrew, means 'house of bread' or house of knowledge, as Jesus himself in the Bible stated that 'bread' is in fact metaphorical for knowledge. From this it can be deduced that Jesus was born in the house of knowledge (the human body). If one remembers the nativity story well enough, it is seen that within the house of knowledge the baby was born in a stable surrounded by animals. Within the human body, this closely resembles the root chakra (our instincts) and the sacral chakra (house-shaped, governed by the Moon and responsible for intuition and pleasure). However, due to the vulnerability placed on the seed here as a result of these powerful energies and urges, the child must travel to a safer country: Egpyt, the place of light (also the solar plexus chakra, powered by the Sun). Here the child is filled with knowledge (power) until being baptised (cleansed) with pure love (at the heart chakra). From here, the prodigal son begins to speak (throat chakra) the truth of God until crucified at Golgotha (the place of the skull) and is entombed for 2.5 days (the third eye chakra). Finally, the son is powerful enough to be able to return to his father in heaven (by way of the crown chakra, energetically supporting Gaia and the functioning of the universe in a give-and-take relationship).

Jesus Christ has also been compared with the Sun, which gives us a new day and new season of harvest cyclically (like the son who rids the world of sin), Orion (the constellation of a man in the sky), historical figures (usually teachers of the Essenes or pharaohs of Egypt) and even as unconditional love which can be felt by all who embrace the heavenly Lord (the Holy Spirit Fire). Thus, Christ is the father, the son and the holy spirit in all forms, both physical and spiritual; macro and micro. As the ancients were masters in the use of symbolism to retell and preserve knowledge, ranging metaphoric visions were used to accommodate this.

Numbers in Mythology

The Bible is still read today, proving our ability to relate to it as the representation of some timeless facts. Throughout this and other sacred texts and symbolism is the use of numbers. Mathematics, as the universal language of energy, remains unchanged through the ages. Plato even called the study of number symbolism: "the highest level of knowledge". Similarly, Pythagoras claimed that *numbers rule all things*. Metaphorically, numbers hold vast symbolism across space and time. Below is a list of just a few of these numerical representations and interpretations.

The Power of 7

- 7 chakras
- 7 cervical vertebrae
- 7 colours of the rainbow (visible light spectrum)
- 7 planets
- 7 days of the week (Sun-day, Moon-day, Mars-day, Mercury-day, Jupiter-day, Venus-day and Saturn-day)
- 7 days of creation
- 7 deadly sins

- 7 sleepers of the Quran, who remain in darkness until the spirit fire awakens them
- In the book of Revelations there are 7 churches, 7 angels, 7 seals, 7 trumpets, 7 plagues and 7 thunders. The resurrection of the dead takes place at the 7th trumpet
- 7 notes of the diatonic scale
- 7 letters in the Roman numeral system
- 7 circles form 'the Seed of Life' in sacred geometry
- 7 tones in the sounding scale of the cosmos
- Ancient (Asian) archaic traditions state that the knowledge regarding the Sacred Heptaparaparshiokh (the Law of Seven) was believed to be from the Atlanteans.

The Power of 3

- The Trinity (Father, Son and Holy Spirit)
- 3 wise men visited baby Jesus
- The Biblical Jonah spent 3 days in the stomach of a fish
- The Biblical Jesus went missing for 3 days at twelve years old
- The Biblical Jesus took 3 men with him during transfiguration
- The Biblical Christ spent 3 days in the tomb after crucifixion
- The Biblical Abraham was commanded to sacrifice his son after a 3 day journey up a mountain
- The Biblical baby Moses was hidden by his mother for 3 months
- The Biblical adult Moses requests his people for a 3 day journey into the wilderness to give sacrifice to God
- The heavenly Jerusalem has 3 gates on each of its four sides

- The Sumerian goddess Inanna spent 3 days in the underworld
- The creator of Sikhism, Guru Nanak Dev, spent 3 days in a river before transfiguration
- The Sun 'disappears' for 3 days during Winter Solstice
- 3 signs in each quarter of the zodiac (each Great Season, which Randall Carlson says correspond with a natural biorhythm of the planet Gaia, discussed in Chapter 2)
- 3 months in each earth season

The Power of 33

- 33 years of Christ's life
- 33 vertebrate of the human spine
- 33 turns in a complete sequence of human DNA
- King David reigned Jerusalem for 33 years
- The Star of David is 3 by 3 (two triangles- the masculine and feminine)
- 3 plus 3 is six; 3 times 3 is nine (3, 6 and 9 are the numbers of the universe, according to Tesla)
- The great solar lords Ra, Horus, Mithras and Jesus (all symbols of the inner Christ- Greek for 'anointed one') were all born of virgins and died at the age of 33

The Power of 12

- 12 cranial nerves (x2 =24; the 24 elders whom sit around the throne of God in Revelation 4:3-4)
- 12 thoracic vertebrae
- 12 archangels of God

343

- 12 disciples of Christ
- 12 signs of the zodiac
- 12 months of the year
- 12 hours of day and night during the equinox (equal light and dark)
- 12 entrances to the highest point of the Great Pyramid
- 12 inches in a foot (the sacred unit of measurement used by the Egyptians)
- 12 year cycle in Asia
- 12 signs of the Chinese zodiac
- 12 sons of Jacob
- 12 tribes of Israel
- 12 is the sacred number of God as 4 elements/ seasons/ corners (angles/ angels) of the Earth multiplied by the trinity equals twelve
- 12 gates guarded by 12 angels in the kingdom of God, according to Revelations
- 12 baskets remained full when Jesus fed the 5000
- 12 days of Christmas

Santa Claus

Other than the biblical tales, the story of Santa Claus is the next most associated with the sacred secretion.

Father Christmas was originally dressed in green and was renowned for his rosy cheeks and flying reindeers. You don't need to look far to see where this story originates: The Eskimos (Inuit). Legend has it that, historically, arctic reindeer would consume mushrooms which would filter through their system and exit as psychedelic urine. Upon consuming this yellow snow, the Eskimos would 'trip', seeing flying reindeer and little elves running around. And there was no way of hiding this altered state of consciousness, evident by their rosy cheeks, glassy eyes, giggling and increased appetite! The white hair from being out in the snow probably didn't help, either. Combine this with the already global celebration of the re-ascension of the Sun after Winter Solstice and the analogy of the 'gift' given by the Claustrum (Claus), which travels down the spine (chimney) before returning up to the brain (North Pole), coated with a play on words from the real-life 'Saint Nicolaus' and you have your mythical Christmas story!

Interestingly, the claustrum, although from a transverse point of view appears like a serpent, from the side it is shaped like a tiny Santa hat. At Christmas time, pine trees (with the esoteric pinecones on them) are brought into the home as a symbol of the rebirth of life in the spring, also representing the power of the pineal gland, whose power is sent down from the heavens by the angel on top (Metatron). Therefore, the celebration of Christmas is, in fact, a celebration of the cycle of life, evident in all life forms, with a little bit of merriness to birth the literal Christmas Spirit (molecule)! [More information can be found in my other book: *Saint Claustrum.*]

FIGURE 27 – The Claustrum

<u>In Islam</u>

The three main Abrahamic religions include Judaism, Christianity and Islam. Interestingly, when all three symbols are put together, you get a clear image of the sacred secret practice: Star, Cross, Moon. A particular 'coincidence' is that the Quran advocates 3 days of fasting each lunar month. Considering that a 'fast' can be described as any kind of cleanse, either from eating altogether or by way of another practice such as 3 days of veganism or even an electronic- fast, this shows resemblance with the sacred practice of preserving the inner Christ. It is compelling to note here that studies show that 3 days of fasting can completely regenerate your entire immune system. This supports the theory of Jesus, in fact, being all-healing as the preservation process boosts the body's immune system.

In Hinduism

Long before the dawn of Christianity, tales of awakening via the Sacred Royal Marriage were encoded in texts from the world's oldest religion: Hinduism. In Hinduism, Shiva (God) and Shakti (Goddess) represent the two essential aspects of the One: the abiding aspects of God's will and the energetical representation on Earth. What's more, nectar (or honey) is said to rain down on the world during the love making of Shakti and Shiva (also symbolised by the sun- male energy- and moon-female energy).

Another renowned Hindu deity is Vishnu, who floats in the ocean (CSF), resting on a great snake, Ananta. Vishnu is awoken by the sound AUM/ OM. As the creation story goes, Vishnu (the preserver and male energy) is ordered by Shiva (the destroyer and female energy) to create Brahma (the creator), who emerges from Vishnu's naval (the solar plexus). Thus, the spirit, which was sleeping within the muladhara (root chakra), emerges from the lotus of the solar plexus with the power to create. The surrounding male and female energies have the power to either preserve or destroy this creation. Interestingly, within the human brain is an area referred to as 'Brahma's Cave' (the third ventricle), which is the same place known to be the internal Tomb of Christ.

In addition to the above, it is also widely believed that the Hindu deity Krishna was the initial Christ (note how Krishna sounds remarkably similar to Kristos, meaning 'bearing Christ'). The legend goes that Mother Earth was burdened by the demon Kings of the planet so went to Lord Brahma (the masculine) in the form of a cow (the feminine) who took to the shore of the milky ocean (CSF) and chanted (vibrated) in order to summon Lord Vishnu (the *preserver* god, by no coincidence, I'm sure). Lord Vishnu promised he would himself incarnate on Earth (as Krishna) and end the tyranny. However, Krishna's life was threatened so he was hidden (saved) until the day he is grown up enough to kill the evil king, Kamsa.

Krishna is often described as a cow herder who enjoys music and playing for fun (rather than sport or gain), which highlights the true meaning of our souls incarnating in human form: to care for the world and have as much harmless fun as possible along the way!

In Sikhism

Alongside Hinduism, another dominating religion in India (where much of the modern philosophy of raising serpent energy is said to have originated) is Sikhism. Guru Nanak founded Sikhism in an attempt to harmonise Islam and Hinduism. What I find especially fascinating, though, is the fact that Guru Nanak had the vision to create the religion following his transfiguration, which occurred after he had spent 3 days submerged in a river (like the sacred secretion preserving for 3 days in the lateral ventricle, bathed in CSF).

Ancient Greece

The word *mythology* often springs to mind stories from the Ancient Greek era. They were prolific storytellers and well-known to have personified vast arrays of natural phenomena within their characters.

One of the most evident for the sacred secretion is that of the birth of Aphrodite. The story goes that the god Uranus was murdered (arranged by Gaia) by his son Chronus (meaning *crown,* like the crown chakra). Chronus threw Uranus' reproductive organs (creative power) into the *ocean behind his back* (just like all humans have their own sea of flowing waters residing around their spinal column). The sea foam (water + air) then mixed with Uranus' blood to birth the goddess Aphrodite (feminine power as the root chakra is known as the crown of the feminine). Aphrodite is the goddess of love and the symbol of the divine feminine, who rose from the waters and brought beauty to Earth.

A prominent Greek mythical substance is that of the golden nectar and ambrosia (the food of the gods), which combine to turn blood into that of **Ichor**. Ichor is the name given to a vibrant, ethereal fluid known to be the *blood of the gods.* In one Greek myth, ichor runs in the single vein (like the central nervous system) of a giant which was ordered by Zeus to protect his daughter. Here, this ichor is clearly representative of the sacred secretion. It can also be seen within the mythological stories of Ancient Greece that this ambrosia/ nectar/ honey substance was used by gods/ goddesses, such as Athena, to anoint others (such as Hercules and Penelope) in order to purify their bodies, giving them knowing and strength for many of life's challenges.

Greek gods were also claimed to be very promiscuous, often impregnating human women. Personally, I believe this to be metaphorical for DNA light transfer (like the sacred secretion), rather than that gods literally *mated* with people.

349

Goddess Athena was one of the most powerful and favoured deities of Ancient Greece. According to myth, Athena's mother (Metis- an oceanid) was impregnated by Zeus and then eaten (consumed/ absorbed) alive and whole. Eventually, Athena was born, rose to the forehead of her father, Zeus, and burst from his third eye in full maturity. She later became the patron of Athens after beating (conquering) Poseidon (god of the ocean) during a challenge of who could bring the most useful gift for the Athenians. Athena won by presenting an olive tree. Interestingly, she was also the goddess of weaving, which is a skill commonly associated with deities of creation, and of wisdom, hence why she was commonly depicted as a serpent.

The Hermetica

The Hermetica are the Egyptian-Greek wisdom texts said to be a recording of the words of Hermes, the messenger of the Gods. A branch of this includes the post-Christian texts called the Corpus Hermeticum, whereby Hermes (AKA Thoth) says to his son Tat: "My son, Wisdom in the womb, conceiving in secret, and the seed is the true good." With Hermes/ Thoth worshipped as a lunar god, many of his functions were derived by association with the Moon powers. Evidence of a sacred river can be seen in religious beliefs worldwide, whether that be the Jordan for Christians, the Nile for Egyptians or the Ganges for Hindus. This sacred river is the internal CSF, flowing through the spinal cord. Furthermore, what is below [on Earth] mimics that above [in the heavens], so this sacred river can also be likened to the Milky Way [stars] whose death [by supernova] gives birth to all of the building blocks of life.

Ancient Egypt

Thoth, as well as being the Egyptian god of wisdom, was also 'Lord of the Moon'. He is also referred to as 'Sin', which holds the potential to be the origin of the phrase "born in sin" as the sacred seed in birthed when the Moon enters your Sun [sign]. In Greek, Thoth is Hermes, of the Hermetic texts, and is also believed to have constructed the great pyramids. From this, the most notable talisman symbol is the Eye of Egypt. The Eye of Egypt, also the Eye of Horus, is an ancient Egyptian symbol of protection, power and health. The myth surrounding the story is that Osiris, king of Egypt, was murdered by his brother Set. Osiris was then entombed by Set (greed, jealousy) and discarded into the River Nile. Hathor (love and nurture) came to Osiris' wife, Isis, and aided her in finding her husband. [NOTE: According to Manly Hall, the sheen of gold in Isis' hair indicates that, while she is lunar, her power is due to the Sun's rays. Thus, as the Moon is robed in the reflected light of the Sun, so Isis, like the virgin of Revelation, is clothed in solar luminosity.] Isis found Osiris' body within the trunk of a tree. So Set chopped Osiris' body into small pieces and scattered them. Osiris' phallus was eaten by a whale (like Jonah from the Bible). Isis and Thoth (the Moon) worked together to restore Osiris long enough for Isis to become pregnant (an immaculate conception by a spiritual father and virgin mother). At which point, Osiris was seen to have conquered death and was reborn as the god of the underworld. Osiris and Isis' son,

Horus, grew to overthrow Set (egotistical emotions) and become ruler of Egypt. During the battle with Set, however, Horus lost an eye, which was torn into six parts and later restored by Thoth. It is this eye which forms the symbol.

Interestingly, the Eye of Horus is mathematically perfect in six parts but add up to a fraction of only 63/64. The missing part is said to represent the magical powers of Thoth; the spiritual secret-ion which returns every 'Moon'. The Eye of Horus is also a precise graphic representation of the inner chambers of the brain, including the corpus callosum, thalamus, pineal and medulla. It therefore shows the area of the brain whereby the spiritual seed is preserved and must be protected. Thus, Horus, born of immaculate conception, reconnects with the father energy by way of sacrificing the 'eye'. With regards to the sacred secretion, the 'eye' is referring to the pineal, which connects us to higher forms of energy, which requires the magic powers of Thoth (the Moon) to fulfil completion.

The Egyptians also tell of a fairy tale whereby a shipwrecked sailor, who landed on an island, rested under a tree for 3 days, then found all kinds of exotic food to fill on before being taken in the mouth of a crystal serpent and permitted to live on the abundant island. This island was called Ka, meaning 'the double', just like the double helix of DNA, the double hemispheres of the brain and even the double of physical and spiritual. According to Bertrand and Bertrand (2017), all matter and energy forms in two parts and seeks the be brought back together again into oneness. This phenomenon is clearly evident within the sacred secretion, whereby the Sun and Moon energies are synchronised into a spiritual seed.

The Pinecone

From the Egyptian Staff of Osiris to the head of the Hindu god, Shiva; Ancient Assyrian palace carvings to the Roman Thyrsus and Pigna, symbols representing the pineal gland can be observed throughout history. There is even a theory that it was a pinecone that was consumed by Adam and Eve from the Tree of Knowledge in the Garden of Eden. It is these endless references to the pinecone and pineal that have led to the common belief that the pineal gland is a spiritual organ; our link to higher levels of reality. This theory is further strengthened when one remembers the break down of the word pineal into PINE-AL (*al* meaning 'god'). The pine-cone shape is evident in symbolism around the world even to this day, such as the pinecone on the pope's staff and the giant pinecone caved in stone outside the Vatican. Clearly, the ancients wanted us to remember the significance of this shape.

Other

In the Welsh Mabinogion, Elen of the Ways (protectress of Earth and the pathways to enlightenment) is described as *filled with golden light* and as a *fairy mistress* who leads heroes and heroines to their initiations. She is also likened to Aluna (the mother goddess of the Kogi tribe in Columbia), who called gold the *immortal blood of the Great Mother*. If

353

we remember that **ichor** was considered the 'blood of the gods' in Ancient Greece, clear resemblance can be seen between this mythological tales concealing the ideology of the sacred secretion.

Down The Rabbit Hole

Before ending this chapter, let's synchronise some of what has been discussed.

Looking at FIGURE 24, it can be seen that CSF is formed within the choroid plexuses of the lateral, third and fourth ventricles (plexuses are bundles of nerves and ventricles are spaces/ chambers which fill with liquid), which are able to produce DMT and hold MAOIs emitted from the pineal. CSF in the lateral ventricles flow into the third, circulate through the cerebral aqueduct, where it crosses the very narrow [path] central canal into the diamond-shaped fourth ventricle before reaching the medulla oblongata. From here it has a number of possible paths. For the sacred secretion, the essential is the flow descending down the spinal cord towards to sacrum. Thus, the spiritual seed [or gift] is conceived [built] in the brain [the North Pole] by the choroid plexus ['coloured network'- elves], connected to the claustrum [Santa Claus]. From here it disperses all around the nervous system [the whole world in one night], travelling down the long road [chimney- the place of fire energy] towards the sacrum [house/ stable] before re-ascending back to the brain- temple [resting place].

When re-ascending, the CSF passes the pituitary [Marys] and optic chiasma [the cross], through the thalamic gate into the thalamus [chamber/ tomb], which relays signals to and from the cranial nerves [disciples], to communicate to all parts of the body and pineal. After preservation, the CSF (homing the sacred secretion) continues towards the neocortex [the throne of consciousness], creating gamma waves which can heighten perception [and vibration].

Summary

The aim of this chapter was to provide a glimpse into how the importance of the preservation process is encoded in mythology. The fact that the metaphorical and symbolical representation of the phenomenon is repeatedly presented across the globe, even before the days of telecommunications, is evident of its discovery by various civilisations, thus laying the foundation for its significance in our ancestral story.

It's worth noting that all major religions of the world strongly advocate equality and the fact that every single human has the right to be a child of Source and light. Regardless of any physical and genetic predispositions, we were all created of immaculate, intelligent design and born with a purpose towards achieving enlightenment. Anybody who says otherwise is clearly misinformed and have not yet found peace with their own shadows. Words cannot describe the contentment and love I feel towards every single living thing since practicing the art of preserving the sacred internal oil, so I know these words to be true. If you ever feel attacked by another's opinion or self-absorbed views, just remember this simple teaching from a book called *I Met a Monk* by

Rose Elliot: If someone tried to give you a present and you did not accept it, who would it belong to? *Them*, still. And anger is the same. If you do not accept another's anger it is still theirs, not yours. So you can continue to go about your business doing the best you can to serve the Father God and Mother Earth, living a life of righteousness without judgement of others. Acknowledging the views of another but not dwelling on them is a skill that will eventually come to all who learn to accept themselves and discover inner peace.

With regards to the mythology of the sacred secretion, one more fact from Manly Hall which I will end this chapter with is that the oldest known story of the *saviour* birth is apparently of Sumerian origin. It states that the daughter of Sin (the Moon) was called Ishtar/ Inanna/ Sophia (female energy and queen of heaven and Earth). She passed down through the 7 gates (chakras) of the underworld (physical form) in an attempt to resurrect her son (seed). There, she was bathed in the Water of Life (CSF) and allowed to pass back upwards (by the will of the gods) through the 7 gates back to heaven (the head). Now that you have glimpsed into the vast codes concealed within tales as old as time, you won't be able to stop having further links revealed to you.

Bibliography and References

Elliot, R. 2015. *I Met a Monk.* Watkins Publishing.

Hamilton, E. 2011. *Mythology: Timeless tales of Gods and Heroes.* Grand Central Publishing.

Hunt, M. 2008. *The Symbolic Significance of the Third Day in Scripture.* Agape Bible Study.

Ketler, A. 2017. Study Shows How Fasting For 3 Days Can Regenerate Your Entire Immune System. Available online at: <www.collective-evolution.com>

Peake, A. 2013. *The Infinite Mindfield.* Watkins Publishing LTD.

Website: www.gnosticteachings.org

Chapter 16

In the Stars

Historically, stories were regularly produced as a means of maintaining knowledge. For example, if a generation of Egyptians realised that the River Nile's annual inundation occurred first as the star of Sirius returned to the early morning sky after 70 days spent below the horizon, then taking note (and creating a visual story to aid the memorability) of this would have been essential for survival, maintaining the Egyptians intuition with the environment. Therefore, from knowing when to sow their seeds to foretelling a flood, before we had clocks and computational technology, the ancients used the stars to tell the time and predict the future.

The first page of the Bible even says: *"Let there be lights in the vault of the sky to separate the day from the night, and **let them serve as signs to mark sacred times**"* to tell the reader right from the start that the text they are about to read is in fact a story guided by the cosmos.

The Bible is full of references to the stars above and their influence on the physical form below. For example. the Son's (Suns) of Jacob- The

Tribes of Israel- are all said by Thomas Burgoyne (2013) to correlate with a zodiac sign:

- Aries- Benjamin
- Taurus- Issachar
- Gemini- Simeon and Levi
- Cancer- Zebulon
- Leo- Judah
- Virgo- Asher
- Libra- Dan
- Scorpio- Gad
- Sagittarius- Joseph
- Capricorn- Naphtali
- Aquarius- Reuben
- Pisces- Ephraim and Manasseh.

The life of Christ is also an easy one to relate back to this phenomenon of personifying stars. For example: The virgin (Virgo) conceives a son of both human and god (Libra). The family is forced to return to their hometown by the Romans (Scorpio). They travel by beast (Sagittarius) until the son is born in the stable of a goat (Capricorn). The son was then 'born' on June 21st (Summer Solstice), evident by the 'brightest star in the sky', which attracted shepherds (Aries) and wise men (Aquarius). King Herod then ordered a massacre of baby boys (Scorpio), which forced the family to flee to Egypt, where Christ was educated on the knowledge of the stars, until the age of 30 (degrees) as a man (Aquarius).

For his first miracle, Christ turns water to wine (symbol of the first harvest). Jesus then performs many miracles as the Fisher of Men (Pisces), including feeding the 5000 with fish and bread (knowledge of the stars). He was also baptised by John (Aquarius) and told many parables, include that of the Two Sons (Gemini) and the Lost Sheep (Aries). The Lamb (Aries) of God's final triumph is his crucifixion on a cross (Libra) between two thieves (of harvest- Scorpio and Sagittarius). At the time of Jesus's death, (the Winter Solstice- Capricorn) the Earth was engulfed in darkness until the body of Christ was laid in a tomb, guarded (Taurus) for 2.5 days.

Likewise, the cosmic crucifixion can be seen in the night sky. On December 21st (the Winter Solstice and shortest day of the year, when dark triumphs light) the Sun passes the constellation Crux (the astral cross) and rests here, hence is 'crucified'. Following this, the Earth is in 'darkness' for 2.5 days until December 25th when the Sun (son) rises again and the days begin to lengthen. Thus, on the 25th of December, the Sun (Son) is reborn. Likewise, Christian countries around the world celebrate Jesus' birthday on December 25th. It is a national holiday and a time to celebrate Christmas. The Christmas holiday is celebrated as the birth of Jesus when, in actual fact, it is instead celebrating longer day time hours after a dark winter (the rebirth of the SUN).

Following the 2.5 days of being preserved within the tomb, Jesus rises again, showing the balance being restored between the physical and the spirit (Libra). After this time, the missing body of the Lord is discovered by the two Marys (Gemini) who spread the word of his resurrection. Finally, the Son rises to heaven to sit upon the throne (of the Summer Solstice- Cancer) to bless his people as the King (Leo) whilst his 12 disciples (all zodiac signs) spread his teachings. The disciples which correspond to each zodiac were detailed in Chapter 10.

And the story doesn't stop there. Once in heaven, recorded in the book of Revelations, the zodiac constellations are repeatedly referenced again, including the lamb (Aries), the lion (Leo), the ox (Taurus), a creature with a face like a man and a rider with a bow (Sagittarius), scales (Libra), the Sun appearing like a sackcloth made of goat hair (Capricorn), locusts like scorpions (Scorpio), human faces and women's hair (Virgo), breastplates of iron (Gemini), and so on.

In addition to the significance of the 12 zodiac signs is that of Orion. In terms of star constellations, Orion is the 'man in the sky' or, according to Adrian Gilbert (2000), the literal ascended Christ. The importance of this constellation is reported by Bauvel and Gilbert (1994), who note that the Giza site of Egypt acts like a giant star-clock, marking the epoch of Zep Tepi ('The First Time' when the gods appeared) and the Golden Age of Orion (when this constellation, from which the Gods came from, was at its lowest point in the sky). Bauvel and Hancock (1996) later suggested that the designers of the Giza Plateau saw the Nile as a reflection of the Milky Way within our own galaxy, so built the pyramids to reflect the Orion constellation ('as above, so below'). As such, Gilbert (2000) claims that the return of Christ to cleanse the Earth is in fact regarded as the return of the constellation Orion, rising in the East ahead of the Great Sphinx (which is happening now!). Hence it can be seen that the return of Christ, as detailed in the book of Revelations, could in fact be representative of the current awakening.

Precession Cycle

Even though the tilt of the Earth stays constant at 23.4 [NOTE: 2+3+4=9] degrees, the orientation is always changing. The physical cause of this shift is mostly due to the Sun and Moon's gravity pulling on the equatorial belt (commonly referred to as the 'bulge') of the Earth. The pull of other planets in the solar system have a very slight influence on this, also. Furthermore, the spinning core rotates at a slightly faster speed than the surface crust, thus creating a series of geodynamic effects that radiate up to the surface. These geodynamics affect the slight wobbling of the Earth's axis (referred to as the 'precession').

The Precession Cycle, also known as the Great Year, is 25,920 years long. The cycle is the result of a motion of the earth itself, a slow circumpolar wobble of the planet's axis of rotation unfolding at the rate of one degree every 72 years. Since the Earth is the viewing platform from which we observe the stars, these changes in orientation inevitably affect the position and rising times of all stars as viewed from Earth. As a result, the Sun spends around 2160 years in each zodiac house. As 2160 x 12 = 25,920, it takes 25,920 years for the Sun to appear to do a full rotation of the zodiac belt, thus this is referred to as a 'Great Year'. The Pole star is simply the star at which the Earth's extended axis, passing through the geographical north pole, points at most directly. So this changes, too. Sometimes there is no pole star at all!

Age of Pisces winter solstice

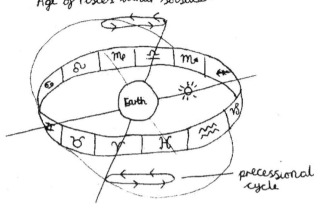

precessional
cycle

Age of Pisces
@ Spring equinox

Age of Aquarius
@ Spring equinox

Spring Equinox ≈ First day of astro-year
and Biblical year (Passover / Aries)

Opposite signs = Complimentary signs.

Pisces – Virgo
Aquarius – Leo.

FIGURE 28 – The Precession Cycle

However, at the March/ Spring Equinox, when day and night are of equal length, the Sun rises perfectly in the East against the background of the 12 constellations. It is the sign that the Sun rises against on this date which is the "Age" we are said to be living in. The zodiac system that most people are aware of is the standard horoscope. This is calculated by the expectation of the Sun to spend around one month in each sign, from Aries to Taurus to Gemini, and so on through to Aquarius then Pisces before returning to Aries. But the slow precessional course of the Sun during the Great Years appears to go in the opposite direction, from Gemini to Taurus to Aries to Pisces to Aquarius, etc. Such discovered recordings of this phenomena include the building of the Great Sphinx to represent the Age of Leo and the Apis (cattle) cults of Egypt, worshipping the Age of Taurus.

Biblically, the family line of Abraham is also said to associate with the Age of Aries (the Ram or Lamb). Such stories as those involving Moses (the lamb) punishing those worshipping the golden calf (previous Age of Taurus) is further evidence of this. Jesus then carried this 'knowledge of the lamb' into his own Age of Pisces (the fish) and taught his followers how to apply this wisdom in order to return to God the father. This is the reason why the ideology of the 'fish' is evident throughout the New Testament (the Age of Pisces). At this moment in time we are within the 'seeding' period, as the Sun shifts from Pisces to Aquarius. This is particularly interesting as, when asked by his disciples where to find him, Jesus replied, "… a man will meet you carrying a pitcher of water; follow him" (Mark 14:13). From this quote, the man with the water pitcher is a metaphor for Aquarius and the modern-day consciousness/ cycle of spirituality.

Similarly, when asked for 'a sign from heaven', Jesus explained: "You know how to interpret the appearance of the sky, but you cannot interpret the signs of the times. A wicked and adulterous generation looks for a miraculous sign, but none will be given it except the sign of Jonah" (Matthew 12:39). This quote shows how all too often humans focus only on what they can physically see. The sign of Jonah is a fish due to the three days he spent in the belly of one and, as mentioned previously, the words of the Bible and the metaphors within it were written during the Age of Pisces- the sign of the fish. Therefore, those in an age able to understand the words of 'the fish' [the metaphors of Christ] will be able to interpret the signs.

Again, the whole universe follows continuous cycles. We are currently in a cycle that is returning to the ways of the ancients; the ways of spirituality, enlightenment and consciousness. It could be this awareness of spiritual re-awakening and Gaia's own internal rhythms that was foretold by the people of the past when leaving such historical artefacts as the Mayan calendar behind. This also relates to the macrocosmic form of the feminine menstrual cycle, whereby Gaia can be seen as cleansing and shedding all that no longer serves whilst setting her attention (ascension) for the next cycle.

Yuga Cycles

Yuga Cycles are a way of measuring time with its origin in Hinduism. Interestingly, it shows incredible similarity to the Precession Cycle. The Yuga, though, are based on the notion that our Sun has a partner star somewhere in the cosmos which it gets pulled to and from. Like the zodiac ages, the Yugas are aware of recording time via star constellations. What is particularly interesting is that, whilst the background of stars moves according to the precession, the star Sirius doesn't. In fact, many believe Sirius to the be partner star of our own Sun. As we reach closer proximity to our partner star, the electromagnetic impulses of Gaia increase in vibration, taking us with it. It is for this reason that ascension and the success of the *light* are inevitable. For those who resonate with the theory of the Nommos described in Chapter 1 (that humans were taught by these aliens from a planet orbiting Sirius) then this could be seen as a return journey home.

Yogic astronomy divides the orbit of the Earth around the Sun into 27 segments called *nakshatras*, which are further divided into 4 segments, altogether totalling 108 (9x12). These are referred to as the Earth's 108 steps through space (Note the significance of the multiples of 3, 6 and 9 here, the *numbers of the universe*, according to Tesla). Currently, the Earth resides within the Material/ Dark/ Iron Age, or Kali Yuga, which is filled with conflict and destruction. Fortunately, it is believed that we are now beginning to ascend out of that Yuga, evidenced by an increase in enlightened beings. We are on the route up towards the golden era of consciousness, but the final years of Kali Yuga may manifest some vast changes in the Earth's character, such as extreme weather.

As of 2025, we emerge into the Energy/ Electrical/ Bronze Age, or Dwapara Yuga. During this era, humans are said to gain more awareness of their own electromagnetic power and to develop the ability to fine-tune energy systems in order to correspond with more subtle matters of creation.

The Big Guy In The Sky

Interestingly, Thomas Burgoyne (2013) relates the star constellations of the zodiac to particular features of the body, which come together to form the man in the sky, the pictorial 'God'. These are:

- Aries- The head and brain
- Taurus- The ears, neck and throat
- Gemini- The hands and arms
- Cancer- The vital organs
- Leo- The heart
- Virgo- The solar plexus
- Libra- The loins
- Scorpio- The generative organs
- Sagittarius- The thighs
- Capricorn- The knees
- Aquarius- The legs
- Pisces- The feet.

[Note the similarities between these and those identified in Chapter 10.]

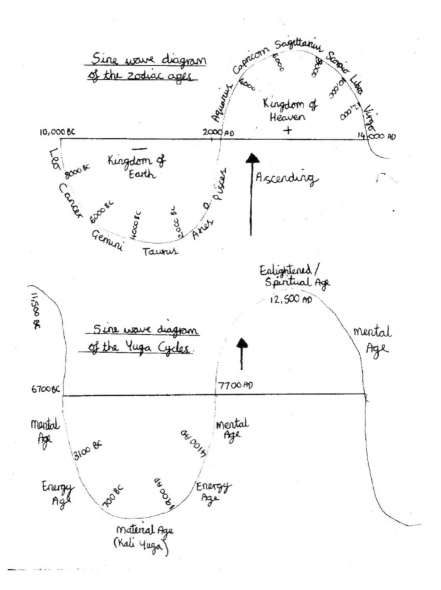

FIGURE 29 – The Zodiac Ages and Yuga Cycles

From this, one can see how worshipping the 'guy in the sky' is in fact a reference to the heavens and the zodiac constellations which make up our closest neighbouring galaxies... the universe. Hence why the stars (Sun energy and givers of light) can be seen as the masculine, whereas the dark space (potential/ womb which nurtures and births creation) is the feminine.

The Son

The Sun is our closest star and giver of all life on Earth, including Gaia herself. Solar gods are evident around the globe and throughout history, as described in Chapter 6. The Bible even states that: 'the Lord God is a Sun and a Shield' [Psalm 84:11]. Thus, the universal aether and giver of all light is God (the father) who provides a prodigal son (the Sun or suns as star constellations) to bless the virgin Mother (Earth- Gaia). This blessing takes the form of a solar, spiritual seed which has the power to heal us all if protected until a time in which it has grown knowledgeable (powerful) enough.

Like a mother protecting a child, the Earth is surrounded by layers of various substances that form the perfect, habitable atmosphere for us. The ionosphere is close enough to be considered part of the Earth's atmosphere. This is where ions and electrons affect radio waves, so is where the majority of our cosmic communication is translated into energy perceivable by the pineal. Most of the electrical activity in the ionosphere is produced from light energy (photons). It is no wonder, then, that this layer of the atmosphere is referred to as the *celestial powerhouse*. At night when there is little photon energy, ions within the lower layer of the ionosphere convert into an abundance of oxygen. From this, the ionosphere layer of the Earth can be likened to the angelic messengers of God, often visiting humans at night during sleep (when oxygen and DMT levels are heightened).

Above the ionosphere is the magnetosphere. Here, the behaviour of charged particles is strongly affected by the magnetic fields of both the Earth and the Sun. The inner layer of the magnetosphere is called the plasmasphere, containing dense plasma. Hence, it can be perceived that the oily (plasmic) substance of the Chrism is released by the solar Sun/son to Earth, delivered by the angels (sacred ions) to those who can save the Christ essence. Interestingly, the combined layers of the Earth's atmosphere and beyond do in fact look like a woman bearing a child, which leads to further evidence for the ancient understanding of cosmic influence when designing such gods as Gaia. What's more, with regards to sacred geometry (described in Chapter 7), the surrounding atmospheres of Earth show remarkable resemblance to the pattern one can create when following the Golden Ratio of Fibonacci's Constant, further evidencing the mathematical proof of the intelligent design of the universe.

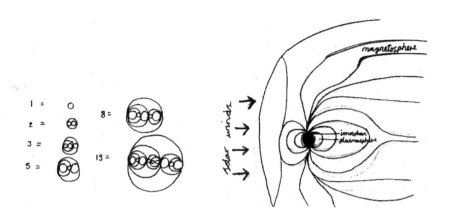

FIGURE 30 – The Earth's Atmosphere Compared to The Golden Ratio

Summary

The human form and all of their creative power is a direct microcosmic manifestation of the wider universe. As the world progresses through its cycles as descension and ascension, we move with it. This age of awakening is bringing the knowledge of the sacred secretion into the collective consciousness again, on both the macro and micro scale.

References and Bibliography

Aderin-Pocock, M. 2018. *Book of the Moon.* Penguin Random House UK.

Bauval, R. and Gilbert, A. 1994. *The Orion Mystery: Unlocking the secrets of the pyramids.* Arrow.

Bauval, R. and Hancock, G. 1996. *Keepers of Genesis.* William Heinemann Ltd.

Bibhu Dev Misra. 2012. The end of the Kali Yuga in 2025: Unravelling the mysteries of the Yuga Cycle. Available online at: <www.grahamhancock.com>

Burgoyne, T. 2013. *The Light Of Egypt: Parts 1 and 2.*

Ekrek, A. 2018. *The Zodiac Oracle.* Arcturus Publishing Limited.

Kerr, K. 2019. *The God Design.* Seek Vision.

McElroy, M. n.d. *Ionosphere and magnetosphere.* Encyclopaedia Britannica. Available at: <https://www.britannica.com/science/ionosphere-and-magnetosphere>

Pratt, L. The Four Yugas. Available online at: <www.bibliotecapleyades.net>

Chapter 17

In History

When one who is familiar with the Bible begins to delve into the history of the Earth and human evolution, questions continuously arise in the mind, such as:

- What if, in the beginning, God wasn't keeping humans ignorant but instead was just letting them be; to test if they were capable of reaching enlightenment?

- What if the snake represented the Moon, which encouraged psychedelic mushroom growth, and the guarding- cherub is the Sun, which stunts it?

- What if the forbidden fruit was psychedelic, and God simply wanted us to find the path within ourselves internally, rather than consume externally?

- What if the consequences given by God are if enlightenment within is not found, as Adam and Eve felt ashamed and tried to hide themselves after?

- What if God did not give punishments but, actually, powers: women given the ability to produce babies and men the skill of working with nature and Mother Earth, whereas the snake had its legs removed so that it can move more freely, like energy?

- What if the metabolising of psychedelics and other state-altering 'drugs' is encoded in our DNA?
- What if the snakes in the ancient texts are just representations of serpent energy in the body, which is why they can be presented as both good and evil, depending on one's true motives?

To date, there is no straight answer to such questions. We can, however, look back at the teachings of philosophers, enlightened in a much simpler time with access to un-tampered inherited knowledge and scripture, to gain some insight into such practices. Once you have an awareness of the preservation of the Christos, the true meaning behind such quotations as that below seem obvious.

"Doth the Sun go his way… Doth the Moon go her way… Doth the Stars go their way… Where the Light of the Sun waxeth brighter… Then do the heavenly forces arise… Made by the Heavenly Father for the increase of the Children of Light… As the sea is the gathering place of the waters, rising up and going down… Thus rise up… [for] the Heavenly Father hath made this eternal and sovereign luminous space… To nourish the Children of Light, the earth is the strong Preserver… The Law is Life.."

(The Essene Gospel of Peace, Book 3)

The Essenes

The Essene Gospel of Peace, Book 3, speaks much of the '*Time of the Great Trees*'. At which time, it is said that the holy religion of the Creator was revealed to Enoch (Metatron), the first follower of the '*Law*'. [Interestingly, trees communicate via fungal systems (mushrooms)]. This time of Great Trees is said to have been destroyed by the Lord after man sinned against him. As such, fire is said to have devoured the pastures and wilderness, another indication of the great catastrophes (from meteor impact [fire] and corresponding ice age that followed [around the Younger Dryas period detailed in Chapter 1]). When reading the Essene Gospel of Peace, one makes constant revelations, linking the information given with current theories about evolution and inheritance.

The Essenes practiced a renewal ritual where they ingested a fluid/ substance that was said to be '*the fountain of life*' and sexual emission of God, which extended people's life spans and awakened them into ecstatic consciousness. I believe this fluid was the sacred secretion.

Within Book 1 of The Essene Gospel of Peace, it is claimed that in the beginning was the WORD, and the Word is the LAW, and the Law is LIFE. I believe this Life to be God's seed, which occupies a pure Temple. According to the Essenes, the Temple is made pure by, first, the Angel of Air (the breath), which removes uncleanliness (acidity), and, second, the Angel of Water (CSF), for "*all must be born again of water... for your body bathes in the river of life*" as no man may come before the face of God (the pineal) whom the Angel of Water did not let pass. The Angel of Water baptises from within to remove

375

uncleanliness, *"like two tombs that outwards are painted fair but within are full of abominations"* (the ventricles). Third and finally, the Angel of Sunlight is said to enter the body in such ways that the Lord may again possess it. Thus, it can be seen that the Lord uses sunlight to enter the body, which combines with the Holy breath before entering the inner waters for cleaning.

It is by LOVE that the holy trinity come together.

Book 1 also describes the ancient practices of the Essenes used to keep the body 'clean' for God to enter. These practices included enemas, sun gazing, fasting, grounding and a raw lacto-vegetarian diet. The text also claims that TRUTH is formed from consciousness + nature + epigenetics. Interestingly, the Essenes recognised that consciousness does not exist in this physical space-time.

From all of the above, it is clear that there are many ways of seeking enlightenment, many different paths that can be followed, although all eventually lead to the same truth. Therefore, the preservation of the sacred secretion is only one spiritual path that can be walked upon in search of this truth. It is for this reason that the practices presented in this book will resonate with some but not for others. It is for this reason that some thrive on vegetables and others do not. It is for this reason that some were born in this generation and others in the last.

Our spirit has a unique path, and only our spirit can guide us down the path that is right for us. In the modern world of technology this can feel over-whelming as there are so many practices all claiming to be the 'true' and 'only' path. In fact, the TRUE PATH is your own. As the

Lord is claimed to have said in Book 1: "*I will speak to you through the mysterious rainbow when you are alone, through the wisdom of the Ancients... When you have seen my Angels, Be still. Know I am God.*"

Book 2 of The Essene Gospel of Peace states that, in the beginning, a covenant was made between God and man, and the holy flame of the Creator entered man, making him the son of God. With this came the responsibility of guarding man's inheritance by making the land fruitful and keeping it holy. It is then claimed that the Law of God was hidden within Moses' breast and kept as a sign to the "Children of Light" (enlightened ones). What I find most intriguing about this comment is that the breast plate of Moses is said to contain 12 stones which are engraved with the names of the 12 Sons of Israel: the zodiac.

I do not have the permissions required to reprint the entire restored fragments of the Essene Book of Revelations, as translated by Edmund Bordeaux Szekely. Instead, I can offer my thoughts on the text and recommend the reader to seek these translations themselves if interested. My own copy is covered in notes made by myself of all of the references to the preserving of the sacred secretion.

These links are clear and bountiful, hence why I am unable to repeat the whole text. To me, it appears that the Essene Book of Revelations is describing the following:

- Oxygen synchronises the mind, body and spirit by opening the pineal;
- The cycle ends in the same place it started (the crown chakra);

- After passing the seven chakras, it reaches the corpus collosum via the CSF;
- The seven stars (our nearest planets, Sun and Moon) are the Angels of the Father;
- The seven candles (chakras) are the Angels of the Mother;
- The spirit of man is the flame which streams between the Father (stars) and Mother (chakras/ earth energy);
- After returning, the left and right hemispheres of the brain become one;
- Bathed in crystal-rich (salty) CSF is the throne of God, surrounded by a rainbow (energy systems) and 13 elders (physical body/ organ systems);
- In God's right hand (hemisphere) was a book sealed with seven seals, which are only able to be opened by one who is 'worthy';
- A 'worthy' one is described as having aligned chakras, breathes clean air, consumes clear water, bathes in natural sunlight, enjoys a life of music and laughter, eats food of the earth, practices good thoughts, good words and good deeds, and understands the mystery of the "Tree of Life in the Endless Sea" and "walks between earth and heaven";
- Once worthy, 'incense' ascends up before God;
- Following the opening of the seven seals, one is described as hearing fire mingled with blood which rises as vapour to the Moon, followed by a great earthquake;
- Eventually, their Sun shall no more go down, neither shall their Moon withdraw itself, for the Law shall create an everlasting

light within (when the body becomes so accustomed to preserving and using the sacred secretion that it can be activated anywhere at will)

- Then the Tree of Life will now bare 14 manner of fruit (two more than previously due to the new pathways and body system being used).

Further evidence of clear metaphoric description of the sacred secretion includes:

- The pregnant woman from Revelations, whose child the dragon is waiting to consume, is said to have in her *"the blood of prophets and of saints"* (From The Essene Book of Revelations)
- If one remembers the necessity of CSF flow and its direct connection to the blood, The Essene Gospel of Peace's description of "the Mother's blood falls from the clouds, leaps up from the womb, babbles in the brooks of the mountains, flows wide in the rivers and sleeps in the lakes" can be understood as a description of the Moon's quantum dew bearing a 'child' within the sacral place.
- Within the Essene Gospel of Peace Book 3 it is said that, for as long as the Sun and Moon endure, there is hope for peace throughout all generations [as our inherited DNA holds the potential to save the seed].

- That the Tree of Life is in fact the cerebellum within the brain stem (The Essene Gospel of Peace, Book 3)
- That the life of the sacred seed is a holy 'Law' of the universe, that can manifest as a baptism of the body and that the law is engraved in the forehead (third eye)
- Only '*pure*' water can mirror the light of the Sun and Moon.
- *"The radiant and luminous Moon keepeth within itself the Seed."* The Essenes then report that, even though the face of the Moon changes, its influence is ever the same, and even though the path of the Holy Law (destiny) of each of the Children of Light is different, the Moon's influence is unchanged in '*essence*' (The Essene Gospel of Peace, Book 3)
- The Moon, Sun, air and stars regulate the '*Holy Order*' [the Christ seed]
- The Essenes also claim that the glorious stars have within themselves the Seed of Life, which reflects into the Eternal Sea [CSF] (The Essene Gospel of Peace, Book 3)

Thus, it seems clear that the ancient Essenes held great knowledge of how to preserve the Christ Oil within and sought ways of retelling this practice through metaphorical print that makes sense to one with ears to hear. What's more, according to Dillon (2003) it is reported that the initiation period for the Essenes was 3 years. This correlates with the time lapse between the baptism of Christ and his ascension to heaven. If true, this could mean that it takes three years of preservation practice before one becomes fully awakened.

The Druids

The Druids were the Shaman of the ancient Celtic cultures. The word *druid* meant 'Knowing the Oak Tree'. These ancient philosophers and teachers from Europe are renowned for their connectedness to nature and nature spirits, such as fairies. In particular, they worshipped the Sun and Moon and based their initiations during specific lunar cycles or solstices and equinoxes when solar influxes were higher. They also celebrated the birth of the Sun God on the dawn of December 25th. Interestingly, they even worshipped the goddess Isis under the symbol of the Moon. It is no wonder, then, that Manly Hall speculated the Druids migrated to Britain from a more ancient civilisation.

The ceremonial robes of an arch-Druid included a crescent- shaped sceptre, symbolic of the 6th day of the increasing Moon as well as the Ark of Noah. According to Manly Hall, admission to Druid ceremonies was via glass boat, symbolic of the Moon, which floated upon the *waters of eternity*, preserving the *seeds* of living creatures within its boat-like crescent. This was also known as the Sacred Ship.

Druids believed that the first settler of Britain came from the '*summer country*', which I, personally, am speculating to have been Egypt, although others have suggested Atlantis. Both seem plausible.

The Druids of Britain were believed to have used magnetism and nature to cure all dis-ease. Their universal remedies included mistletoe (incredibly magnetic and grows on oak trees, hence the Druid sacred deity was worshipped through oak) and serpent eggs (as these attract astral light in a reportedly special manner- although I think this is metaphorical for the spiritual egg/ Christ seed).

Symbolism from Druidry that shows clear resemblance to much of the ideas already covered in this book include that the sacred colours of Druidry were green, blue and white (the upper chakras), the circle was the universe, the oval was the mundane egg, wings were the motion of the divine spirit (such as that recognised within the symbol of Kundalini) and the cross meant regeneration (much like it did for the Egyptians; the cross and serpent were both sacred to Druids).

In alchemy, the term 'seed' means spirit, as spirit is like an ever-present seed which can grow and flourish. Thus, the seed of spirit is sown in the womb of matter and by an immaculate (pure) conception, the progeny is brought into being.

Ancient Egypt

When one thinks of Ancient Egypt, the first thoughts are typically around the imagery of pyramid structures. What isn't so prominent is the understanding of how these worked. The ancient pyramids contain 'dark rooms', where it is believed that initiated would go and retreat as part of their path towards ascension, typically for three days (of darkness). Such theories become more evident when considering that pyramids are built on places of high electromagnetic activity from the Earth, are aligned with specific star constellations, have running aquifers and are adorned with sacred symbology. What's more, the pyramid shape (pointed top) is also associated with increased energy influx, as demonstrated within Tesla's scalar energy experiments. Being in a dark room for this amount of time not only stimulates the body's natural DMT production but having these increased frequencies would have raised one's capability exponentially.

It is recorded that Ancient Greeks, including Hippocrates, travelled to Egypt to learn about their *sacred oils*. Further evidence of the Egyptian advocation for the sacred secretion can be seen here:

In this image, we can see an initiate being blessed with fluid from Thoth (the Moon god) and Ra or Horus (the Sun god). The Ankh (key of life) pours from their anointing.

Here, we can see a royal woman, who has fish scales/ tail for legs and a pinecone at her feet, being anointed with two oils from what appears like a large mushroom. To the right, the hieroglyphs also appear to be showing a drop of liquid being emitted from the head of a serpent, whose body is above a woman with water on her head and who has two energies coming together around the moon below her.

Within this depiction, feminine and masculine energies appear to be working together to produce a liquid, under the influence of the pictorials of star constellations above.

Here, Thoth, the Moon god, is holding two entwining rods in one hand and is using the other hand to *feed* the initiate the key of life (ankh).

The centrepiece in between them also shows two pillars supporting the ceremony.

The Ancient Egyptians are renowned for using imagery as their form of written communication. Nowadays, such forms are referred to as *art* and considered to be of visual beauty, only. However, even modern art is commonly encoded with vast information waiting to be uncovered, which is what the next chapter dives into.

Summary

Identifying the evidence for the sacred secretion in historical texts is by far the most difficult due to the amount of evidence that would have disappeared over the years, either by natural means or by those in power in order to suppress the masses. This chapter has identified some of the key ideas, although I am sure that much more proof will continue to emerge as we move through our cycle of enlightenment and into the age of energy. More modern evidence will be examined in the next chapter.

Bibliography and References

Billington, P. 2011. *The Path of Druidry.* Llewellyn Publications.

Carey, G. and Perry, I. 2013. *God-Man: The Word Made Flesh.*

Dillon, J. 2003. *The Essenes in Greek sources: Some reflections.* In: Jews in the Hellenistic and Roman Cities (pp. 117-128). Routledge Taylor & Francis Group.

Golb, N. 1989. The Dead Sea Scrolls: A new perspective. *American Scholar.* 58(2):pp.177-208.

Hall, M. *Secret Teachings of All Ages.*

Szekely, R. 2018. *The Essene Gospel of Peace: Books 1-4.* Re-Printed by AudioEnlightenment.com

Chapter 18

In the Art

As well as storytelling, humans are profound artists. From the cave paintings left by Stone Age people to the stain glass art of the Metropolitan Cathedral of Saint Sebastian, imagery has always been a form of expression used by humans to record knowledge and to become creators. With the sacred secretion in mind, the most famous works are by the one and only Leonardo Da Vinci.

Leonardo Da Vinci

Leonardo Da Vinci was not only a prominent artist but he also had a keen interest in astronomy and anatomy. From analysis of Da Vinci's life works, I believe he was an active preserver of the Christ Seed and attempted to communicate this knowledge into his art, which could also trigger DNA activations depending on any light code intent that he may have held. This chapter hopes to bring to light evidence of this. As I do not have the rights to re-print any of his works, I will title the pieces I discuss throughout this chapter so that you may do an internet search on them for yourself.

The Madonna of the Carnation (1478): Here, Leonardo draws the baby Jesus with his mother, who is holding out a red carnation flower, possibly symbolising the blood sacrifice he will have to make later or as a symbol of her womb awakening.

The Benois Madonna (1478): A young mother (virgin) is illustrated here offering a white flower (a crucifer) to the baby, which alludes the sacrifice of Christ. Both have halos to show their higher mental functioning. Interestingly, the landscape once evident in the window was painted over for reasons unknown.

The Baptism of Christ (1478): This piece of art is astounding and full of symbolism. Above is a white bird surrounded by light, being given to Christ. From this direction there is a black bird flying to the left into a pine tree (pineal) and one on the right flying into two conifers (the two lobes of the pituitary). Centrally, Jesus is being baptised by light from above, with a cruciform as a halo, hands in the prayer position and feet submerged in the river Jordan. To the left of Christ is John the Baptist holding a staff. The staff has a cross on the top and the bottom is in the river. Just below the cross on the staff is a small structure which holds uncanny resemblance to the brain stem. To the right of Christ are two angels, a male and female, holding clean garments, ready to clothe to purified Son of God.

The Annunciation (1478): In the distance of this painting are large mountains and water, similar to that within The Baptism of Christ, painted in the same year. Could da Vinci have been communicating two events paralleled in time? This seems more plausible when one notices the sun-like halo over the woman's head (Sun energy), the gold drape covering her naval area (solar plexus) and the clear drapes (CSF) covering the red stand (blood) which holds a book (knowledge). The woman is welcoming a white angel (Moon), who is holding up two fingers (lines of energy) and holding the same white flowers that are engraved into the woman's white lectern (spiritual body). Fascinatingly, closer inspection of the lectern appears to be representing a body, with two feet at the base and a shell-shape at the top, covered in spirals (vortex energy). To me, this picture instantly appeared to be representative of the delivery of the Christ (baptised in the Jordan) oil to the physical body.

The Adoration of the Magi (1481): Although the purpose of this altarpiece appears to be an easy one to interpret based on the baby Jesus and Mother Mary at the centre, surrounded by adoring worshippers, my attention was caught by the figure on the far right looking off the page. It is suggested that this person is a self-portrait of Leonardo at age 30. If so, it seems more than coincidental that the self-portrait is not only of a person the same age as Jesus at baptism (purification), but the figure is also looking away from the immense imagery at the centre of the page, as if showing that everyone else is looking in the wrong direction (or interpreting incorrectly).

The Virgin of the Rocks (1486): Here, the virgin Mary has a golden drape covering her solar plexus (like in the Annunciation) and is holding the baby St John, who is praying to the baby Christ. The baby Christ is pointing at John with two fingers and is being held by the angel Gabriel, who is also pointing at John with one straight finger. In the middle, Mary holds the baby John with her right hand and is holding her left hand directly over the pointed finger of Gabriel and the baby Jesus, who also happens to be sitting with his legs crossed over. This picture appears, then, to be illustrating the Christ seed preparing to enter the solar plexus. Da Vinci produced a second version of this image (clearly, it must have been of significance to him) at around 1508. A key adaptation is that baby John is now also holding a staff.

Homo Virtruvianus (1490): Leonardo had a fascination with human anatomy and spent much of his later career studying the human body, both internally and externally, possibly in search of internal evidence of the Sacred Royal Marriage. His drawings depict the perfect design of the human figure and its corresponding likeness to the rules of sacred geometry.

Allegory on the Fidelity of the Lizard (1496): This sketch shows a lizard and a snake battling ahead of a man sleeping under a tree. To me, this appears to be representing the reptilian part of the brain trying to fight against the serpent energy.

The Last Supper (1498): Probably the most astounding painting of Da Vinci's is that of the Last Supper, whereby Jesus and his disciples are sitting at a long table. Santos Bonacci and Manly Hall both claim that within this picture the disciples are using hand gestures to symbolise their corresponding star constellation. And from inspection, I agree. As mentioned in Chapter 10, by paying close attention to the hand gestures of each follower of Christ, the disciples begin with Aries (the start of the astrological year) and follow through to Pisces (the end of the astrological year). In Da Vinci's painting, one can clearly see Judas (Cancer), who has spilled salt, sitting by Peter (Leo), Mary Magdalene (in place of John to show a clearer depiction of Virgo) and James (Libra). From this, Leonardo's fascination with spiritual practices seems evident.

Leda and the Swan (1508): Inspired by Greek mythology whereby the god Zeus, in the form of a swan, seduces a woman named Leda who later gave birth to an egg bearing twins. As swans are frequently used to symbolise purity and Leda gave birth to an egg rather than a live child, this image could be symbolic of god-energy entering the body and producing the spiritual egg. Interestingly, Leda's hair is also plaited and dangles in serpent-like shapes. Thinking astrologically, though, with the swan as Sagittarius, the eggs as Gemini and Leda as Virgo (see Chapter 5 for a reminder of zodiac symbolism), then one would not have to look far to see that these would be the other three dominating constellations during the Age of Pisces. Virgo and Pisces complimented each other during the Equinoxes and Sagittarius and Gemini complimented each other during the Solstices.

Raphael Sanzio da Urbino

Raphael was influenced by the work of da Vinci (and possibly learned the same philosophies). Some of his most notable paintings are:

Mond Crucifixion (1502): This image shows the crucified Christ, with the Sun to his right (rising in the East) and the Moon to his left. Under the Sun and his right hand, a red-winged angel is capturing the blood pouring from him. Under the Moon and his left hand, a blue-winged angel is capturing the blood pouring from him. There is a body of water behind Christ, centrally, and both Marys plus John the Evangelist and Saint Jerome are at the base of the cross. This phenomenon could be related to a person's light codes harvesting the cosmic influences from the plasma of the body.

Coronation of the Virgin (1504): This painting depicts two distinct scenes. The higher, spiritual part of the photo shows the virgin Mary being crowned by Jesus whilst angels are playing music, whereas the lower, earthly half show the apostles gathered around the empty tomb of Mary, whose body has been raised to heaven. Thus, Christ will crown all who are able to bring their body to the place of the Lord (higher states).

Madonna of Foligno (1511): My personal favourite piece of art out of them all. In the centre is Mother Mary holding the baby Christ. They are framed by the Sun and borne by a cloud of angels. Immediate below them is a rainbow and another angel who appears to be holding a blank plaque.

Observing the scene are John the Baptist pointing up, St Francis of Assisi pointing down but looking up, Sigismondo de' Conti dressed in red and St Jerome dressed in blue. This painting could be seen as the initial prophecy, with the blank plaque showing that the true interpretation is up to the observer.

The School of Athens (1511): This painting shows a number of philosophers, including Plato, Aristotle, Socrates, Pythagoras and Ptolemy, to name a few. It depicts distinct branches of knowledge. Even Da Vici has been painted as a model of Plato. Many believe this to be showing the high regard that Raphael held for the painter. Personally, though, I think Raphael was communicating the idea of Da Vinci being divinely inspired.

The Transfiguration (1520): The piece is considered Raphael's finest work, although it remains unfinished by him. Within this painting are a vast number of events happening at once. Obviously, Christ transfiguring into pure white is dominating the piece centrally. Other key figures include Moses, Elijah, James, Peter and John, whom were present during Christ's transfiguration. Below, Jesus' other nine disciples are trying and failing to heal a possessed man, looking into a book for the answers rather than at Christ. Thus, this piece appears to be showing that our connection to Christ and associated healing abilities lies between Heaven and Earth (within ourselves).

Michelangelo

Another world- famous artist who worked alongside Da Vinci was Michelangelo. Michelangelo was predominately a sculptor during his artistic career, however, he was commissioned to paint the ceiling of the Sistine Chapel. Michelangelo incorporated a variety of key Biblical stories in his mural of art. Note, however, that Michelangelo was condemned by Pope Paul IV at the time for his developed belief in spiritualism and direct communication with God, without the need for a church. The Pope even stopped Michelangelo's pension and defiled his paintings to conceal their original form. Yet, the mural of art upon the ceiling of the Sistine Chapel is still as popular today as it always has been.

The Separation of Light from Darkness (1512): God is central in this painting, separating the light from the dark, and is framed by two shields (one above and one below) and four sleepy angel (one in each corner). This painting clearly shows the human spinal cord and brain stem leading up to the centre of God's chest and throat. Thus, the 'voice' of God is the 'brain' of man, who was given the intelligent power to separate the metaphorical light from dark. What's more, further down in the image one can see that God's robe twists at the waist, revealing the optic nerves from two eyes, hinting at the connection between light and optical function when reaching out to God.

The Creation of Adam (1512): Michelangelo's *Creation of Adam* is one of the most replicated religious paintings of all time. It depicts God as an elderly white-bearded man wrapped in a red cloak and surrounded by 12 angels, reaching out to Adam on the left. The fact that Adam and God are yet to touch shows that God is awaiting our return with open arms. The twelve angels also likely represent the 12 signs of the zodiac which hold God's power. The most intriguing part of this image, however, is the fact that the cloak of God is swaying in an unnatural way, which very clearly resembles the human brain.

The mural by Michelangelo is known to secretly depict a range of human organs within the various forms of God. For this reason, it is believed that the meaning behind this mural is not of God giving intelligence to Adam, but rather that intelligence and observation of the human body makes it possible to lead without the necessity of the church directly. That is, that we all have a unique ability to communicate with God through our own human form, created by intelligent design.

Other Notable Piece

Alchemy (1738): This piece within Clavis Artis Volume 2 clearly shows the masculine and feminine coming together in sacred union within a vase, with a pinecone emanating from the top. To the left is a single star flower (constellation) and to the right are two twinned flowers (the pituitary). Many of the piece with Clavis Artis appear to present imagery regarding enlightenment via the sacred secretion and endocrine alchemy. Simply type '*Clavis Artis*' into your internet search engine and witness these for yourself.

The Black Madonna of Montserrat, Spain: Here, the virgin mother holds a globe in one hand (Earth energy) and her other is around a child on her lap. This child points up to the heavens (cosmos) with his right hand and is holding a pinecone in his left. Both are wearing crowns as signs of their sovereignty and enlightenment.

Moving Art: Films and movies are able to elicit emotional responses and encode subliminal messaging within the subconscious without a person even realising. I particularly find it simple to elicit connections to the sacred secretion with *fictional* moving pictures such as Star Wars and Harry Potter, both of which demonstrate the power of energy use and intent in order to create light.

Summary

This by no means exhausts the vast artistic works that show the story of the internal Christ but opens up the doors for further study. As the right side of the brain is swayed towards visually stimulating means of communication, the manifestation of this phenomenon by way of both artists and authors seems to be God's way of ensuring that this message is accessible to all. And who knows, maybe these artists channelled source energy and have depicted light codes within these visuals, awaiting the students *with eyes to see* to uncover them and awaken!

References

An Artabras Book. *Leonardo Da Vinci.* Reynal and Company.

Cremante, S. 2006. *Leonardo Da Vinci: The Complete Works.* A David Charles Book.

Porter, R. 2013. A reflection and analysis on the 'Creation of Adam' Sistene Chapel Fresco. Available online at: <biblicaltheology.com>

Suk, I. and Tamargo, R. 2014. Concealed neuroanatomy in Michelangelo's separation of light from darkness in the Sistene Chapel. 66(5):pp.851-861. *Neurosurgery.*

www.michelangelo.net

Chapter 19

In English

Within this chapter, I have sought to explain what I believe is happening at the time of the sacred secretion in one clear swoop.

Distant star constellations (including the zodiac belt) communicate with our own Sun via stellar signalling. These influence the solar winds emitted by the Sun, which pass through the plasmic magnetosphere of Earth until translated by the electron-rich ionosphere into light language comprehensible by Earth. To accommodate for changes in solar-communication, sodium molecules (cell salts) are produced in the body in order for balance to be maintained throughout the year. At birth, a more direct impact from these solar winds would have caused the plasma (blood) in our own bodies to adapt in an attempt to restore this balance. Correspondingly, energy from the dominating stellar signalling at this time would have been used to restore synchronicity, generating a magnetic signature and claustrum blueprint.

Throughout the next twelve years of life as the human organism matured, signals from arrays of cosmic forces would have charged and influenced the body. Notably, at age twelve, the pineal gland is said to be fully developed. Thus, the sacred seed can begin the early stages of preservation. (It's no wonder that teenagers have vast mood swings, rebel against the system and want to sleep so much!) At which time, a lot of learning happens.

Some take longer than others to repent past life karma and reach a stage of enlightenment and spiritual maturity which can consent to the impregnation of the heavenly gift. Eventually, though, as an adult, when our closest cosmic body, the Moon, reflects energy from our dominating star sign, magic happens. As lunar frequency begins its journey into your star sign (starting with the void period just before), this electromagnetic signal travels through the layers of Gaia (as if literal angels are delivering a heavenly saviour) to the body of all resonating antennas. At such a time, bio-magnetite molecules respond magnetically, exciting the brain. The claustrum releases its neuropeptides to the pineal and pituitary (hence, using neural somatostatin- its 'body'- to spiritually link both the mother and father), stimulating them to release their sacred secretions (milk and honey; nectar and ambrosia). Further signals are sent to the choroid plexus (elves) dictating which ions (gifts) to transport into the CSF from the blood, which pass into the third ventricle (the womb).

This vibrant water then flows past the cerebellum (Tree of Knowledge) and medulla as it descends down towards the lumbar base of the spinal cord. Here, at the base of the spine (above the root chakra, the *animal* instincts), the triangular sacrum (the five-fused vertebrate with a 'stable' appearance that holds our sacral chakra, responsible for pleasure-seeking) holds the fluid just long enough for the cascade of chemicals to intertwine (as a result of the crossing over of the ida and pingala energies) and react to birth the 'Christed substance'. From here, it must reach the land of light (the solar plexus), protected and empowered by the gifts of the Magi (the three cell salts required to balance the composition and electromagnetic sensitivity of the salt-fuelled CSF) and the loving-mother hormones from the pituitary (vasopressin to harmonise electrolyte balance in the holy waters and oxytocin for a feeling of love, calm and tranquillity) in order to survive its fragile *infancy* stage. The sacred secret-ion is then 'uncoiled' (awakened) and propelled back up the spinal cord by the sacral pump (a regular rhythmic motion).

As this vibrant fluid, homing the protected Chrism, travels back up 30 of the spine's vertebrate, electrified by the motion of the moving waters (like an aquifer), the fluid containing the spiritual seed reaches the back of the throat [chakra]. From here, the holy waters pass the 'olives' (hence the orthodox idea of baptism by 'olive oil' to 'light the lamp' – Leviticus 24:2; Exodus 29:7; Exodus 30:23; Matthew 25:4) and the final 3 vertebrae. Eventually, the electromagnetic internal waters direct the Christ oil until it 'climbs the highest mountain' (the pyramids) and transfigures before the eyes of the prophets (previously invisible genetic potential).

Once combined with the input from the vagus nerve (The Tree of Life, allowing for improved oxygen transport as this nerve stimulates the lungs to breath), the Christ seed becomes 'holy' (whole- the spirit molecule) and is 'betrayed' (which translates as 'double crossed') by the directional flow of the ida and pingala energies and is crucified at

Golgotha (the place of the skull) between two thieves (the eyes). In anatomy, this is referring to the CSF passing the optic chiasm (the cross-over made by the two optic nerves from the eyes). This crucifixion is ahead of the two parts of the pituitary gland; hence, the two Marys who witnessed the 'death'. CSF then flows back through the subarachnoid space into the dural sinuses towards the heart (the centre of the body's electromagnetic field) and returns to the blood (the blood and water leaving Christ's pierced body).

Now circulating within the blood and electromagnetic field of the body, the spirit molecule awakens the holy men (ancestral receptor sites). In an alkaline body, this spiritual essence within the blood plasma can return again to the brain (signalled by the bio-magnetite) through the filtration system of the choroid plexus. After passing the substantia nigra (in darkness) the essence reaches the lateral ventricle covered by the septum pellucidum (Latin for 'translucent wall') and is concealed behind the rock-like thalamus (Christ was clothed in white and laid inside the Tomb, sealed with a rock) and bathed constantly in electromagnetic CSF and lunar light codes, increasing in power. [Interestingly, if the thin membrane- septum pellucidum- sealing the lateral ventricle is removed during a dissection, the observer would find what appears to be a small body- the 'head and body' of the caudate nucleus- with the claustrum above its head, where a large neuron referred to as the 'crown of thorns' resides from.]

The Moon's magnetic effects on the magnetite of the brain and the hormone inhibiting enzymes from the Claustrum signal the Christ energy to remain dormant for 2.5 days. During these days of preservation, the chemicals within the fluid are vulnerable to being consumed by the blood (physical limitations) and inhibited before reaching their full potential.

[Strategies on how to support the preservation of the sacred secretion are analysed in Part 3.]

After the preservation period, the oil has refined into the mystical ichor fluid which triggers the emergence of the *three layers of Christ* [1 John 5:8], evident in the *water* (CSF- neurotransmitter), *blood* (hormone) and *spirit* (the light code energy field- quantum DMT). Once pure and increased in power, the Christ energy can be reborn via the corpus callosum (pure white, myelinated nerve fibres connecting the left and right/ physical and spiritual/ logic and creative brain hemispheres- hence the *white* robes left upon the rock in the tomb) and stimulate the cranial nerves, notably the vagal tone, thus increasing oxygen and alkalinity levels throughout the body.

At this point, increased oxytocin from the heart expands this chakra centre and enables the 'felt' experience associated with peace and harmony, supporting the anchoring in and embodiment of these higher frequencies of love. At the same time, effective vasopressin release increases vibrant water levels in the body, allowing for more light to be held, which supports light body activation. Action potentials are also sent throughout the body, opening pathways to allow ions to flow into cells that support healing and regeneration, as well as increased receptor sites for upgrades to the pineal and its brewed metabolites. Moreover, surges of electrons are sent through the body, regulating its voltage,

and the CSF around the pineal stimulates the piezoelectric effect, leading to an upgrade in the body's charge; allowing one the ability to tap into the Christos Fractal Family of Light (Christed consciousness codes) and into the 5D realm and beyond.

Here, it can be seen that an entire chakra/ energy system upgrade occurs. This stimulates more vibrant secretions, including Thyroid hormone which is responsible for how much energy we generate by switching up Mitochondria energy production within our cells, further enhancing light body embodiment and activations. Spirits and light beings may also see your inner light and know whether they can communicate with you are not.

This process enhances communicative ability of the whole body, flipping the switch and turning up the DMT thermostat. The receptor sites (holy men) previously awakened can now receive the 'truth' and reconnect to father energy (Source- a living light code). At which point, your senses are overtaken. As it is reabsorbed again into the cardiovascular system, new blood is produced and the thalamic gate (to heaven) opens, allowing the energy to move through to the thalamus and access the Reticular Activating System (responsible for our levels of wakefulness and experiencing greater levels of awareness, hence the term "waking up"). This arouses the neocortex (the front, human part of the brain) which vibrates into higher brain wave patterns. We are now operating at a higher level. This further stimulates the pineal, causing it to vibrate rapidly, producing luciferin (inner light) which aids communication between all parts of the body- physically and spiritually- and increases the energy influx to and from the crown chakra (source).

Furthermore, as we become more aware of our reality and sensitive to the energies within our environment, Conscious Guardian Angels (spirits entangled to us that are vibrating on a higher plane) will be able to interact with us easier and we may even become more clairvoyant and psychic. Our vibrant energy will also influence electromagnetic frequencies within our physical world. Due to this, we are more susceptible to 'messages', often in the form of synchronicities such as repeated number patterns and visits from wild creatures ("The Lord worked with them and confirmed his word by the signs that accompanied it"- Mark 16:20). You will see synchronicities and understand them to be a sign that you are on the right path, resonating with Gaia and Source. Because of this increased intuition, trust the messages that you receive and your initial thoughts and instincts. As Jesus said to his followers: "When they arrest you, do not worry about what to say or how to say it, for it will not be you speaking, but the spirit of your father speaking through you."

You will feel more connected to the cosmos through an increased sensitivity to energies and higher planes of existence. The universe will literally be able to communicate with you and your awareness of reality will be at a level high enough to interpret it. The sacred secretion is therefore a spiritual conception, of a 'virgin', if you will, as the book of Revelation states: "A great and wondrous sign appeared in heaven: a woman clothed with the sun, with the moon under her feet and a crown of twelve stars on her head. She was pregnant... Then an enormous red dragon appeared with seven heads... The dragon stood in front of the woman who was giving birth, so that he might devour her child the moment it was born." When analysed metaphorically and numerically, it can be seen that this passage is explaining that you will give birth when the Moon is in your sun sign, as the Moon is at the foot of the main constellation, out of the 12 that crowned you and influenced the stellar mineral- cell salts that clothed you at birth, when you were pure (a virgin). It is then, through the mastery of our own energy field and egotistic desires, that we can conquer the dragon, the lower self, that would otherwise consume the child/ seed.

That's not to say, however, that all will be of peace, love and light after successfully preserving one sacred secret-ion. As more light is drawn into the body, more shadows (trauma, stored negative thoughts and emotions, un-serving habits, debilitating relationships, karmic bonds, etc) are brought to the surface in order to be cleared. This is an essential part of the process, though, as releasing shadows enables more space in the body to hold light. Beings who ascend to higher levels of consciousness are also able to clear the karma/ karmic cycles of others. This happens because your DNA activations and biophotonic exchanges begin to trigger others as DNA codes are shared (discussed in Chapter 6). Sometimes, though, being in such a position can be exhausting if you have not yet learned to protect yourself from 'energy-vampires' (people who may be drawn to you for help but not yet in control of their own sovereign vibration or whose egos release feelings of pleasure at making you feel bad). Protecting yourself can be done simply by wearing protective crystals such as Tiger's Eye or Orgone, or by regularly partaking in Kundalini, visualisation or meditative practices which clear your field. It will also mean that some people and situations are forced to leave your life as they are no longer a vibratory match, so try to see all that is unfolding as happening *for* you rather than *to* you.

Basically, as we ascend and our DNA reconstructs to hold more light, it may feel like being the shuttlecock in a game of badminton as the body is constantly learning to navigate through dimensions. At which time, it is important to just allow the experience to play out and observe your needs. If the body needs more rest, grant it. If it needs more fruit, consume it.

Summary

In short, the sacred secretion is the name given to the scientific description of the physical release of Christ light codes and DMT, as well as the spiritual description of the religious story of Jesus. By taking back control of our past conditioning and increasing our understanding of collective consciousness, we become 'enlightened'. And through enlightenment we find true peace and happiness. But, just as a mother during pregnancy follows rules to keep a baby healthy, we must do the same for the spiritual child. By preserving the 'seed' within the nutritionally- dense environment, we allow it the opportunity to grow. We give it life. Therefore, the many stories of Jesus healing are, in fact, testimonies for how the sacred preservation can heal one's body and soul, from healing sight and speech to awakening the dead (cells) and finding clarity. By preserving the sacred secretion and increasing its charge during the 2.5 days that the Moon is in our star sign each month, we can trigger a highly vibrant fluid and frequency throughout our body that improves our consciousness and psychic awareness. Eventually, enough cell receptor sites and DMT- producing genes can be re-surfaced to enhance this accessibility constantly. At which time, one can consciously tap into this source energy via self-communication, such as intuition and meditation.

The purpose of the secretion of this claustrum oil is for healing. By empowering ourselves and nurturing the solar seed into strength and consciousness, we not only heal ourselves, but we send healing to the larger organism (Gaia), which in turn signals greater healing to the even larger consciousness (God- the universe). However, as humans have developed in the image of the gods, we have acquired free will. Therefore, the Christ spirit cannot merely enter our bodies and control our actions. As conscious organisms, we must make the choice to raise this secret-ion and connect to the larger energetic-functionings of the universe.

The art of preserving the spirit molecule is a lifeline provided by the cosmos in the most beautiful, metaphoric way in order to ensure that only those who have the cosmic understanding and spiritual maturity to give consent for their temple body to be used for the increase of sacred energy in this way, can. By choosing to engage with Christ consciousness, you give power to the light. It feels apt here to finish with a quote from one of the most powerful (fictional) wizards of all time: *"Happiness can be found in in even the darkest of times, if one only remembers to turn on the light" – Professor Dumbledore.*

Summary of Part 2

Within his book 'Aion', Carl Jung (1959) endeavours to describe the connection between astrology and the human soul, providing an interpretation of a piece by Sendivogius, whereby water is described as "the hiding place" of a treasure. This treasure, influenced by celestial forces, is said to be the "fire" element of awakening. Nowadays, this *treasure* is commonly termed 'the sacred secretion'. Awareness of the inner Christ residing and rising in all of us as part of a natural biorhythm of the human body is a phenomenon that has been concealed within the art and literature of mankind throughout history. This knowledge is now coming to light again, encouraged by the 5D upgrades of the collective consciousness. Therefore, preserving the sacred secretion is a spiritual process that connects the microcosm of man to the macrocosm of the universe. In order to enhance this connection, various structures and tools have been used. Part 2 of this book aimed to tie together all of the science described in Part 1 in order to elicit a range of interpretations and presentations of this spiritual practice and to illustrate evidence for its advocation from a range of sources. Next, in Part 3, I endeavour to describe some of my own tried-and-tested practices for preservation.

References

Jung, C. 1959. *Aion*. Bollingen Foundation.

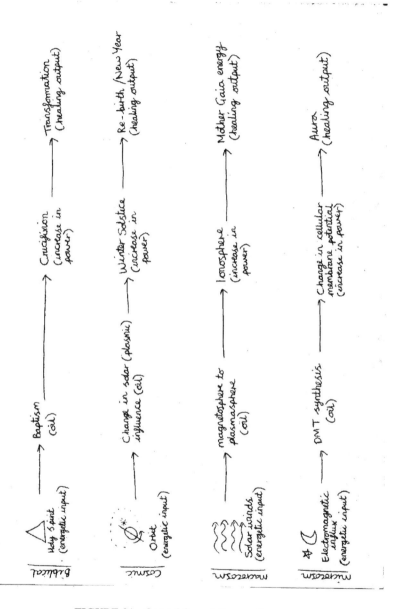

FIGURE 31 – Sacred Secret Connections

Victoria Loalou
THE ART OF PRESERVATION

Part 3

The Process of Preservation

Victoria Loalou
THE ART OF PRESERVATION

Chapter 20

Preserving the Secret-ion:
a Recipe

It is essential to preserve the sacred secret-ion in order to allow it to increase in energetic vibration, particularly during the 2 and half days of 'rest'. Some people don't even realise that they are doing this and all happens behind the scenes due to their lifestyle being so supportive. Preservation is made by healing ourselves physically, psychologically and spiritually so that we may *"Prepare the way for the Lord [by] mak[ing] straight paths for him"* [Mark 1:3]. In the modern world, we are heavily bombarded by media and advertisements, as well as hormonal manipulations (such as MSG fooling our brains into believing that rotten 'food' tastes good). Consequently, preserving the Christos is a conscious process and one that should not be taken lightly. Even the tales of Jesus himself speak of temptation and mood swings, but it's perseverance that is key (and a little forgiveness for yourself when things don't go as planned).

This chapter is a collaboration of the laws given by Jesus in the Bible for how to connect with God- consciousness and the scientific knowledge that we now have. I have also included references to my own beliefs, based on my own research and successful (and unsuccessful) practices. In the next chapter, an attempt has been made to put all of these ideologies together in the form of a preservation diary.

For now, let's explore some key points with regards to preservation.

Decalcify the Pineal

This is the most crucial factor. As the pineal is the 'throne' of God, it must be free to do its alchemical work in order to both produce, save and signal the return of the Chrism. There are two key aspects of decalcifying the pineal gland. The first is to prevent any further calcification and the second is to remove the existing calcification. Ways to de-calcify and awaken your pineal include:

Ways to de-calcify and awaken your Pineal include:

- Getting outside in the Sun

(Vitamin D is necessary to mobilise calcium throughout the body; grounding to the earth at the same time will also help to reset your circadian rhythm and provide healing frequencies to the whole body. Sunlight also aids the body in maintaining its natural electric charge)

- Sleeping in complete darkness

(This is when the Pineal produces melatonin and brain waves slow to a healing-state. It is also recommended that blue-light blocking glasses are worn after sunset in order to support the body in maintaining an accurate circadian rhythm.)

- Meditation

(This triggers the Pineal Gland to produce melatonin and DMT, thus making visions more easily obtained; meditating specifically on the idea of a healthy, fully functioning Pineal will also send the necessary signals into your body of what is required of it.)

- Filtering water

(To reduce toxins; I predominately use a distiller which I can then re-mineralise and bless. Leaving water out in the natural sunlight can also be effective at structuring it in a way that is preferable for absorption by the body.)

- Using a non-fluoride toothpaste

(To reduce intake of fluoride; at the very least, thoroughly rinse the mouth after brushing. Currently, I use a mix of bicarbonate soda and mint extract before swishing with coconut oil.)

- Consume an Iodine supplement

(This removes heavy metals and toxins from the body and supports hormone regulation. A high quality sea-weed based product from less-polluted waters is usually best, such as Icelandic Sea Kelp.)

- Eat organically

(glyphosate shuttles aluminium into the pineal and binds to minerals so that they cannot be absorbed)

I also regularly affirm that: *"My pineal is healthy and fully functioning at the optimal level for ascension of the collective consciousness."*

Mitochondria as the Mother Ship

In simple terms, molecules from the food we eat combine with oxygen and light as part of the mitochondrial electron transport chain to produce energy (adenosine triphosphate- ATP) which the body uses to stay alive. [INTERESTING NOTE: The inner mitochondrial membrane responsible for energy production is twisted into structures called cristae, which are serpent-shaped.] When grateful, we tell our body that we're safe. Dr Martin Picard, a mitochondria researcher, claims that people with the most mitochondria enzymes in their morning blood have a higher positive affect when they woke up. Furthermore, as mitochondria are responsible for energy production in the body, the quantity and quality of these organelles within us dictates our mood, our ability to heal and our overall physical appearance. Mitochondria can even be paralleled to Mother Mary as they are passed down through the mother's ancestral line only.

Studies have shown that magnetic exposure enhances nutritional intake and changes molecules within the body (as we already know). As discussed throughout this text, magnetic influence pulls apart ions and changes the chemical composition of various molecules, such as salt. Mitochondria are no exception from this, as these tiny organelles are reported to react more to electromagnetic fields than diet, so the negative impact of EMFs such as 5G, as well as the positive effects of practices such as grounding, are increasingly paramount. In addition, the glymphatic system of the body (the clearance pathway for CSF) requires well-functioning mitochondria in order to work effectively.

A point I absolutely love is also that mitochondria is believed to be the true name of the midichlorians described within the 'fictional' Star Wars movies. As more midichlorians in the body meant a stronger connection with force energy, one could speculate whether the creators of this genius series had some insider knowledge that they were trying to communicate! Especially as Anakin himself was said to have been born from immaculate conception, also.

According to Magenta Pixie (2019), who transmits information from a collective consciousness called Nine, raising this serpent energy provides a higher charge to the mitochondria, thus emitting a liquid plasma. This then begins to spin at such a high frequency that 'fire' is created and carbon-based DNA is alchemicalised into silicate-based (crystal) DNA. Following that, the pineal gland is flooded with 'liquid plasmic light' (quantum DMT), which emits a frequency synchronised with the Schumann resonance. In her book, Magenta Pixie claims that soul-families incarnate in large clusters. During the incarnated life in human form, if one of those souls enlightens their mitochondria in this way, the rest of the soul-family begin to resonate, also. In this way, we strengthen, heal and empower each other by means of awakening to become a larger (spiritual) organism. It is due to this connection that different methods of enlightenment have developed as soul-families can be at differing points within the ascension and with varying life-missions from each other. As mitochondria have a plasma membrane, and potentially emit a liquid-plasma-light which raises up the body, the mitochondria bear much comparison to ourselves on a smaller scale, as they also use the energy from their macro-organism to literally empower and enlighten both themselves and their larger organism, for the greater good of all. One form of energy goes in and another form of energy comes out in a reciprocal relationship between the microcosm and the macrocosm.

In short, mitochondria (from a physical mother) produce light (energy) which becomes pure and strengthened when ascended (up to the pineal-the throne of the father), awakening dormant-DNA (ancestral knowledge, both physical and spiritual) which can save the world (by means of awakening further soul-families and strengthening the Schumann resonance [Earth's shield and defender]). In this way, the mitochondria can be seen as mini-suns inside of us and we can be seen as mini-suns for Gaia; Earth Stars, if you will.

Dave Asprey first coined the term 'biohacks' some years back as a way of grouping practices which can be manipulated in order to stimulate a particular response from the body. Here is a list of a few biohacks which can be put into your daily routine in order to increase mitochondria levels:

- Cold Thermogenesis – This was made famous by Wim Hof, who showed how cold exposure can increase norepinephrine (noradrenaline) in the brain fivefold. Due to such, the body is able to better handle stress, heal damaged cells, improve signalling between neurons and increase resilience levels, which correspond with improved mood, energy and focus. According to Rhonda Patrick, the shock of the cold also stimulates mitochondrial reproduction as a way of enhancing survival as they burn more energy to turn into heat (basically,

416

the mitochondria panic because of the cold, so produce more of themselves so that they are more likely to stay alive if they encounter that cold again). Taking a cold shower for a few minutes a day is an easy practice for this biohack. Interestingly, a cold shower in the morning wakes you up, but a cold shower at night helps you to sleep!

- Heat Exposure – Heat acts as a mild stress signal on the body and triggers adaptation, such as increased mitochondrial capacity. Low EMF saunas are an effective means of accommodating these. (Spa day? I don't need telling twice!)

- Sleep – The brain detoxes during sleep, ridding the body of products that are damaging to mitochondria.

- Sunlight – Vitamin D is necessary for mitochondrial function and even promotes mitochondrial biogenesis.

- Red and Near-Infrared Light Therapy – These enhance the efficiency of mitochondrial energy production and improve cellular communication.

- Nutrients – Like all living things, mitochondria require certain nutrients for optimal function. These include B-vitamins, minerals (e.g. from fulvic mineral drops and Celtic sea salt), polyphenols (micronutrients found in most everyday foods such as tea, coffee, fruits and veggies), coenzyme Q10 (abundant in animal products but also found in beans, nuts and fermented foods) and creatine (rich in meat and fish but also found in vegetarian sources such as milk, peppers, shallots, mushrooms, tomatoes, cranberries and seeds), to name a few.

- Fasting – According to Adaes (2019), reducing calorie intake is the most successful way to enhance longevity and increase mitochondria efficiency.

- Exercise – When we work out it stresses our muscle mitochondria which signal for more energetic demand from the rest of the body. The body responds by signalling for increased mitochondria production. Exercise also increases biophoton exchange and loosens muscles to be able to hold more light energy, supporting the building of a grounded light body.

- Meditation – Stress can alter mitochondria structure and function. As a way of managing stress, meditation is essential. Meditation can also upregulate genes that are linked to healthy mitochondrial function (Adaes, 2019).

I also affirm to myself that: *"Health optimising mitochondria thrive and are constantly increasing in my body"* and that *"my aura is my shield"* from health deteriorating frequencies, such as 5G.

Meditation

In the beginning angels would appear and communicate to biblical prophets such as Joseph in *dreams*. Nowadays, we know that when the physical body is engaged in meditation, our brain waves mimic those of a dreaming state. Furthermore, meditation has proven to calm the mind, improve concentration, promote rational thinking, boost the immune system, heal disease, reduce stress, increase happiness, slow aging and raise the physical body's astral vibration.

Daily meditation is needed when taking control of your own mind, even if it is just for 1 minute each morning. This is particularly true during the 2.5 days of preservation, where meditation should last much longer. As the preservation days are a time of rest, it is obvious that regular meditating is one of the most crucial factors and directly influences every other point this chapter makes. Whilst the Chrism is resting, it is gaining energy. Meditation allows this energy to become more concentrated and vibrationally more powerful as the body is told to focus on this strengthening. The flow of CSF is further enhanced by mindful breathing due to the fact that it stimulates the rhythmic movement from the sacrum bone and skull, thus further energising the resting oil. It takes 12 hours for a complete circuit of CSF through your body, making conscious breathing and regular meditating essential during the preservation days so that the sacred secretion is flushed with a more energised and vibrant fluid. Furthermore, on the surface of the pineal are tiny hairs called Cilia. If CSF is accelerated by rhythmic breathing, the hairs are 'tickled', which further stimulates the pineal.

It can also be useful to listen to mantras and music during meditation to enhance the tranquil experience. Scientific studies have proven that vibrations at the appropriate frequency literally clean the cerebrospinal fluid, which bathes and constantly purifies the brain. This is due to the fact that the vibrations exert a massaging effect on the brain and facilitate the secretion of metabolic chemicals into the CSF. Vocalisation also has this effect, which supported the speedy mass evolution of the human species shortly following the development of speech. Frequencies at 432 hertz or 528 hertz are best as our bodies resonate at these frequencies, although there are many others that can alter and manipulate the vibrations of our cells in order to achieve a specific outcome. (For example, listening to 396 hertz to deal with grief or 639 hertz for re-connecting within a relationship.)

In addition to the above, as the breath controls psychophysiological and neurophysiological systems of the body, when you inhale your heart rate increases slightly and blood vessels constrict, thus activating the sympathetic system. When you exhale, heart rate decreases slightly and blood vessels dilate, returning the body to parasympathetic. From this, one can see the continual, subtle pulsation associated with the breath. Learning to control breath can therefore give an individual the power to control their body. Disciplined use of the diaphragm when breathing also massages the vagus nerve, hence stimulating every organ of the body. Alternate nostril breathing is effective for the same reasons. According to Dawson Church (2018), meditation increases levels of circulating stem cells, dissipates plaque on the brain, improves memory and attention, boosts serotonin, repairs DNA, regulates inflammation, boosts the immune system, repairs skin, bone, cartilage and muscle cells and enhances neural connections. What's more, as mentioned in Chapter 3, meditation even grows telomeres, which slows aging and increases longevity.

When I know that it is approaching the time in which the Sun and Moon energies will align and deliver the pre-cursors to the sacred secretion into my body, I make sure that I conduct a visualisation during my meditation that sets my intent. You don't need to know exactly when this alignment happens (e.g. if you are worried about the transition from Tropical to Sidereal) as you can use your intent to talk your body through the process regardless of exact timing.

Personally, I sit in meditation and tell my body that the incoming cosmic frequencies are going to change, that the Moon will soon be entering our dominating Star sign, and that it will be that time again for the coming together of the masculine and feminine energies in order to birth the sacred secretion. At this point, I would begin talking my body through the process of raising the Chrism, visualising an essence of light in my sacrum, which raises up my spine, passing each chakra, towards the brain stem. From here, I would imagine the sacred oil passing between the eyes (the place of crucifixion). I then tell my body that this precious substance must be preserved and purified within the tomb of the brain. Finally, I would remind my body that, after a few days, when the Moon energy leaves and our resonance shifts again, the sacred secretion can be released in order to heal and upgrade the body to its next stage of spiritual development, ending the visualisation with an image of my being surrounding in pure light and feelings of love.

By conducting a visualisation/ meditation in this way, you are making your body aware of the approaching shift, reminding it of how the process of preservation should plan out whilst setting your intention and consenting to the light body activation. Now, your own intention for each preservation may be different (e.g. healing trauma, releasing karma, accessing light codes for physical upgrades, etc) so feel free to set any specific preferences of your own during the meditation, instead.

The main purpose of this is to talk your body through the act so that it knows what you want it to do when the time comes and which strands of DNA to activate. During the days of preservation, I simply remind my body to preserve the sacred secretion and keep it safe, as well as meditating on the achievement of my intent. If you are unsure, guided meditations are available from my website (www.victorialoalou.com). The benefits of meditation are enhanced further when combined with yoga practices.

Kundalini

Every person's energetic signature is different, regardless of whether you call it DNA, genetics, light codes, water drops, cosmic heritage, it is your personal blueprint, and you made the choice to design it that way, just like when you start a video game and you design your character and navigate particular paths depending on what outcome you want. Ultimately, your soul will eventually try all outcome- because why not! So there are many 'spiritual' practices which aim to provide awakening or enlightenment. Depending on your soul inclination, you will be drawn to some more than others. And just like the energy we absorb from food, these practices may be good for most people or just a few. The most fun part of this game of life is learning which works for you. One of the easiest ways to test this is through the feeling of resonance. When something is right, you *know* it- you *feel* it. A practice similar to preserving the sacred secretion is that of Kundalini yoga.

According to Barbara Clow (2013) the Kundalini rise is a spiritual purification process. The rising of Kundalini has been likened to the preservation of the sacred secretion due to the vast similarities between the intentions of both and the ideology of raising dormant energy. 'Kundalini' comes from the Sanskrit word for *coiled* and is seen as a serpent- goddess energy in everyone which needs to be awakened and developed in order to realise spiritual potential. Practitioners call Kundalini yoga the *yoga of awareness*, because they claim it increases self- knowledge and unleashes the creative potential that exists within every human being.

Kundalini refers to a form of primal energy located at the base of the spine. The name derives from the ancient Hindu goddess Kundalini, a fiery female serpent that lays coiled up, asleep in the cosmic ocean, until awakened by the vibrational chanting of OM/ AUM. Once awakened, she rises up to merge with Shiva, the male energy. On a macro-scale, this story can be likened to Moon energy within the appropriate star constellation [Milky Way- cosmic river], which combines with the male energy of the Sun. On a micro-scale, this story shows similarities to the magnetic Moon energy pulling the inner Christ Oil up towards the Creator [brain]. Further clarification lies in a similar tale, whereby nectar [honey] is said to rain down on the world from the love making of Shakti and Shiva, much like the Solar [golden] Seed that enters one's body via the connecting Sun and Moon energies.

In the physical body, the Kundalini resides in the spine. The two nerve channels that intertwine around the spinal column are called the Ida (the lunar) and the Pingala (the solar). At first from the head, the Pingala and

Ida nerves release the male and female energy. These coil towards the base of the spine, acting as conductors of the Kundalini. As they intertwine, the vibrating nerves flow through each of the 7 main energy centres which align vertically down the spine. Each of these chakras is associated with a basic colour from the spectrum of light and is located at a gland in the human body, which determines the hormonal functions. From bottom to top, these chakras are referred to as Mulahara (red), Svadhistana (orange), Manipura (yellow), Anahata (green), Vishuddhi (blue), Anja (indigo) and Sahasrara (violet).

Once it reaches the base of the spine, the lunar and solar energies connect. It is then, between the Mulahara and Svadhistana chakras, within a triangular bone known as the *sacrum* that the Pingala and Ida energies unite. At this point the energy rises again and increases in vibration, unblocking and re-aligning each of the chakras on its return journey back to the top. As each chakra is awakened, the level of consciousness is elevated. Finally, when it reaches the head, it produces an "extremely profound transformation of consciousness", according to the Kundalini Master: Saraswati. This is due to the energy empowering the vibration and functioning of the pineal gland.

All biological consciousness is chemical in nature- it is controlled by the secretion of hormones and electrical communication in the brain. Therefore, when we directly raise the Kundalini, it increases the alchemical production of these chemicals; altering awareness.

The strength of this energy can be risen through meditation, yoga, chanting and righteous living. During Kundalini yoga, stagnant energy is released from the nervous system so that new and vibrant energy can flow in. It also improves the flow for Kundalini energy as is rises back to the skull. An important component of Kundalini yoga and meditation is mental focus as it deepens your awareness of the present moment. Concentration is to be fixed on the third-eye point (between the brows, where the Anja chakra lies). This stimulates the production of Kundalini energy and, thus, the secretion of chemicals from the pineal (including DMT). At the same time, the individual person must remain aware of their breath and posture so that the energy flow is not blocked. It can also be useful to listen to mind-guiding mantras (which can be found abundantly on the internet).

As everything in the universe is a form of energy, and sound is vibrating energy that our ears deliver to the brain, each mantra has its own quality, rhythm and effect. This is based on the frequency of the sound and its vibrational effect on individual chakras. Those who achieve awakening through Kundalini practice claim to feel an electric current running up their spine, like a serpent, towards the cerebellum of the brain, which is shaped like wings. Also, structurally, the snake is simply a head and spine which move in a wave-like motion. Consequently, the symbol for Kundalini is a pair of snakes entwining around what appears to be a staff, through each chakra energy centre, with a set of wings and a crown floating above the serpents' heads (similar to images of dragons). I will here emphasise that it is always recommended that Kundalini yoga is practiced in the presence of a master practitioner, as even the most minute disposition could cause an array of physiological problems.

For beginners who would like to try to access this energy but have not yet found an appropriate yoga class, some simple breathing and chanting can stimulate the vagus nerve (the nerve connecting the brain to every organ in the body) and CSF flow in an easier way. Mantak Chia has some excellent videos on YouTube for this. If you're very lucky, you may even have a professional in your area who teaches Kundalini Dance! Dancing is an excellent way to increase energy flow in the body. By moving and swaying to feel-good music, your body releases floods of mood-lifting hormones, including those that boost the immune system, and releases stagnant energy; opening you up to influxes of those newer, more resonant frequencies. Swaying your hips and waving/ spiralling your body to a specific hertz frequency also triggers cell resonance. This is why dancing works as Feng Shui (energy clearing and transmuting) for the body.

Remain Calm and Control Your Emotions

This practice compliments the meditation example detailed previously as the focus is on self-control. Jesus said that, "Anyone who is angry with his brother will be subject to judgement. First go and be reconciled to your brother, then come back and offer your gift." He emphasises settling matters quickly and moving on. This is so that the body doesn't become over-excited by the negative emotions. Therefore, during the days of preservation, focus needs to be given to allowing bodily functions to remain in a parasympathetic state (natural, secure). This is the part of the autonomic nervous system which targets the automatic functions- such as breathing, digestion and biorhythms. However, when we become angry or stressed, various chemicals (such as adrenaline and cortisol) kick in within our body that throws us into survival mode (Fight-or-Flight). Consequently, our physical body shuts down the parasympathetic system to increase the energy that it can put into the sympathetic to get us out of danger and ensure our survival. Unfortunately, these reactions prevent the body from preserving.

In the Bible it says that: "a man's enemies will be the members of his own household." These enemies are our dominating thoughts, our ego and the physical senses. Additionally, it is asked: "Why do you entertain evil thoughts in your hearts?" Instead, those within the Bible praised God who had given such authority to men as to control their physiology. As a result, during the preservation days, it is important to remain focused on positive thinking and seeing reality for what it really is, rather than through the eyes of our ego and deceiving physical senses. This is due to the fact that emotional control is absolutely vital when becoming enlightened. It not only keeps the body healthy as it prevents the over- release of stress chemicals, but it also enables us to remain objective.

It must be made cleared, though, that emotional control is not the same as *always happy*. The human body is designed to feel emotion; it is our feedback loop. Trying to ignore this will only cause suppression of energy, which equates to 'shadows'. Instead, it is recommended that energy is allowed through, to be felt and witnessed. That doesn't mean you have to play with and feed it as this can give it power. Rather, just observe it. Say hello and let it go. If lots of negative emotions arise, just sit with them and nurture your body in any way in needs or call in any

427

guides, ancestors or archetypes to support you as you could be working through a purge of shadows (a dark night of the soul) that need releasing and cleansing in order to clear your ascension path. The human body is intelligent; trust that it can do what it needs to.

Abstain from Immoral Sexual Behaviour

Mary conceived the Son of God whilst a virgin and the Bible states that Joseph had no union with Mary until she gave birth to the son, thus abstaining from sex. It should be noted, however, that 'virgin' historically simply meant *pure* and was used to describe a woman who had awakened her womb magic (see Chapter 9). Sex with a loving, honouring partner was always seen as *clean*, so did not affect this purity or 'taking' of virginity. Sex that was not conducted in this way, that was of selfish pleasure rather than joined matrimony, was deemed *immoral* or *adulterant* to the divine honouring of sacred union.

With regards to immoral sex, like the negative effects from becoming angry and stressed mentioned within the previous point, participating within such behaviours excites the body and takes the mind's attention away from being relaxed, focusing on the production of pleasure hormones such as dopamine. Instead, this sexual energy needs to be harvested.

We know that the sacred secretion is an internal alchemy and the process of turning one substance into another, such as carbon under pressure becoming a diamond. Moreover, science has shown us that thoughts, feelings, emotions and energy transfer play a crucial role in the makeup of our physical world. Thus, Sexual Alchemy is using this magic to turn sexual energy into manifestation energy. Therefore, during the days of preservation, abstaining from sexual desires will both hand the control over to the parasympathetic nervous system and allow a heightened creative awareness.

Abstaining for sexual behaviour is also common in Shamanic practice prior to performing a ritual, as a way of directing energy. As discussed in Chapter 9, abstinence is recommended the first time one attempts to preserve the sacred secret-ion. When a person, after some practice, is able to successfully channel and use this energy whilst in such a euphoric, altered state, then this can be used when necessary to increase the electrical charge of the body and sacred sex or sexual meditation may be put into practice successfully without negatively affecting the spiritual seed. Mantak Chia and Johnathan White have great content available online for exercises that improve and strengthen this clarity.

Crystal Elixirs

Crystal elixirs are basically just water that has had its structure and vibration adjusted by crystals. Crystals can hold thoughts as well as vibrations of emotions, music, colour and sound, so fully clearing, cleansing and charging the crystals used is essential. The potency of this can also be strengthened through colour-solarising the water (leaving the water in the Sun in coloured glass that reflects the desired chakra being targeted). As water has its own vibration and crystals are perfect electromagnetic influencers, crystal elixirs allow us to consume vibrant water that our own body can use for healing and re-structuring. Telling the crystal your intention for it within the elixir is good practice as thoughts can also alter the structure of water and the frequency of crystal, too. Crystals such as quartz are even used to store information and convert one form of energy into another, evidencing their energetic memory and transformational power.

Care must be taken, though, as some crystals are toxic for ingestion. Generally, the quartz family are safe (for example, using rose quartz for soothing the heart chakra or amethyst for the third eye), but always check if a crystal is safe to leave in water, first. Otherwise, just leaving the crystal next to the water or in a grid around the glass bottle is also very effective. Although elixirs only need a few minutes, they can be left longer for higher influences, such as during a full moon, new moon or when the Sun is in a particular star sign. Preparing lunar water in this way was historically known as *drinking the moon* and was considered a healing balm to restore health and infuse the soul with feminine (intuitive) light.

Orgonite is particularly effective at altering energies as it resonates with the Schumann Resonance. Hence, placing one in each corner of the room or home creates a grid that helps to eliminate radio waves and dirty electricity whilst cleansing the room's energies. Orgonite coasters can be used to charge water in a less-intrusive way than standard crystal-elixirs. [Alicia of ayaorgone.com sells some amazing hand-made orgonite (which she even has quality checked) and neutralises them with a sun ring. At the time of publication, she is also accessible on

Instagram @ayaorgone]. Personally, I have a range of orgone jewellery that I wear in order to support my body's resonance with Earth energies.

In addition to crystal elixirs, water can also be infused with solar and lunar energies in order to produce desired light codes. This is incredibly simple. All you need is a glass bottle or jar. You fill this with water and then hold it whilst setting your intention for it (e.g. to cleanse the heart chakra). This is then set outside (even better if you can place it on the earth to ground it) either in the Sun or Moon and left for at least 12 hours. You can then safely consume this water with all of those desired light codes. Obviously, certain parts of the solar-lunar cycle hold more potency for particular codes.

I always set a glass out during my sacred preservation (yes, for the whole week!) with the intention of bringing to me any downloads that I need in order to upgrade to the next stage of my activation. As solar energy structures water into the fourth phase of EZ (discussed in Chapter 4), this water is more readily absorbed and used by the cells of the body, making it the perfect delivery driver of cosmic light codes.

Maintain a Balanced Alkaline Body

As 90% of serotonin is produced in the gut and both the foods you eat and how you eat them contribute to the body's acidity levels, a natural diet whereby healthy digestion is supported is essential. During the days of preservation in particular, the body needs to put as much energy as it can spare into relaxing, resting and increasing the vibrational potency of the stored CSF. However, an alkaline diet shouldn't be a 2.5 day thing. For the full benefits, it should become part of normal, daily routine.

["Blessed is anyone who does not stumble on account of me" - Matthew 11:6]

That's not to say that you necessarily need to cut out your morning coffee (although a dash of reishi mushroom tea added to this has a reported cascade of improved health benefits), but just being more mindful of what and why you are eating will have a profound effect. Personally, I've never felt better since switching to a predominately alkaline diet and can seriously feel the effect on my energy levels when I have a 'bad' day. A study conducted by Rudolph Wiley in 1987 even showed how an alkaline diet reduced or eliminated psychological, stress-related, psychosomatic and psychogenic symptom severity in over 85% of participants.

Alkaline foods are mainly those that grow 'on the land around you', such as fruits, vegetables, beans and nuts. Strictly no alcohol (as this inhibits vasopressin) or dairy (as so much conventional dairy is full of added sugar and hormones)! For me personally, following a Paleo-Vegan diet for the 2.5 days works. Some people even choose to do a complete 3-day fast whilst preserving, although I wouldn't recommend this to anybody who hasn't practised building up to it, first.

Preservation Laws

Preservation is made by healing ourselves physically, psychologically and spiritually so that we may *prepare the way for the lord*. From the words of Jesus, preservation is enhanced from following his LAW:

1) Do not get angry. Love your enemies.

2) Don't commit adultery, even mentally.

3) Pray and meditate.

4) Fast and remain alkaline.

5) Store up treasures mentally.

6) Give to the needy (love thy neighbour).

7) Do not worry about tomorrow.

8) Do not judge or you too will be judged.

9) Do not be a hypocrite by telling others to do what you are not.

10) Ask and it shall be given.

11) A good tree produces good fruit.

12) Enter through the narrow gate.

It can be seen very clearly how these relate to the laws of chrism preservation and, hence, should be followed. Jesus then said that, "everyone who hears these words of mine and puts them into practice is like a wise man who built his house on a rock." So hear these words and follow the rules of preservation that were lost for so many centuries but are now coming to light in the Age of Aquarius. From research and personal experience, I have found the following to be the most effective ways of preservation, to date:

1) Practise the art of having a positive, growth mindset. (Learning the rules of the Law of Attraction are particularly beneficial here.)

2) Practise being grateful and emitting love as these are the highest forms of positive vibration.

3) Pray and meditate to calm the mind and enhance oxygen intake (a key component of the DMT molecule).

4) Maintain an alkaline diet, eating Paleo if you can (the less effort your body has to put into digestion and de-toxifying, the more it can focus on healing and preservation).

5) Engage in feel good activities, including exercise, to increase purification levels.

6) Commit to acts of kindness to promote feel-good hormones and a vibrant aura.

7) Be present and live in the moment to raise your unique awareness and wider perception.

8) See the bigger picture in life so that righteous actions are increased.

9) Practise what you preach so that no awkward-feeling hormones are dropped into the blood stream or conflicting energies.

10) Live with expectation, knowing that you are on the right path for you right now.

11) Eat organically to reduce the intake of toxins, such as pesticides and heavy metals.

12) Incorporate moments of deep breathing throughout the day, in nature if you can, to increase oxygen levels for the synthesis of those all-important DMT molecules and to restore the body to its natural relaxed state.

13) Reduce EMF exposure as these can negatively influence the natural cycle that should be running according to lunar energy, not your Wifi box. I would recommend keeping your phone on airplane mode, turning the Wifi off at night and grounding/ earthing as much as possible away from interfering fields such as phone towers to re-sync your body with the Earth's natural PEMF, as equally influenced by astronomical bodies such as the Sun and Moon.

Regardless of your unique spirit-path, these guidelines for preservation are appropriate to all, whether to raise the sacred oil or even just to optimise mental and physical health. Enhanced pineal activations will also reveal the living blueprints of your soul. These are all different to support the different pillars of the ascension and cycles of Gaia. It is for this reason that, when something doesn't resonate, we should consider this as a positive, as it confirms a truth for you. This process is a slow and steady one, upgrading as an amount just right for your moist optimal ascension timeline.

References and Bibliography

Church, D. 2018. *Mind To Matter*. Hay House.

Clow, B. 2013. *Astrology and the Rising of Kundalini*. Bear & Co.

Jindrak, K. and Jindrak, H. 1988. Mechanical Effect Of Vocalization Of Human Brain An Meninges. 25(1): pages 17-20. Medical Hypotheses.

Pixie, M. 2019. *The Black Box Programme and the Rose Gold Flame as Antidote*. Independently Published.

Chapter 21

My Preservation Diary

During the early stages of my spiritual development, I remember explaining to my partner that when I get really into a deep meditation, I hit a point where I can't go any further. I described it as feeling like I just needed to 'tip over', but an un-explainable feeling similar to anxiety prevented me from being able to. The emotions of excitement, confusion and disappointment brewed within me until I read *DMT and the Soul of Prophecy.* Here, on page 41, Rick Strassman (2014) described my exact feeling at that point in every meditation. Yet, it was being analysed in correspondence to his volunteers' experiences on DMT. This consolidated for me that the emotion I was feeling was due to not having enough endogenous DMT in my system to be able to 'let go' and reach those higher states. It is my belief, then, that by preserving the sacred secretion for long enough to turn up the thermostat, one can tune into the cosmic field of knowledge, just like the prophets and messengers of God recorded throughout history.

That said, every single human body is unique and different, so although this chapter specifies some of my personal practices, it is necessary for one to adapt these to their own body. What's more, this is my personal diary, but even this alters on a monthly basis depending on how I feel physically and what I want to focus on spiritually, so never feel like this is a set-in-stone way of living for the rest of your life. Eventually, it will become second-nature and you will receive the right information from your body and the universe on what you need to practice each month.

You can set intentions for each monthly journey, too, if you are trying to manifest something in particularly or nurture a specific project. Personally, I like to just tap in and tell my body to use this Christed essence for the greater good of myself and the collective, to support the transmutations of shadows into light. Once you've set an intention, you can just go about your everyday business and rituals, holding the knowing that the metaverse will bring you into alignment with circumstances and situations that will influence the spirit-molecule's chemical brew in a way that best supports your intentions. Obviously, these can sometimes be tests of will from your shadow self, so it is important that you learn to really embody your own knowing so that you are aware of the difference.

As an Intermittent Fasting- Paleo-Veggie (and part-time Ketogenic) dieter, I consume a majorly alkaline- balanced diet in my day-to-day life. It is during my 2.5 day preservation period, that I will fast more, depending on how my body is feeling at the time. It is absolutely essential that you listen to your physical-self and prepare for any cleanse. If not managed properly, cleansing can cause serious health issues. In the days building up to the preservational cleanse, I try to eat more mindfully and alkalise as much as possible. For 48-72 hours prior to my preservation days, I also minimalise my caffeine intake and meditate more frequently. It is good practice during this preparation time to be more positive by monitoring your thoughts and staying present. I wear a small mushroom ring on my little finger, which reminds me to come back to the moment each time I see it.

At the end of this chapter I have included a table of a possible run-down of a basic preservation for me (again, remember that this is very generalised). Although this isn't necessary, when I started I wanted a plan that I could build upon and personalise. Therefore, there is a blank column here where you may make your own notes about things you think will/ will not work for you, or ideas that download into your energy field whilst you read.

As preserving the sacred secretion is a purification process, it's best to build up to your ideal physical vehicle so that you do not get lots of detoxing effects (often manifesting as physical illness). I was the world's worst for poor diet and was on a straight path to diabetes when I discovered the sacred secretion, so I speak from honest experience when I say that it is easier to start by adding the 'good' stuff in rather than completely cutting all of the 'bad' stuff out. Eventually, you won't even crave that chocolate or TV show anymore because it will no longer resonate with your path. So just start simple with those aspects of cleansing that are achievable for you right now and gradually build up.

It has taken me years to get to this point in preservation, and I'm still learning and adapting constantly. As your thoughts generate more power than your diet, it is important that you remain as calm and stress-free as possible during the cleansing days in particular. It is meant to be a time of rest and detoxifying; both physically and mentally. Therefore, if fasting is making you miserable, remember that this isn't maintaining an alkaline environment. Feeling happy and positive is far more important than resting the digestive tract. And, epigenetically, your body may just not be able to fast well! Instead, your body may be able to raise the oil in other ways, depending on its own genetic imprint, such as via the fruitarian route or by simply being mindful and not overindulging. Preservation is a gradual progress, and not one to be taken lightly. It takes preparation, commitment and time to unknot previously limiting thoughts and habits in order to strengthen newer, healthier ones. But good things come to those who wait and building up the DMT thermostat gradually is necessary for gradual evolution.

If you are in a position where you are able to fast and sun-gaze during the preservation days and feel good during this: perfect. If not, don't sweat it. Everybody is different and can preserve at different levels. My body now craves the preservational cleanse and I feel good when I get there, my monthly bleed has even synchronised with my preservation time, so this is a really powerful cleanse and purification phase for me. But it has taken a lot of trial, error and practice. Learning to control your mind and body is the first step and should be part of daily life, not just during the preservation days. I remember a particular bank holiday weekend when the Moon entered my star-sign but I had social plans on every day, including a music festival on the Saturday. At times like these, when the pros of preservation do not outweigh the cons, just do what you can. That weekend, I just tried to laugh as much as I could and was extra grateful. I saw no synchronicities but won £40 on a scratch card: so was still winning at life!

My point is, go at your own pace and listen to your body; you'll know whether the messages are from the healing Universe or the devouring Dragon. And as every soul-family's genetic blueprint is different, how my body saves the seed may be different to yours. It can also be difficult to explain this phenomenon to those who are in a complete state of ignorance or who have no interest in the subject. Therefore, it can be easier to merely say that these days are 'cleansing days' to avoid any negative comments that may cause conflicting emotions at this time. As it says in Matthew 6:17-18: *"But when you fast, put oil on your head and wash your face, so that it will not be obvious to others that you are fasting, but only to your Father, who is unseen; and your Father, who sees what is done in secret, will reward you."* Thus, sharing your knowledge with those who are ready to hear it is always a good idea as it is likely divine timing and entanglement which has brought you together. However, knowing when to protect your own self-worth is just as important. Like it said above, only the Father needs to see what is done in order to reward you.

It is difficult to describe the emotions felt after a successful preservation of the sacred secretion, but I will try my best; just remember that your biorhythms run differently to mine and your soul may be seeking very different levels, so you may well experience very different clues. But for me, typically, following the re-birth, my senses become heightened (I literally feel as though I am aware of every electron whirling around me), my dreams become far more vivid, my meditation sessions become more intense and I see more synchronicities such as number patterns and songs on the radio (during one preservation period, I was meditating outside and the same bird kept flying passed and around me, over and over). In addition, I feel more in-sync with the world and a strong sense of understanding, as if I know that I am doing the right thing. Since beginning my journey of monthly preservation periods, I have noticed that I am able to reach the 'higher states' during my meditation sessions (you know, the ones that feel like an orgasm in your head) much quicker. Here, I feel more connected to the universe and come out of the meditation full of euphoric love. It is during the preservation days and the few that follow that I tend to receive more specific communication from the universal energy field. These messages have included the titles and cover pages for my books, people I need to reach out to and even confirmations to thoughts and ideas that I had been considering.

Signs that you are upgrading include, but are not limited to:

- Memories (past life, ancestral, Akashic) being activated
- Increase synchronicities presenting themselves
- Light-headedness and tingling (although these can also be signs of toxic electromagnetic influence or environmental poisoning, so tap into yourself to feel if these are positive or negative symptoms)

- The heart feeling open and prolonged feelings of love and gratitude
- The physical senses feeling more powerful and brighter
- Being aware of elementals and light beings, such as fairies
- Rushes of warmth through your body
- More powerful meditations
- Vivid dreams
- Vast life changes as energies shift
- Changes in food cravings
- Increased thirst
- A strong desire to be outside

As I started to hold more light, I remember becoming increasingly frustrated at trying to verbalise what I could see and feel in my body, rather than simply being able to send and receive these (the DNA blueprint of telepathy) as well as having to physically travel (the blueprint memory for bilocation and teleportation). I would also go through stages of feeling like eating was incredible effort (the genetic markings for sun-eating and photosynthesising). Whilst delving deeper into myself and the spiritual literature, it became evident that these were just the awakening memories from a time when such phenomena were not only possible but were the norm.

If all of this seems too much to take on, note that it has taken ups and downs to get to this point in my life and, as with everything, your body may react differently to mine and have varying requirements. I may not even have it right myself as I'm still learning all of the time, as every single human being is. Listen to your body and your soul and follow the path that makes you feel most connected. If nothing else, make these days a time to focus on YOU. Note, though, that it is essential not to 'push' anything to happen when attempting to reach enlightenment. I learned this the hard way. After having a very successful meditation session one day whilst on holiday, I spent months pushing and pushing, trying to force my mind into reaching this higher state again, as it truly was the best emotional experience of my life. It wasn't until researching the sacred secretion that I began to 'let go'. Lo and behold; these are now regular occurrences of mine. So don't force it. Take your time.

For more information on when the Moon will enter your star sign, you can find a table for each on my website, www.victorialoalou.com, or you can follow www.moontracks.com. You can also download the following apps:

- TimePassages (this uses your location to detail the exact time that various cosmic bodies, including the Moon, are dominating according to the Tropical zodiac system)
- SkyView (this is great for identifying specific constellations and seeing where cosmic bodies are according to the Sidereal system)
- Deluxe Moon (this is good for comparing the location of the Moon, Sun etc within all three zodiac systems described in Chapter 5). You can also skip into the future in order to make note of when your future preservation periods occur.

Remember, many people successfully preserve the sacred secretion without even being aware of it, evidencing that there is no wrong way or right way: you will just *know*.

	V.L.	**NOTES**
Preparing the way for the Lord. Typically two to three days before the start of the rest days.	• Reiki massage to clear energy blockages • Meditation for mental preparation • Alkaline eating to purify • Grounding to enhance connection with Gaia • Increase melatonin intake (usually Tart Cherry Juice) • Minimise caffeine intake to enhance the parasympathetic state • Consume more water to cleanse and flush • Stimulate mitochondria production, e.g. through exercise, saunas • Partake in yoga practice to increase CSF flow (and delivery of the oil) • Set intentions for the practice	
Rest days. About 2.5-3 days.	In addition to the above: • Fast for as long as comfortable each day • Increase meditation and mindfulness practices to provide moments of rest • Breathing techniques to increase oxygen levels	

	• Allow longer for sleeping, having afternoon naps when possible • Ground more and walk in forests to improve oxygen quality • Sun-gazing to increase Vitamin D levels and pineal health	
Re- Awakening. A further 2 days (allowing for transition between different astronomy systems).	In addition to the above: • Identify any revelations from the last few days • Keep a notepad by the bed to note any interesting dreams • Consume the crystal elixir brewed whilst the Moon and Sun sign were connected	
Other notes	• No alcohol as this prevents the release of vasopressin. • Particular focus should be given during the month of birth when the Sun is also in your star sign, thus aligning all three energies (the sacred trinity), as the spiritual seed will be particularly strong and potent at this time. • DANCE! Dancing is a beautiful way of increasing energy flow in the body, including CSF, and lubricating your joints. It also provides a massive mood boost!	

FIGURE 32 – Preservation Plan

Summary of Part 3

According to Jordan Peterson (2018), order and chaos must co-exist. Accepting this fact opens one to the possibility of transforming chaos into order. So, in a world where we are constantly bombarded with negative news stories, one must realise that accepting defeat is not an option, and we must all step up out of the chaos so that we can create order. This is also one of the key principles when aspiring to 5D consciousness: acceptance.

There are countless adaptations to the spiritual practice of preserving the sacred oil, which has caused a lot of controversy regarding the 'true' way to God. However, if anything this highlights that there is no *true* way; we are all unique and for valid reasons. We cannot create an entire macro-organism from one type of blood cell or variant of cristae in mitochondria or species of bacteria. Each have different purposes, motives and realms of consciousness and are essential for overall health, performance and awareness. In the same way, a vast range of humans manifest, too.

Part 3 of this book aimed to detail some of the common strategies and techniques used to preserve the inner Christ. In addition, examples are given of some of my own routines that could offer a starting point for anybody unsure of the first steps in their journey. As well as what is presented in this book, my best efforts are put into trying to keep my website (www.victorialoalou.com) and Instagram (@victorialoalou) updated with all that I learn along this life journey, so checking in with these is recommended for regular updates.

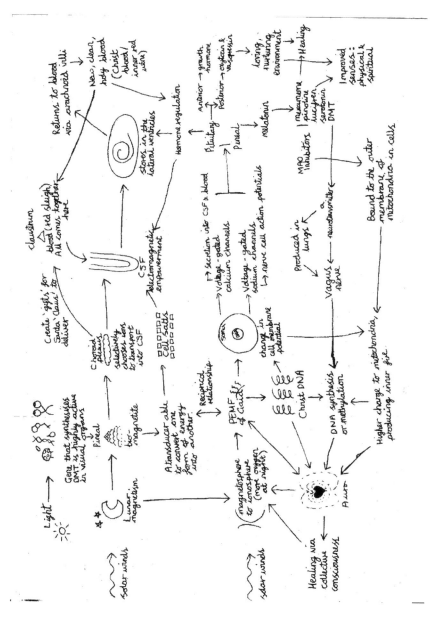

FIGURE 33 – Summarising Concept Map

Conclusion

In this fast-paced modern life, so many people have become distanced from their true nature. We lost our power and understanding of the natural rhythm of being human. Our intuition became dormant and our insight irrelevant. We swapped ritual for routine and forgot that we, too, are a part of nature. There is a time for rest and a time for play, a time for high-energy and a time for reflection. It is the following of cycles that enables us to grow. When we fight against this flow, life can lose meaning and purpose. Preserving the sacred secretion is a chance for you to take time, just once a month, to re-calibrate; to really *feel* your power and connection. After all, living in love and awe is the ultimate devotion to God, creation and yourself. In the Gospel of Mary, God is the *good* and the good is not separate from us.

The sacred secretion is both an oily and plasmic substance that equates to quantum- DMT for both humans and Gaia. When the masculine and feminine energies (and corresponding physical biochemicals) of the human body intertwine, the awareness-enhancing 'child of light' is born and raised to crucifixion, in order to cleanse the body of sin (and cellular damage). By preserving this substance, the Christos is empowered. Following awakening and ascension, a person's spiritual signature is strengthened. Over time, the repetition of this practice, alongside the encouragement of such amongst others, gives power to the collective consciousness of the Earth.

From the research presented in this book, it can be seen that raising and preserving the sacred secret-ion is one of many paths one could take in achieving enlightenment and reconnecting with their collective soul-family. What separates raising the Chrism in this way from other spiritual practices is its strong connection to the cosmos and the alignment of our closest celestial body (the Moon) with that of our life-giving star (the Sun) and our nearest influencing astronomical bodies (the planets and zodiac belt). By synchronising our own microcosmic body with the larger Mother Gaia and further expanding macrocosmic life of the Father, we are not only able to access support from the universe, but we also give back by strengthen it. Just like each human relies on the smaller organisms that are the building blocks of themselves, so is each living thing on this planet an organism supporting to health of Gaia.

I recently heard a beautiful theory from Randall Carlson which resonated with me tremendously. He stated that humans are indeed the Guardians of Earth, as detailed within the creation story of the Old Testament. When one considers the fact that the natural cycles of the universe means that the Earth in bombarded with asteroids and meteors every few thousand years which devastates most life, and that the planet is in itself a larger living organism trying to survive and protect the life it has created as a macro-Mother, it seems obvious that the planet would manifest an organism with intelligence that would benefit the whole world by inventing technology (physically or spiritually) that would divert such a catastrophe.

Consider yourself, for a moment. You are a conscious being, who increases the consumption of nutrients and supplements which support the health of beneficial smaller organisms within yourself, e.g. sauerkraut for Bifidobacteria. In this way we are consciously influencing the types of organisms that manifest within our own living cells in order to generate coherence. In accordance with the Law of Polarity, there must be negative to balance the positive. Without an awareness of what makes us feel bad, we would be unaware of what makes us feel good. It is the slow and steady awakening of one's self that leads to so much good that the bad becomes irrelevant. And that is where Randall Carlson claims we are moving towards now. Ignorance is no longer bliss and the vast majority of humans no longer want to throw plastic into the oceans, kill animals for pleasure or cut down forests. As a species, we are waking up.

To summarise, Gaia is a living organism which is consciously manifesting more intelligent life in the form of humans, who are required to work as guardians to protect the rest of the planet. Just like the organisms residing within our own human-bodies depend on each other, so does all life on Earth. The planet's manifestation could have been of terrestrial evolution (through such phenomena as bringing man and mushroom/ DMT together for neurogenesis) or extra-terrestrial (if Gaia had called for help by way of signalling the consciousness of other worldly beings to spore the planet) origin. Either way, the planet needed support in maintaining perfect health and upgrading to the next level of consciousness so it sought the supplementary material required to do so; just as we would on a microcosmic level.

Although there are some occasional errors in judgement which may cause a slight turn for the worst (like rogue cells turning into cancer) our worst days are always our biggest lessons. After all, once rock-bottom has been hit, the only way left to go is back up. According to Dennis McKenna, we are being helped along the way by the sentient beings of Earth who are still physically rooted into the Mother. He even believes that it is the plants who think they have domesticated humans due to the fact that they communicate with us chemically and are spreading all around the world (such as the availability of ayahuasca in vast countries, not just Peru, nowadays) in order to support Gaia (her healing and ascension) like our own chemical messengers between cells.

Randall Carlson believes the Earth has nurtured the evolution of an organism smart enough to develop machines which can prevent the bombardment and destruction of the planet's life via cosmic collision, which has happened so many times before in history. Thus, even though there is no doubt that there are corporations and 'families' (some would even claim *reptilians*) which exert their influence on the planet through fear mongering, power and control, history teaches us that good always prevails. And it always will. In the words of Matt Kahn: *The light has already won.*

This is further evidenced by the increased resonance between planets and constellations and the return of energies such as those from Chiron, Sedna and Aquarius, which remind us that we are currently going

451

through an era of purging, both individually and collectively. Materialism and the dark agendas from the past have dominated and encrypted our light DNA, but our prayers are being answered. Due to the fact that we reside within a slice of the matrix which currently abides by the laws of time, it has felt like a slow movement. Now, however, we are reawakening at incredible speed. Our power and ability to work together collectively has been underestimated. We are collectively recalibrating our light bodies with the frequencies of Gaia and Source and returning to a reciprocal relationship, focused on love, gratitude and trust. Our souls, from whatever parts of the matrix they have previously gained knowledge from, chose to incarnate here to support the upgrade of Gaia by reactivating our own energies and working with those of other way-showers. When enough of us are ionising and radiating energy within ourselves that emit the 5D resonance and beyond, Gaia's ascension will accelerate and the forces that live from the dark will no longer be able to survive on the planet.

Within the Gospel of Mary, Magdalene explains that, at the end of the Age (of Pisces), all will return to being one and connected, as a fractal of the original, divine blueprint (DNA). She describes how the good enters your heart and returns from your heart back to source. The heart is our true treasure which we must build up in heaven (the divine energy field). This is why the Egyptians favoured the heart over the brain. Mary Magdalene continues, stating that Christ is within and must be sought from the inside, at which point, we become free from the chains of forgetfulness.

This is similar to the book of Revelations, which describes the end of the Age of Pisces as now. We are part of a huge shift in consciousness as part of the interconnected collective consciousness of Gaia. We are light, descended into physical form on this planet with a great mission. Just like you may choose those organic blueberries over the croissant for breakfast for the greater good of your body, Gaia has chosen us as the living organisms to support her own vehicle upgrade. Simply being aware of our existence, supporting others and taking action to both give and receive resonance from the Earth and its ionosphere is enough. We may not all be destined to be prophets who will live forever in physical history books, but we will all sleep in peace knowing that we are collectively strengthening the Earth with our own energy; like mitochondria in the macro-form. We are the force; whether we choose to use that to serve the light or the dark is a choice of free will. The preservation of the sacred secretion within oneself affirms that we are here in the image of God; we are the children of light; we are the guardians of Gaia; and we will not let her down.

God bless

X

Glossary

Akashic Record

Collective cosmic memory.

Anatomy

The structure of organisms and their parts.

Astrophysicists

Scientists who study the relationship between physics and astronomy.

Atom

The basic unit of matter and the defining structure of everything.

Bio-Magnetite

Magnetite minerals in the brain that respond to electromagnetic influences.

Black Hole

Densest known matter in the metaverse.

Cell Salts

Salt-like compounds that increase the conductivity of CSF.

Cerebrospinal Fluid

A clear, colourless liquid that flows along the nervous system, cushioning the brain, circulating nutrients filtered from the blood and removing waste from the brain.

Chakras

Energy centres within the body that vortex.

Chrism

Another name for the Sacred Secretion.

Christ Oil

Another name for the Sacred Secretion.

Claustrum

A thin sheet of neurons in the centre of the brain. Where the Secretion begins its journey.

Conditioning

A learned procedure that elicits a biological response that is paired with past experiences.

Constellations

Star clusters that form an image.

Cortisol

A steroid hormone often referred to as the 'stress hormone'.

Cosmic Womb

The spiritual and energetic birthing portal at the centre of the metaverse. Correlates with black holes.

CSF

An abbreviation for Cerebrospinal Fluid.

Decalcification

The process of removing excess calcium build up.

DMT

A natural molecule produced by every living thing. It can be synthesised as a powerful psychedelic drug.

Earthing

The act of putting bare feet on the earth to absorb nutrients and release toxins.

EMF

An abbreviation of Electromagnetic Fields

Endocrine Alchemy

Spiritual science behind the teachings of alchemy, with the 'lab' being the human body.

Essenes

A historic civilisation who taught the way of the sacred secretion preservation.

Equinox

When the length of day and night are equal.

Gaia

The name given to the collective energies of Mother Earth and all of its connected organisms that depend on one another as a complex, integrated system.

Gnosis

Referring to a direst 'knowing'.

Gnostics

A collection of religious ideas and systems which originated in the first century AD.

Great Year

The length of time it takes the Sun to travel around the entire zodiac.

Grounding

See 'Earthing'.

Ida

A nerve channel on the left side of the body (also see 'Kundalini' and 'Pingala').

Ion

An atom with unequal protons to electrons.

Ionosphere

At atmospheric layer of the Earth.

Kundalini

A form of spiritual practice in which energy is preserved and risen in the main chakras, usually through yoga and breathwork.

Law Of Attraction

The natural law of the universe that governs how like attracts like.

Magnetosphere

At atmospheric layer of the Earth.

Mass

How we measure the amount of matter.

Matter

Physical substance; the stuff in the universe. It occupies space and has mass.

MCT Oil

A medium-chain fatty acid compound that is easily digested and used by the body for energy.

Medulla

A long stem-like structure that makes up part of the brain stem.

Melatonin

A molecule naturally produced in the body that has many responsibilities, including the regulation of sleep cycles.

Meditation

The practice of calming the mind.

Mindfulness

The act of living in the moment and being present.

Mitochondria

Tiny organelles that reside in every cell of the human body.

Molecule

A combination of atoms.

Neurons

Cells within the central nervous system that carry messages as electrical impulses.

Neurotransmitters

Chemical messengers within the body which transmit signals through neurons.

Oil of Gladness

Another name for the Sacred Secretion.

Particle

A minute portion of matter.

PEMF

Abbreviation for Pulsed Electromagnetic Fields.

Photons

Light particles.

Physiology

The study of the functions and mechanisms of the body.

Pineal Gland

A small structure in the brain that secretes hormones and chemicals into the CSF, notably melatonin.

Pingala

A nerve channel of the right side of the body (also see 'Kundalini' and 'Ida').

Pituitary Gland

A small structure in the brain that produces many hormones, such as oxytocin, and stimulates other glands to produce other hormones.

Plasmasphere

At atmospheric layer of the Earth within the magnetosphere.

Precession

A change in orientation of the rotational axis of a rotating body, such as planet Earth.

Priestess

A woman who devotes her life to embodying spiritual teachings and performs ceremonies and rituals whilst practicing the feminine healing arts.

Receptors

Chemical structures that receive and transduce signals.

Revelations (The Book Of)

A book within the New Testament that occupies the central place in Christian eschatology.

Sacred Secretion

The process of preserving DMT charged CSF to reach higher planes of thought.

Serotonin

A molecule naturally produced by the body that has many responsibilities, including adjusting our mood.

Shakti

From the Sanskrit word meaning 'life force'. Also the name of the Tantric goddess for creation.

Shamanism

Practice that allows a practitioner to reach altered states of consciousness in order to interact with the spirit world and bring healing.

Solstice

When the Sun appears to reach is most Northern or Southern peak relative to the equator.

Vertebrae

An irregular bone with a complex structure in the spinal column.

Witch

A healer and wise woman in a community, usually able to travel to other dimensions and use communication with ancestors, spirit animals and nature to bring healing and wisdom.

Womb Awakening

Reconnecting the physical womb with ancestral wombs, the Earth Womb and Cosmic Womb.

Yeshua

The original Hebrew spelling of Latin name Jesus. Referring to a Biblical figure.

Zodiac

An area of the sky that is followed by the Sun's annual path. The paths of the Moon and visible planets are also within the Zodiac.

About the Author

Victoria Loalou is a primary school teacher from Essex, England, with a Master's Degree in Mental Well-being and a desire to support the developing minds of the next generation. Victoria's vision board for the future includes involvement with a group of professionals to develop a teacher well-being programme, aimed at developing positive psychology within schools across the country, as well encouraging support groups between pupils in schools which promote self-empowerment and sisterhood/ brotherhood. Her dream is for children to have a more positive self-image and outlook of the world so that they feel more empowered to pursue their dreams, whilst spreading kindness and love.

Alone, Victoria could only impact 30 children a year.

Together, we can impact thousands.

So if the words of this book resonate with you, please follow Victoria Loalou's Instagram page [@victorialoalou] for regular updates and advice regarding the natural laws of the universe, holistic health and positive well-being (and, of course, the sacred secretion). By building a community together, we can increase the collective consciousness, enlighten one-another and support the strengthening of the conscious field of Gaia.

Victoria Loalou is always open to feedback regarding the theories provided within her books. Please contact her directly via her personal Instagram page (@victorialoalou) or email (info@victorialoalou.com) for any queries.

Also by Victoria Loalou

Saint Claustrum

A short, sweet but enlightening book about the origins and symbolisms behind the traditional Christmas celebrations.

Bibliography

Aberts, B., Hopkins, K., Jonson, A., Morgan, D., Raff, M., Roberts, K. and Walter, P. 2019. *Essential Cell Biology.* 5th Ed. WW Norton and Company.

Adaes, S. 2019. Mitochondria: 10 ways to boost the powerhouse of your cells. [online] Available at: <draxe.com>

Aderin-Pocock, M. 2018. *Book of the Moon.* Penguin House.

Alberts, B., Hopkins, K., Johnson, A., Morgan, D., Raf, M., Roberts, K. and Walter, P. 2019. *Essential Cell Biology. 5th Ed.* Norton & Company.

Allegro, J. 1970. *The Sacred Mushroom and the Cross.* Hodder and Stroughton Limited, London.

Al-Khalili, J. 2012. Quantum: A Guide for The Perplexed. Orion Books.

An Artabras Book. *Leonardo Da Vinci.* Reynal and Company.

Anderson, S. with Cryan, J. and Dinan, T. 2017. *The Psychobiotic Revolution.* National Geographic.

Asprey, D. Biohacker: How To Become The Ultimate Super Human [podcast]. *London Real.* 6 October 2019.

Axe, J. 2019. *Keto Diet.* Orion Spring.

Axelrod, J. et al. 1983. The Pineal Gland And Its Endocrine Role. NATO Advanced Science Institutes Services.

Banks et al. 2017. Telomere length and salivary DNA methylation after 48 hours of sleep deprivation. *Journal of Sleep Research.* 26(S1): p.11.

Barnard, N. Your Body In Balance: Will a Vegan Diet Improve Your Health? [podcast]. *London Real*. 27 October 2019.

Bassano, M. 1993. *Healing With Music and Colour*. Red Wheel.

Bauval, R. and Hancock, G. 1996. *Keeper of Genesis*. Heinemann.

Bauval, R. and Gilbert, A. 1994. *The Orion Mystery: Unlocking the secrets of the pyramids*. Arrow.

Becker, R. and Seldon, G. 1985. *The Body Electric*. Harper Collins Publishers.

Bertrand, A. and Bertrand, S. 2017. *Womb Awakening*. Bear and Co.

Bikman, B. Physiological Effects of the Ketogenic Diet [podcast]. *Take Control of Your Health*. 14 April 2019.

Billington, P. 2011. *The Path of Druidry*. Llewellyn Publications.

Blanco, D. 2019. *Our cells are filled with 'junk DNA'- Here's why we need it*. [online] Available at: <www.discovermagazine.com>

Boland, Y. 2016. *Moonology*. Hay House.

Bonacci, S. *Chemistry of the Living Tissues- The Twelve Zodiacal Cell Salts*. Available online at: <https://universaltruthschool.com/syncretism/celltissue-salts/>

Bonacci, S. Secret of Secrets: The Elixer of Life, hiding in the Bible. *MrAstrotheology*. [YouTube] 14 August 2012

Bonacci, S.Santos Bonacci talks on Cell Salt Deficiencies and Facial Diagnosis. *Circle Healing Network*. [YouTube] 15 February 2016

Borowsky, B., Adham, N. and Jones, K. et al. 2001. Trace Amines: Identification of a Family of Mammalian G-Protein- Coupled Receptors. *Proc Natl Acad Sci USA*. 98:pp. 8966-8971.

Brogaard, B. 2013. *Remembering Things From Before You Were Born*. Available online at: < https://www.psychologytoday.com/intl/blog/the-superhuman-mind/201302/remembering-things-you-were-born>

Brogaard, B. 2015. Q&A: Berit Brogaard on Unlocking Your Brain's Superhuman Abilities. Available online at:<https://www.inverse.com/article/5716-q-a-berit-brogaard-on-unlocking-your-brain-s-superhuman-abilities>

Brogaard, B. and Marlow, K. 2015. The Superhuman Mind. Hudson Street Press.

Brogaard, B. 2016. Can We Access The Memories Of Our Ancestors Through Our DNA? Available online at: <https://www.vice.com/en_au/article/ypv58j/genetic-memory>

Bryson, C. 2006. The Fluoride Deception. Seven Stories Press. US.

Burgoyne, T.2013. The Light Of Egypt, Volume 1 and 2. Martino Publishing.

Bynum, E. 2012. Dark Light Consciousness. Inner Traditions.

Campbell, D. 2001. The Mozart Effect: Tapping the power of music to heal the body, strengthen the mind and unlock creative spirit. William Morrow And Company.

Carey, G. The Zodiac and the Twelve Salts of Salvation. Republished 2013 by Martino Publishing.

Carey, G. and Perry, I. God Man: The Word Made Flesh. Republished 2013 by Martino Publishing.

Carey, N. 2012. The Epigenetics Revolution. Icon Books.

Card, D. 2004. Facial Diagnosis of Cell Salt Deficiencies. Kalindi Press.

Carlson, R. 2017. Catastrophes of Ancient Earth. [podcast] Earth Ancients. 17 August 2017.

Carlson, R. 2018. New Evidece of Catastrophic Global Floods. [podcast] Earth Ancients. 11 August 2018

Carlson, R. 2019. Cataclysms, The Holy Grail and The Holes in The Human Story. [podcast] The Higherside Chats.

Chang, P. 2019. Word Magic. Esoteric Knowledge Publishing.

Chang, S. 1986. *The Tao Of Sexology.* Atlantic Books, London.

Chavez, J. 2017. *Questions for the Lion Tamer 1.* Independently Published.

Chavez, J. 2018. *Questions for the Lion Tamer 2.* Independently Published.

Chia, M. 2018. Mantak Chia- Sexual Energy. *London Real.* Available on YouTube and on the London Real podcast. 28 January 2018.

Chopra, D. 1989. *Quantum healing: exploring the frontiers of mind/ body medicine.* Bantam.

Church, D. 2018. *Mind To Matter.* Hay House.

Colleen, A. 2016. *10% Human: How Your Body's Microbes Hold The Key To Health and Happiness.* William Collins.

Cooper, J. 2016. *Chinese Alchemy.* Hodder and Stoughton.

Cowan, T. Dr Mercola Interviews Dr Cowan on the New Biology of Water [podcast]. *Take Control of Your Health.* 13 October 2019.

Cozzi, , N., Mavlytov, T., Thompson, M. and Ruoho, A. 1999. Indolethylamine N-methyltransferase expression in primate nervous tissue. *University of Wisconsin: School of Medicine and Public Health.*

Cremante, S. 2006. *Leonardo Da Vinci: The Complete Works.* A David Charles Book.

Crick, F. and Kock, C. 2005. What is the function of the claustrum? 360 (1458): p. 1271-1279. Philosophical transactions of the Royal Society of London B: Biological Sciences.

Currivan, J. 2017. *The Cosmic Hologram.* Inner Traditions.

Dean, C. 2017. *The Magnesium Miracle.* Ballantine Books.

Dean, J. et al. 2019. Biosynthesis and Extracellular Concentrations of N,N-dimethyltryptamine (DMT) In Mammalian Brain. *Scientific Reports.* 9:9333.

Devlin, T. 2011. *Textbook of Biochemistry.* 7th Ed. Kaye Pace Publications.

Dicknett, L. and Prince, C. 1997. The Templar Revelation. Touchstone Publishing

Dillingham, C. et al. 2017. The claustrum: considerations regarding its anatomy, functions and a programme for research. 1:p1-9. Brain and neuroscience advances

DiNicolantonio, J. 2017. *The Salt Fix: Why The Experts Got It Wrong And How Eating More Might Save Your Life.* Piatkus.

DiNicolantonio, J. Importance of Dietary Fats [podcast]. *Take Control of Your Health.* 13 November 2019.

Dispenza, J. 2017. *Becoming Supernatural.* Hay House.

DK. 2017. *How The Body Works.* Penguin Random House.

Dobbs, D. 2005. Zen Gamma. Available online at: <www.scientificamerican.com>

Domenig, S. 2015. The Alkaline Cure: The amazing 14 day diet and mindful eating plan. Modern Books.

Donoghue, B. 2013. Cosmic Christmas The World Has Missed: Santa Claustrum. Video.

Eden, G. 2016. *Chnoubis.* [online] Available at: < www.spellsandmagic.org>

Ellis, R. 2002. *Jesus: Last Of The Pharaohs.* Independently Published.

Emm, D. *12 Cell Salts.* Three videos available on YouTube: <https://www.youtube.com/watch?v=QsswcMX7nqk>

Emyrs, C. 2007. *Revelation of the Holy Grail.* Aurora.

Falde, N. 2019. *Acoustic Levitation: Floating on a Wave of Sound.* Available online at: www.ancient-origins.net

Farrow, L. 2013. *The Iodine Crisis.* Devon Press.

Faulkner, R. 1969. *The Ancient Egyptian Pyramid Texts.* Utterance 412-442. Oxford University Press. Aris and Phillips reprint edition.

Fenton, D. 2018. *Hybrid Humans.* Independently Published.

Fletcher, E. n.d. 5 Ways Meditation Can Help You Have Mind-Blowing Sex [online]. Available at: <www.mindbodygreen.com>

Franzis, B. 2012. *Taoist Sexual Meditation.* Energy Arts Inc, California.

Frecska, E. et al. 2013. A Possible Sigma-1 Receptor Mediated Role of Dimethyltryptamine in Tissue Protection, Regeneration and Immunity. *Journal of Neural Transmission.* 120(9): pp.1296-1303.

Furlong, D. 2003. *Working With Earth Energies.* Piatkus.

Gaia, 2015. *How To Align With Planetary Energies.* Available online at: <www.gaia.com>

Gariaev, P., Tertishny, G, and Leonova, K. Journal of Non-Locality and Remote Mental Interactions. Available online at: < https://www.slideshare.net/INVERTONE/the-phantomdna-wave-p-garjajev-v-poponin>

Gerber, R. 1988. *Vibrational Medicine: New Choices for Healing Ourselves.* Bear & Co.

Geyer, C. 2019. Telomeres: Are they the Fountain of Youth, or markers for the benefits of living well? *Journal on Active Aging.* 18(2):p.26-32.

Gilbert, A. 2000. *Signs in the Sky.* Bantam Press.

Gottschall, J. 2012. *The storytelling animal: how stories make us human.* Mariner Books.

Grant, B. n.d. *Magnetism and Plant Growth- How Do Magnets Help Plants Grow.* Available online at: <www.gardeningknowhow.com>

Gaves, K. 1875, *The World's Sixteen Crucified Saviours.*

Griffiths, R. et al. 2017. Psilocybin-occasioned mystical-type experience in combination with meditation and other spiritual practices produces enduring positive changes in psychological functioning and in trait measures of prosocial attitudes and behaviors. *32(1):pp.49-69.* Journal of Psychopharmacology.

Grinberg et al. 1994. The Einstein-Podolsky-Rosen Paradox In The Brain: The Transformed Potential.

Gundry, S. 2017. *The Plant Paradox.* Harper Wave.

Gundry, S. Healthy Aging Begins and Ends in the Gut [podcast]. *Bulletproof Radio.* 27 June 2019.

Hackathorn, J., Ashdown, M., & Rife, B. 2016. The Sacred Bed: Sex Guilt Mediates Religiosity and Satisfaction for Unmarried People. *Sexuality & Culture.* 20(1):pp. 153-172.

Hall, M. 1928. *Secret Teachings of All Ages.* Reprinted in 2004 by Jeremy Tarcher.

Hall, M. *Brilliant Hidden Messages- Da Vinci's "Last Supper".* Available online at: <https://sagaciousnewsnetwork.com/brilliant-hidden-messages-da-vincis-last-supper/>

Hameroff, S. and Penrose, R. 1996. Consciousness Events As Orchestrated Spacetime Selections. *Journal of Consciousness Studies.* 3(1):pp.36-53.

Hamil, J., Hallack, J. and Baker, G. 2019. Ayahuaska: Psychological and Physiologic Effects, Pharmacology and Potential Uses in Addiction and Mental Illness. 17(2):pp.108-128. *Current Neuropharmacology.*

Hancock, G. 2001. *Fingerprints of the Gods.* Century.

Hancock, G. 2015. *The Divine Spark.* Hay House UK.

Hancock, G. 2015. *Magicians of the Gods.* Coronet.

Hanuise, C. et al. 2006. From The Sun To The Earth: Impact Of The 27-28 May 2003 Solar Events On The Magnetosphere, Ionosphere and Thermosphere. *Annales Geophysicae.* 24(1):pp.129-151

Harrell, K. and Dudek, R. 2019. *Anatomy.* Wolters Kluwer.

Hayes, M. 2004. *The Hermetic Code in DNA.* Black Spring Press.

Hernandez-Kane, K., & Mahoney, A. 2018. Sex Through a Sacred Lens: Longitudinal Effects of Sanctification of Marital Sexuality. *Journal of Family Psychology.* 32(4):pp.425-434.

Hermes Mercurius Trismegistus. *The Divine Pymander.*

Hill, N. 1937. *Think And Grow Rich.* Reprinted in 2015 by Mindpower Press.

Hof, J. 2015. *The Wim Hof Method Explained.* [pdf] Available online at: <www.wimhofmethod.com>

Hopkins, D. 2017. *Sacred Geometry and the Flower of Life.* [podcast] The TruthSeekah Podcast. 1 December 2017.

Horowitz, L. 2011. *The book of 528: prosperity key of love.* Tetrahedron Publishing Group.

Hugo J Niggli, H. et al. 2005. Laser-ultraviolet-A-induced ultraweak photon emission in mammalian cells. J *Biomed Opt.* 10(2):024006.

Hunter, C. 2010. *The art of hypnosis.* Crown House Publishing.

Jacob, M. and Presti, D. 2005. Endogenous Psychoactive Tryptamines Considered: An Anxiolytic Role For Dimethyltryptamine. *Medical Hypothesis.* 64(5):pp. 930-937.

Jacqueline, M. and Ungerlerider, S. 1991. *Mental practice among Olympic athletes.* Golding First.

Ji, S. 2013. The Human Body Emits, Communicates with, and is Made From Light. *GreenMedInfo LLC.* Available online at: <www.greenmedinfo.health>

John St Julien Baba Wanyama. 2015. The Sacred Science Of The Pineal Gland- The Greatest Secret Never Told: The Sacred Secretion. Video.

Jones, M. and Flaxman, L. 2009. *11:11 the time prompt phenomenon: the meaning behind mysterious signs, sequences and synchronicities.* New Page Books.

Jung, C. 1960. *The Structure and Dynamics of the Psyche.* 2nd Ed. Routledge.

Jung, C. 1969. *On The Nature Of The Psyche.* Ark Paperbacks.

Jung, C. 1974. *Dreams.* Princeton University Press.

Kerr, K. 2018. *The God Design.* Independently Published.

Kirschvink, J. 1992. Magnetite Biomineralization in the Human Brain. *Proc Natl Acad Sci.* 89:pp.7683-7687.

Know, L. 2018. *Mitochondria and the Future of Medicine.* Independently Published.

Ko, Y. and Suszak, K. 2014. Epigenomics: The science of no-longer-"junk" DNA. 33(4). *Seminars in Nephrology.*

Kobayashi, M., Kikuchi, D. and Okamura, H. 2009. Imaging of ultraweak spontaneous photon emission from human body displaying diurnal rhythm. PLoS One. 4(7):e6256.

Kolb, B., Whishaw, I. ad Teskey, G. 2016. *An Introduction to Brain and Behavior.* 5th Ed. Macmillan Education.

Land, S. Dr Mercola Interviews Siim Land on Metabolic Autophagy [podcast]. *Take Control of Your Health.* 15 September 2019.

Lane, N. 2005. *Power, Sex, Suicide.* Oxford.

Lee, W. and Rosenbaum, M. 1987. *Chlorella: The Sun-Powered Supernutrient and its Beneficial Properties.* Keats Publishing.

Lee et al. 2011. Entangled Macroscopic Diamonds At Room Temperature. *Science.* 334(6060):pp.1253-1256.

Levy, J. 2018. *4 Steps to Achieve Proper pH Balance.* Available online at: <www.draxe.com>

Levy, J. 2018. *Get More Tryptophan for Better Sleep, Moods and Fewer Headaches.* Available online at: www.draxe.com

Lewis, D. 2015. *Saint Germain on Advanced Alchemy.* Meru Press.

Liberman, J. 1991. *Light: The Medicine of the Future.* Bear and Company.

Liggett, D. and Homada, S. 1993. Enhancing visualization of gymnasts. *The American Journal Of Clinical Hypnosis.* 35(3):p.190-197.

Lohmann, K. and Johnsen, S. 2000. The Neurobiology of Magnetoreception in Vertebrate Animals. *Trends in Neuroscience.* 23(4):p.153.

Lipton, B. 2014. *The honeymoon effect: The science of creating heaven on earth.* Hay House UK.

Lorius, C. 2011. *The Sacred Sex Bible.* Godsfield Press, London.

Makukov, M. and Shcherback, V. 2015. **In**. Discovery CSC. *The Planetary Science Journal Karus, the 'Wow' signal of intelligent design.*

McKanzie, C. 2017. *Mystery of Our Coded DNA- Who Was The 'Programmer'?* Available online at: < http://www.messagetoeagle.com/mystery-of-our-coded-dna-who-was-the-programmer/>

Marieb, E. and Hoehn, K. 2013. *Human Anatomy and Physiology.* 9th Ed. Pearson Education.

Martini, F., Nath, J. and Bartholomew, E.2015. *Fundamentals of Anatomy and Physiology.* 10th Ed. Pearson Education Ltd.

Mason, R. *The Serpent As Divinity.* [online] Available at: <http://www.reptilianagenda.com/research/r020600a.shtml>

Mayor, S. 2009. Unravelling the Secrets of Aging. *British Medical Journal.* 338:a3024.

McKenna, T. 1992. *Food of the Gods.* Rider.

McKenna, . 1994. Ayahuasca Increases Serotonin Receptor Sensitivity in the Brain.

McKeown, P. 2015. *The Oxygen Advantage.* Piatkus.

Mendillo, M. et al. 2018. Comparative Ionospheres: Terrestrial and Giant Planets. *Icarus.* 303:pp.34-46.

Mercola, J. 2017. *Fat For Fuel.* Hay House.

475

Mercola, J. Eat Like a Carnivore [podcast]. *Take Control of Your Health.* 7 July 2019.

Mexico. *Pyramid of Kulkulcan at Chich'en Itza.* [online] Available at: <atlasobscura.com>

Mishra et al. 2013. A multicellular randomized control trial of a plant-based nutrition program to reduce body weight and cardiovascular risk in the corporate setting. 67(7):p.718-724. *European Journal of Clinical Nutrition.*

Montagnier, L. 2010. DNA Between Physics and Biology [video]. Available online at: < https://www.mediatheque.lindau-nobel.org/videos/31544/dna-between-physics-and-biology-2010/laureate-montagnier>

Montagnier, L. 2011. DNA "Teleportation". Summary available online at: < http://www.rexresearch.com/montagnier/montagnier.htm> Full article: Montagner,L. et al. 2011. DNA waves and water.

Montagnier, L. et al. DNA Waves and Water. Available online at: <http://www.rexresearch.com/montagnier/montagnier.htm>

Mousa, Haider Abdul-Lateef. 2016. Health Effects of Alkaline Diet and Water, Reduction of Digestive-tract Bacterial Load, and Earthing. *Alternative Therapies in Health & Medicine.* 22:p.24-34.

Murphy, C. et al. 1993. Long-Range Photoinduced Electron Transfer Through a DNA Helix. Science. 262(5136)

Murphy, J. 2008. *The power of your subconscious mind.* BN

Myers, B. 2013. *PEMF: The 5th Element of Health.* Balboa Press.

Na, S. et al. 2016. Changes In The Earth's Spin Rotation Due To The Atmospheric Effects And Reduction In Glaciers. *Journal of Astronomy And Space Sciences.* 33(4):pp.295-304

Narby, J. 1999. *The Cosmic Serpent.* Orion Books.

NASA. 2013. *Earth's Atmospheric Layer.*

Niggli, H. 1993. Artificial sunlight irradiation induces ultraweak photon emission in human skin fibroblasts. J *Photochem Photobiol* B. 18(2-3):pp.281

Norton, S. n.d. *What is oxalate and how can it impact your health?* [online]. Available at: <www.sallyknorton.com>

Norton, S. Dr Mercola Interviews Sally K Norton on Oxalate Toxicity. *Take Control of Your Health.* 10 November 2019.

Ober, C. 2014. Earthing: The Most Important Health Discovery Ever. Basic Health Publications.

Ori, J. 2017. *How Do Magnets Work in Saltwater?* Available online at: <www.sciencing.com>

Paungger, J. and Poppe, T. 2013. The Power Of Timing: Living In Harmony With Natural And Lunar Cycles. Wisdom Keeper Books.

Peake, A. 2013. *The Infinite Mindfield.* Watkins Publishing LTD.

Peate, I.and Nair, M. 2017. *Fundamentals of Anatomy and Physiology.* 2nd Ed. John Wiley.

Penagos, Hector, Carmen Varela, and Matthew A Wilson. Oscillations, Neural Computations and Learning during Wake and Sleep. 44:pp.193-201. *Current Opinion in Neurobiology.*

Perez-Alcazar, M. Culley, G. and Illes, S. .2016. Human Cerebrospinal Fluid Promote Neuronal Viability And Activity Of Hippocampal Neuronal Circuits (In Vitro). 10:54. Frontiers In Cellular Neuroscience.

Peterson, J. 2018. *12 Rules For Life.* Penguin Books.

Pinkha, M. 1997. The Return of the Serpents of Wisdom. Adventures Unlimited Press

Pimentel, D. and Pimentel, M. 2003. Sustainability of meat-based and plant-based diets and the environment.78:s660-663. *American Journal of Clinical Nutrition.*

Pixie, M. 2019. *The black box programme and the rose gold flame as antidote.* Independently Published.

Pocock, G. and Richards, C. 2008. *The Human Body*. Oxford.

Pocock, G., Richards, C. and Richards, D. 2018. *Human Physiology*. 5th Ed. Oxford

Pollack, G. 2013. *The Fourth Phase of Water*. Ebner and Sons Publishers.

Popp, Γ. et al. 1984. *Biophoton emission. New evidence for coherence and DNA as source. Cell Biophys.* 6(1):pp.33-52.

Poporin, V. 1995. The DNA Phantom Effect. Available online at: < https://www.bibliotecapleyades.net/ciencia/ciencia_genetica04.htm>

Proctor, B. 2016. *The 11 Forgotten Laws*. [video] Available on YouTube.

Rabinowitch, T. 2013. Long term musical group interaction has a positive influence on empathy in children. *Psychology Of Music*. 41(4):p.484-498.

Redd, N. 2017. *What Is a Wormhole?* Available online at: <https://www.space.com/20881-wormholes.html>

Rodwell, M. 2016. *The New Human: Awakening to Our Cosmic Heritage*. New Mind Publishers.

Rodwell, V., Bender, D., Botham, K., Kennelly, P. and Weil, P. 2018. *Harper's Illustrated Biochemistry*. 31st Ed. McGraw-Hill Education.

Rose, A. et al. 2018. MSR1 repeats modulate gene expression and affect risk of breast and prostate cancer. *Annals of Oncology*. 29(5):pp.1292-1303

Ryan, S., McNicholas, M. and Eustace, S. 2011. *Anatomy for Diagnostic Imaging*. 3rd Ed. Saunders Elsevier.

Sackett, C. et al. 2000. Experimental Entanglement of Four Particles. *Nature*. 404:pp.256-259.

Saladin, K. 2017. *Human Anatomy*. 5th Ed. McGraw-Hill Education.

Saladino, P. Kick Veggies to the Curb and Go Full Carnivore [podcast]. *Bulletproof Radio*. 27 August 2019.

Sangiah, S., Gomez, M. and Domino, E. 1979. Accumulation of N,N-Dimethyltryptamine in Rat Brain Cortical Slices. *Biol Psychiat*. 14:pp.925-936.

Satija, A. et al. 2017. Healthful and unhealthful plan-based diets and the risk of coronary heart disease in US adults. 70(4):pp.423-425. *Journal of American Coll Cardiol*.

Schwabl, H. and Klima, H. 2005. Spontaneous Ultraweak Photo Emission From Biological Systems and the Endogenous Light Field. Forsch Komplementarmed Klass Naturheikd. 12(2):pp.84-49.

Scranton, L. 2006. *The Science of the Dogon*. Inner Traditions.

Scranton, L. 2014. *China's Cosmological Prehistory*. Inner Traditions.

Scranton, L. *2018. Decoding Maori Cosmology*. Inner Traditions.

Shananhan, C. 2016. *Deep Nutrition*. Flatiron Books.

Sherson, J., Julsgaard, B. and Polzik, E. 2005. Distant Entanglement of Macroscopic Gas Samples. *NAII*. 189: pp.353-372.

Sidorova, A. 2018. *Planets and Subtle Body: How Planet Energies Are Related To Chakras*. Available online at: <www.exemplore.com>

Stacey, F. and Hodgkinson, J. 2013. *The Earth As A Cradle For Life*. World Scientific.

Steifel, L. et al. 2014. The claustrum's proposed role in consciousness is supported by the effect and target localization of Salvia divinorum. 8:p.20. Frontiers in Integrative Neuroscience.

Strassman, R. and Qualls, C. 1994. Dose Response Study of N,N-Dimethyltryptamine in Humans. Part 1. Neuroendocrine, Automatic and Cardiovascular Effects. *Arch Gen Psychiat*. 51:pp. 85-97.

Strassman, R., Qualls, C., Uhlenhuth, E. and Kellner, R. 1994. Dose Response Study of N,N-Dimethyltryptamine in Humans. Part 2. Subjective Effects and Preliminary Results of a New Rating Scale.. *Arch Gen Psychiat.* 51:pp. 98-108.

Strassman, R. 2001. *DMT: The Spirit Molecule.* Park Street Press.

Strassman, R. 2014. *DMT and the Soul of Prophecy.* Park Street Press.

Suleyman, S. 2015. *Cell Biology and Genetics.* Elsevier Ltd.

Sutton, N. 2014. What Are Biorhythms? Helping You To Know Yourself. Spiritual-Awakening.Net.

Tennant, J. 2010. *Healing Is Voltage.* 3rd ed. Independently Published.

Timmermann, C., et al. 2019. Neural Correlates of the DMT Experience Assessed with Multivariate EEG. *9:a16324.* Nature.

Thompson, A. 2016. The Logic- Defying Double- Slit Experiment Is Even Weirder Than You Thought. Available online at: <www,popularmechanics.com>

Three Initiates. 2017. *The Kybalion.* Independently Published.

Tuso, P. 2015. A plant-based diet, atherogenesis and coronary artery disease prevention. 19(1):pp.62-67. *The Permanente Journal.*

Van, M. 2019. Deep Sleep Optimization (parts one to five). Available online at: <https://www.drmichaelvan.com/category/sleep-optimization/>

Van Der Hoeven, J. 2014. *The Awen Alone.* Moon Books.

Veenig, J. and Barendregt, P. 2010. The Regulation Of Brain States By Neuroactive Substances Distributed via The Cerebrospinal Fluid: A Review. 7:1. BioMed Central: Cerebrospinal Fluid Research.

Verny, T. and Weintraub, P. 2002. Tomorrow's baby: the art and science of parenting from conception through infancy. Simon and Schuster.

Virtue, D. 2009. *The Crystal Children.* Hay House UK.

Walker, M. 2018. *Why We Sleep.* Penguin, London.

Wallace, D. 2009. Mitochondria, bioenergetics and the epigenome in eukaryotic and human evolution. 74:pp.383-393. *Harb Symp Quant Biol.*

West, P. 1984. Biorhythms: Your Daily Guide To Achieving Peak Potential. Thorsons.

Wheatley, M. 2014. *Divining Ancient Sites.* Celestial Songs Press.

White, J. 2019. Semen Retention: Harnessing Sexual Energy [YouTube]. Available online 12 July 2019.

Widmaier, E., Raff, H. and Strang, K. 2016. *Vander's Human Physiology.* MvGraw-Hill

Wilcock, D. 2018. Secrets Of The Pineal Gland. Video.

Wiley, R. 1987. Biobalance: the acid/ alkaline solution to the food-mood-health puzzle. Life Science.

Williams, M. and Penman, D. 2011. *Mindfulness: Finding peace in a frantic world.* Piatkus.

Wise, A. 1995. *The high performance mind: mastering brainwaves for insight, healing and creativity.* GP Putnam's Sons.

Wolfe, D. 2009. *Superfoods.* North Atlantic Books.

Wrangman, R. 2010. *Catching Fire: How Cooking Made Us Human.* Profile Books LTD.

Yin, B. et al. 2016. Claustrum, consciousness and time perception. 8:p. 258-267. Current Opinion In Behavioural Sciences.

Yudelove, E. 2000. *Taoist Yoga and Sexual Energy.* Llewellyn Publications.

Yurdagül Zopf, Dejan Reljic, & Walburga Dieterich. 2018. Dietary Effects on Microbiota—New Trends with Gluten-Free or Paleo Diet. *Medical Sciences.* 6(4):p.92.

Zeng, H. and Xu, W. 2015. *Enzymic Assays of Histone Methyltransferase Enzymes.* Epigenetic Technological Applications.

"There's a dance only you can do,

that exists only in you,

here and now,

always changing,

always true.

Are you willing to listen with fascination?

If you are,

it will deliver you

unto the self you have always dreamed you could be.

This is a promise."

– Gabrielle Roth